SAILORS

English Merchant Seamen 1650–1775

———e·e———

PETER EARLE

Methuen

Published by Methuen, 2007

1 3 5 7 9 10 8 6 4 2

First published in the United Kingdom by Methuen, 1998

Methuen Publishing Ltd
11–12 Buckingham Gate
London SW1E 6LB

www.methuen.co.uk

Methuen Publishing Limited Reg. No. 3543167

ISBN 10: 0-413-77634-4
ISBN 13: 978-0-413-77634-1

A CIP catalogue record for this book is available from the British Library

Typeset by MATS, Southend-on-Sea, Essex
Printed and bound in Great Britain by
Bookmarque Ltd, Croydon, Surrey

'The seamen here are a generation differing from all the world. When one goes into Rotherhithe and Wapping, which places are chiefly inhabited by sailors, a man would be apt to suspect himself in another country. Their manner of living, speaking, acting, dressing, and behaving, are so very peculiar to themselves. Yet with all their oddities, they are perhaps the bravest and boldest fellows in the universe.'

Sir John Fielding, *A Brief Description of the Cities of London and Westminster* (1776)

Contents

Preface

Preface

This book is a social history of the sailors who worked England's merchant ships some three hundred years ago. It is organized topically, with different chapters on such subjects as the sailor's origins and training, his possessions, work, discipline, mortality and so on. The book is mainly based on the verbal testimony of the sailors themselves as given in courts of law, especially in the High Court of Admiralty. Quotations from this testimony, sometimes discreetly edited, are scattered through the text to enable readers to be able to hear the actual words of the sailors of the past. Ships' papers, such as logbooks and account books, have also been very valuable, as have the journals and memoirs of contemporary sailors and travellers, especially Edward Barlow whose fascinating *Journal* opens a window on life at sea in the late seventeenth century.

The book's main focus is on the period from 1670 to about 1740, but it strays outside these limits from time to time. Not a great deal could have been said in any detail about sailors' work and their chances of surviving a voyage without logbooks and muster rolls, of which there are not many surviving before the 1760s and 1770s, while the shipping paper *Lloyd's List*, whose reports on marine casualties provided much of the material for the section on shipwrecks, did not begin until the 1740s.

No doubt many readers will have preconceptions about sailors and may believe that their lives were more than likely to be short, brutal and extremely unpleasant. Read on! The book does reflect such negative aspects of the lives of sailors, but not exclusively. If the lives of sailors had been so truly awful as they are often painted, it would have been a wonder that so many thousands of men and boys should have gone willingly to sea. Shipboard life was not all doom and gloom, storms and tyranny, and the book will show the good side of the sailor's life as well as the bad, the harmony and comradeship on board most ships, the attractions of travel and adventure, the delight in a difficult job well done, the joys of fine-weather sailing when it was a 'wonder how any man can be such a lubber as to stay at land'.

My thanks are due to the libraries and record offices where I have worked and to participants in seminars and conferences at which I have given papers on my work in Britain and the Netherlands. Very special thanks are due to Dr Nicholas Rodger who read the much longer original version of this book and saved me from some lubberly errors. Thanks also to many friends and colleagues who have generously given me references to useful books or interesting documents. Finally, I acknowledge with thanks a grant (R000234603) from the Economic and Social Research Council which has helped to sustain me through the three years of researching and writing this book.

CHAPTER ONE

The Sailor and his World

CHAPTER ONE

The Sailor and his World

'I have used the seas above forty-five years and have been in almost all habitable maritime parts of the world.'[1]

Sailors must be the most familiar to the modern eye of all working men of the seventeenth and eighteenth centuries. Their images abound in television, film and historical novels. There they are, barefoot, bronzed and pigtailed, running up the rigging, performing acrobatics on the yards, staring from the tops into the blue or stormy yonder on their way to romance and adventure. There they are, handkerchiefs knotted round their heads, loose breeches flapping, cutlass in their hands and pistols in their belts, as they storm across the decks of an enemy ship or drive their captain and officers into the sea in a frenzy of mutiny.

Shipwreck and mutiny, piracy and plunder, rum, sodomy and the lash, these are the images of the early modern sailor which have come down to us. But these images, whether they reflect the truth or not, are nearly always drawn from sailors in the Royal Navy or from pirates, those devil-may-care favourites of children of all ages. The sailors serving on merchantmen, who form the subject of this book, are far less familiar, men who usually appear in films and novels only as the victims of pirates or of the press gangs who provided the navy with its crews. Few people today know much

about the ships which carried England's trade, except perhaps the
stately East Indiamen, and then only because they carried treasure,
or the slave ships whose human cargo remains a subject of
fascination and pity for social historian and novelist alike. And
most people know even less about the crews of these ships, humble
and now forgotten men who carried coals from Newcastle or
brought home to their native land wine and oil, sugar and tobacco
to make life more bearable for their stay-at-home contemporaries.
These men are the subject of this book.

What sort of life did they lead? One might imagine it was a life
of poverty, brutality and great hardship, toiling in leaking sailing
ships across the oceans, subject not just to the storms and threat of
shipwreck with which the modern sailor is familiar, but also to the
threat of capture by the numerous predators who plied the seas and
to the arbitrary discipline of captains and boatswains ready with
lash and cane to drum their crews into obedience. These men had
few mechanical aids, no electronic wizardry to tell them where they
were, no wireless to call for aid, no cans to preserve their food. They
ate salt food, slept when they could in crowded leaking forecastles,
lived in damp, smelly clothes and relied on muscle, common sense
and knowledge of the sea to carry their ships across the globe. They
were cheated and short-changed by officers and shipowners; duped
ashore by victuallers and prostitutes; abused and reviled by those
who made their living on the land. What sort of men were these?

Few contemporaries knew much about merchant sailors, unless
they were sailors themselves or sailed on their ships. Sailors were
seen almost as a race apart, as Sir John Fielding noted when he
crossed the social and imaginative frontier between the East and
West Ends of London and went into Rotherhithe and Wapping,
places 'chiefly inhabited by sailors, [where] a man would be apt to
suspect himself in another country. Their manner of living,
speaking, acting, dressing, and behaving, are so very peculiar to
themselves'.[2]

We cannot follow Sir John and see, hear and smell England's
sailors for ourselves, but we can still try to determine what was
peculiar or unpleasant and what quite ordinary in their manner of
living and behaving. Our guides will be travellers who occasionally

described the highlights of their maritime experience, but the main source will be more humdrum, the verbal testimony given by sailors themselves in a law court whose main function in peacetime was to hear their grievances.[3] What they said was written down by clerks and it is these words spoken by sailors some three hundred years ago which should give this book its salty tang. Sailors spoke of everything, of poor treatment, the incompetence of others and a thousand other grievances, as well as allowing a curious historian to discover what were the 'customs of the sea'. The reader will slowly discover what these customs were but first a few words should be written to set the background for this maritime world of the seventeenth and eighteenth centuries.

Which lands did English sailors visit as they sailed the seas? Experience varied, as will be seen, but between them the sailors in this book went just about everywhere from the Americas to the coast of China, but not yet to Australia and the Pacific. During the period considered, England became the world's greatest trading nation, as well as its most successful naval power. Such expansion meant that the variety of employment open to England's sailors grew as well. Much of the growth was in truly oceanic long-distance trades, above all to the West Indies and the American colonies, to which an ever increasing number of sailors plied to bring back sugar, tobacco, rum and a multitude of other products to satisfy the increasingly varied demands of the English market. Further north in the Atlantic, cod-fishing on the Newfoundland Banks provided another major source of work for the English sailor while, in the freezing waters of the Arctic, whaling became an important specialist trade after 1750.[4]

The trades across the Atlantic were sadly linked to the period's greatest crime in modern eyes, the slave trade from Africa to the Americas. This trade, now condemned by all nations, will play a fairly prominent part in this book, since it not only employed increasing numbers of sailors, several thousand a year by the end of the period, but was also associated with somewhat unusual and often very unpleasant conditions of service. This was also true to some extent of service in the longest of all long-distance trading ships, the East Indiamen which sailed to ports in Asia and were the largest, most heavily manned and beautiful of all English ships. They traded to ports in Arabia, India, south-east Asia and, increasingly, to China to bring home goods which made English diet and dress even more exotic – silk and cotton textiles, coffee and tea and beautiful china to drink it from as well as a host of other things.

These long-distance trades were certainly exotic, but there was plenty of work nearer home, and sometimes not so near home as in the many voyages undertaken to the 'Straits', that is of Gibraltar and so into the Mediterranean, to Spain, Italy and the Middle East and many islands and places in between. These ships brought home cotton, silks and other textiles, but the great bulk of the trade which filled the ships was food and drink for the English table, wine, olive oil, oranges and lemons, currants and much else besides. Other ships traded to the Atlantic coast of western Europe or across the Channel to fetch the products of France, the Low Countries and Germany, all trades which were major employers of English sailors. And, finally, very large numbers sailed across the North Sea to bring back the products of Russia, Scandinavia and the Baltic, the most important in terms of shipping tonnage and hence of sailor employment being the trade in timber which mainly came from Norway.

Not all sailors spent their lives voyaging abroad, be it to near countries such as Holland or far ones such as China and Brazil. At the beginning of the period studied, nearly two-thirds of all sailors never went far from home, since they were employed in inshore fishing and in the coasting trades around the British Isles. Later this proportion had fallen, but not by all that much, despite the huge increase in long-distance trade and shipping. Customs officers actually counted the numbers of sailors doing different types of work in the 1770s and found that there were some 30,000 working in ships sailing overseas and as many as 20,000 (40 per cent of the total) in inshore fishing and the coastal trades.[5] Coasters carried a huge range of goods – foodstuffs, raw materials and manufactured goods – but the largest single employer of English sailors throughout the period was the coastal trade in coal, down the east coast of Britain to London and later from north-west ports to many places but particularly to Ireland. Coasting might seem less exciting than a voyage to China, but it employed very large numbers of sailors and this is reflected in this book, which has much to say about those who sailed in coasters and especially that 'nursery of seamen', the east coast colliers.

English ships were sailed mainly by British, Irish and colonial sailors since the employment of foreigners was restricted by law to a maximum of one-quarter of the total crew. Such laws were relaxed in wartime but, in peacetime, they were observed and in fact most ships employed much less than the quarter of foreigners permitted.[6] So most of the sailors considered here were English or at least British, but just how many there were at any one time is difficult to say. They were rarely counted and it would in any case be difficult to say just what constituted a sailor since many people only went to sea as part-timers and were mainly employed as fishermen or in occupations ashore. In very rough terms, there were probably rather less than 30,000 English sailors in 1660 and rather more than 50,000 in 1770, not counting those serving in the Royal Navy.[7]

Such numbers mean that the trade of sailor was one of the most important in eighteenth-century England, but growth in numbers was modest considering the very large increase in English trade and shipping tonnage, which roughly trebled in the period studied here. This means that over time fewer sailors were needed to work each hundred tons of English shipping, a major increase in productivity which has been noted by many maritime historians.[8] This improvement in efficiency may of course have been achieved at the sailors' expense by making them work harder, though they did not complain much about this. But if sailors did not work harder, how did each sailor manage to work more tons of shipping? Experts suggest three main reasons. First, ships got bigger and, generally speaking, larger ships need less men per hundred tons though this was not true of the largest ships of all, the East Indiamen, which had very much the same manning ratios throughout the period. Then there were a few technical changes, not many but enough to make ships easier to handle with fewer men. And finally, ships began to need less men because the seas became safer in the course of the period. At least until the 1720s, ships sailing any great distance south or west had to carry many more men than necessary to sail the ship just to provide defence in the not unlikely event of attack by predators such as corsairs and pirates.[9]

Practically every aspect of life at sea, such as life expectancy or the nature of the work, varied considerably depending on the trade in which the sailor was engaged. Size of ship and size of crew are two good basic examples. In the early 1770s, there were about 6,000 ships with a combined tonnage of just under 600,000 tons.[10] The average ship was thus a modest 100 tons, but the range ran from 20 tons for small coasters to nearly a thousand tons for the largest East Indiamen. The average crew at the same time was between eight and nine men, no bigger than many households of the day, but again the range was enormous, from the master, man and boy who worked small coasters through the typical fifteen or twenty or so who crewed the ships in the colonial trades to over one hundred men on East Indiamen. It does not take much imagination to appreciate that life aboard ship must have been very different as one of three than of a hundred. Workload, the work itself, and familiarity with one's mates were all totally different. And, in general, it is true to say that the larger the crew the more likely there was to be trouble aboard the ship.

Length of voyages varied as much as did the size of crews. A small ship trading in the River Humber and on the east coast completed fifty-four voyages in the three years 1726–28, while another averaged one round trip a month between London and Maldon in Essex in the 1680s. A veteran of the Newcastle coal trade claimed that the average round trip to London and back took six weeks, while a ship bringing timber from Norway would make about four voyages a year, lying up in her home port in England during the winter when Norwegian ports were usually frozen up.[11]

Such brief absences from home can be compared with the experience of sailors sailing across the oceans. The round trip to America or the West Indies and back rarely took less than six months and often took eight or nine, much of the time being spent loading in American ports and creeks, while a slaving voyage from

England to England via West Africa and America typically took about a year. A voyage to the Mediterranean could be quite speedy if it simply involved the carriage of a cargo out and back, but English shipping also played an important part in the internal carrying trade of the region and such port-to-port trading within the Mediterranean could involve an absence of two years or longer. A long time away from home was the invariable experience of sailors serving on the ships chartered by the East India Company. A typical voyage from London to the east and back to London lasted between eighteen months and two years but trading within Asia could extend such times to three years or more. Many sailors found long voyages attractive, since they provided a continuity of work difficult to obtain in short-haul trades, but confinement on board ship for such a long time posed a variety of problems unlikely to be encountered by sailors engaged in voyages of a few weeks or less.

The word 'voyage' here means the contractual voyage which a sailor was engaged to serve, which will be discussed later, normally beginning and ending in England. Times at sea, without a break in a port, known as 'passages', were obviously much less. A passage across the Atlantic typically took between seven and ten weeks, though misfortunes often led to much longer times at sea, causing shortages of food and water and discontent aboard. English merchant ships were not yet engaged in the long passages round Cape Horn to the Pacific, so the only trades in which sailors would expect to spend any longer at sea were those to the East Indies. East Indiamen nearly always stopped somewhere before reaching their destination, small islands round the African coast being the commonest places, but these were still very long passages likely to test to the limit the harmony of a crew. A typical run from London to the Comoro Islands (in the western Indian Ocean) was between sixteen and twenty weeks, twice as long as across the Atlantic. Continuous passage times coming home were less but still very long before the crew anchored with relief in Table Bay or St Helena, the normal places of refreshment on homebound voyages. Passage times to St Helena from the last place of call in India or south-east Asia were normally between twelve and sixteen weeks;

any longer would almost certainly mean a very long sick list.[12]

Crew size and length of voyage were two important variables governing the lives of sailors, but there were many others as will be seen in detail in later chapters. A sailor was, for instance, much more likely to die (and indeed be flogged) in the course of a voyage if he served on a slave ship or an East Indiaman than if he sailed to North America or the Baltic Sea. Desertion was common in the West Indies and the Mediterranean, but not in the Baltic or in western Europe. All this means that if one wants to say that sailors were likely to die, desert or be flogged in the course of a voyage, as many writers do, it is necessary to specify the type of voyage. And, before one can generalize with confidence, one should remember that relative numbers in different trades changed over time. Total crews working on slave ships, for instance, grew from a few hundred in the 1650s to over 5,000 men in the early 1770s, while numbers on East Indiamen quadrupled from about 1,500 to 6,000 in the same period.[13]

A sailor's main job was to help to sail, load and unload and maintain his ship, but such work itself varied enormously from trade to trade. Sailing in coastal waters or in the Irish Sea and North Sea was very different and often much more dangerous than sailing across the Atlantic, while sailing in the north Atlantic was a very different experience to rolling along before the huge swells of the westerlies in the south Atlantic where fears of being overwhelmed by waves might be mitigated by daily runs of two hundred miles or more.

Sailors in many trades had to do rather more than sail, load and unload. One very important trade was that in salt cod from Newfoundland 'to a market' in south-west Europe or the Mediterranean. Some English ships simply sailed to Newfoundland and picked up a cargo of cod caught by settlers. But many others sailed to the Banks 'to take and cure fish', which means that they caught and preserved the cod themselves and did not leave until the ship was full. They left England in March, picked up a cargo of salt somewhere on the Atlantic coast of Europe and then spent months in or off Newfoundland catching, splitting, drying and salting cod until, their holds full, they sailed for a port in southern Europe and returned home very late in the year with a cargo of wine, oil or dried fruit for the English market.[14]

Such work required 'extraordinary labour and pains', according to one veteran and such was also the lot of the whaling crews who sailed from English ports in March or April to hunt their prey in the floating ice off Spitsbergen and Greenland. Whaling may be condemned today, but these men were not to know that and they certainly earned their wages the hard way. They were indeed some of the finest seamen in the world. The whales were chased through the floating ice in small open boats and then struck with hand-held harpoons 'an instant before the boat touches [the whale]'. The whale was then played for hours, even days, with thousands of feet of line, until at last the huge, dead creature was towed back to the ship and then 'made off', the most time-consuming task of all in which the blubber was cut up into small pieces for storage in barrels. A lucky ship might be back in port with a full cargo ready to be boiled down early in July; others returned in August or September, while an unlucky few never returned at all, to be reported later 'lost in the ice'.[15]

The lives of sailors were thus quite varied. Some men spent years away from home as one of the very large crews of East Indiamen, stopping briefly for periods ashore in such exotic locations as Sumatra or St Helena. Others spent years sailing up and down the east coast of England as one of the small and heavily worked crews of colliers, men whose recreation would be enjoyed in more homely places such as Sunderland or Scarborough. English sailors might spend most or some of their working lives catching cod on the Grand Banks, whales in the Arctic or men, women and children on the west coast of Africa. Others plied to Alexandria for cotton, Norway for timber or, more prosaically, to the ports of Kent and East Anglia for foodstuffs to feed the metropolis.

Not all a sailor's life was spent at sea and, although many had no permanent home, most sailors felt that they belonged to a certain home port where they might have friends and relations and perhaps a wife and children and where they would know the whereabouts of the best lodging-houses and alehouses. There were over seventy active ports around the English coastline, but most were very small and most of England's sailors when not at sea lived in a dozen or so of the larger ports.[16] London was much the most important and its eastern parishes housed the greatest concentration of English sailors during their spells ashore. London controlled well over half of all of England's trade and shipping until 1700 and the forest of masts below London Bridge was one of the city's great sights. This dominance was challenged in the eighteenth century. The rise of the Atlantic trades favoured first Bristol and then Liverpool, which rose from virtually nothing to become the second most important port, while Hull and other east coast ports made inroads into London's share of the trades of the North Sea.

London sailors engaged in every trade and had a monopoly of some, such as the East India trade and the trade to the eastern Mediterranean, but the other ports specialized to some extent. Liverpool and Bristol were the major provincial slaving ports and both also engaged extensively in direct trade with the American colonies. The larger east coast ports such as Newcastle and Hull concentrated on the coal trade, fishing and the trades of the North Sea, though their mariners often sailed further afield. Hull, Whitby and Newcastle all became whaling ports after 1750, for instance, while Yarmouth retained an important trade to the Mediterranean. Shipping in the south-east was of course dominated by the trade of London, but there were many smaller ports such as Harwich, Dover and Southampton and these specialized in trade and passenger services across the Channel, in fishing and in the coasting trade, especially to London. Finally, a mass of mostly very small ports in the south-west, all the way round the coast from Poole to Ilfracombe, concentrated on the trades to south-west Europe and on the trade in cod from Newfoundland to the Mediterranean.

What sort of men used the seas to make their living? Sailors have tended to get a bad press from their stay-at-home contemporaries, to be 'deemed almost the refuse and offscourings of the earth' as Herman Melville (of *Moby Dick* fame) noted in his novel *Redburn*. They were necessary if nations were to have navies and trade to thrive, but the men themselves were regularly denounced as idle, drunken and many other things, especially when they were ashore. 'There is nothing more idle and dissolute', wrote the novelist

Henry Fielding. "'Tis their way to be violent in all their motions', claimed Daniel Defoe. 'They swear violently, whore violently, drink punch violently, spend their money when they have it violently . . . in short, they are violent fellows, and ought to be encourag'd to go to sea, for Old Harry can't govern them on shoar.'[17]

Attitudes sometimes changed radically when the sailor did go to sea. 'In their element', admitted Henry Fielding, 'there are no persons who live in the constant practice of half so many good qualities. They are . . . perfect masters of their business, and always extremely alert and ready in executing it, without any regard to fatigue or hazard'. Few others praised sailors quite so fulsomely, but many echoed the virtues singled out by Fielding. Janet Schaw, for instance, a Scottish lady who sailed as a passenger in the 1770s, remarked on 'the warm hearts we generally meet with in sailors'. 'Do you want a man of heart', wrote a Frenchman. 'A man of work, industrious and ready for everything? Take a sailor. The true sailor fears nothing and refuses nothing.'[18]

Once one starts to look, it is easy to find people in the past saying both rude and pleasant things about sailors and such anecdotes and quotations are the raw material of social history, which can of course be selected to make any point the author wishes. A captain, for example, was described as 'a sober, worthy man, and a compleate seaman', a carpenter's mate was 'as ingenious a man as could come between stem and sterne of a ship' and even a humble ship's boy was 'a very pretty boy at his worke'. But no ship's company was likely to consist entirely of such paragons. There were also those described by their shipmates as 'very often in a lazy fit', 'negligent and carelesse', 'noe seaman' or 'a very drunken idle fellow', while the master himself might be a man who did not know his job.[19]

One could collect a few hundred such quotations to reflect the characters of the several tens of thousands of English men and boys who sailed the seas during the period of this book, but such industry would simply reinforce the impression given by the handful of quotations above. There were some good captains and sailors and some bad ones, just as there were good men and bad men in any occupation ashore. Even the very best of sources can take us very little further forward. John Pyke, an officer on the *Rochester*, was unusual in including in his journal brief descriptions of some of his humbler shipmates and his observations provide a range of sailor types from an officer's point of view. Hansome Brown, for instance, who fell out of a boat and was drowned, 'was a dilligent lad in his business . . . and, by his civill deportment, he became generally beloved, but he was unhappy in loveing strong liquor too well and he had at this time drunk too much'. John Fowler also had a drink problem. 'When he is sober he is a very usefull hand, and is a good sailor, but he will be drunk as often as he can.' John Perrey and Arthur Fletcher, by contrast, were not only good sailors but sober ones, Perrey being 'a very civill fellow, ready to oblige and serve every body according to his power', and Fletcher 'good natured to everybody, active and of a frugall temper'. Another man, however, who drowned when he fell overboard at sea, was not mourned for long. 'He was a sloathfull coarse fellow and unfitt for any buisnesse.'[20]

Generalizing from these five pen-portraits, one might say that most sailors on the *Rochester* were competent, hard-working and obliging but there were a few bad apples and drink was a problem aboard the ship. Readers may well feel by the end of the book that this is reasonably true of English sailors as a whole. Many, perhaps most, ships' crews included one or more difficult sailors, 'unfitt for any buisnesse'; many ships had at least one tyrannical or incompetent officer. But the vast majority of ships' companies, the silent majority, sailed the seas in reasonable harmony, reached their destinations in safety and provide no more evidence of their passage than their names in a list of the crew. Some, however, have left rather more evidence of their existence and it is to them that we must turn now to find out why sailors went to sea, where they came from and what sort of training they received to fit them for the rigours of a life at sea.

CHAPTER TWO

Bred to the Sea

Bred to the Sea

'Not liking to live at home, he went
to Sea.'[1]

Why did people choose to become sailors? The writers of memoirs
tend to give rather romantic reasons for their decision to go to sea.
John Nicol, a cooper's apprentice, 'had read Robinson Crusoe
many times over and longed to be at sea . . . while my hands were
hooping barrels my mind was at sea and my imagination in foreign
climes'. Edward Barlow 'had always a mind to see strange countries
and fashions'. Nicholas Owen also thought that 'the hopes of
seeing strange countrys' was a major reason, but suggested
'expectation of gain' as another motive.[2]

Gain was clearly important to many. Sailors were not badly paid
and there was a good chance of promotion for the competent. Such
a chance to move up in the world was not easily available in other
occupations open to the poor. Economic motivations were
strongest in wartime when competition from the Royal Navy
always forced the wages of merchant seamen up to very high levels
and drew many young men away from their previous landbound
lives, such as John Robinson, a pipemaker who signed on as cook
of a collier in 1692.[3]

Many of these men were hardly real sailors. Robert Willis of
Newcastle was aged fifty when in 1690 he described his employment record over the past seven years. 'He hath worked about the

coal workes, sometimes done husbandry (farming) work, sometimes gone to sea with the fishermen and sometimes gone of short
voyages.' His sea service was not very great, three voyages from
Newcastle to London and back, but others were more adventurous,
such as Thomas Cradding, a Londoner who was also fifty when he
appeared in court in 1705. 'I was bred a warehouse keeper to a sugar
baker but have used the seas at times for thirty years as steward
being no sailor, and served two voyages to the East Indias in the
Golden Fleece and one voyage thither in the *Asia*.'[4]

Gain, adventure, a desire to see the world, were among the more
positive reasons for going to sea. For others, the decision was very
much a *pis aller*. They took refuge in a ship because the land had
nothing to offer or was positively dangerous, the sea providing a
convenient bolthole for many a runaway apprentice, deserting
husband, debtor or fugitive from justice. John Charlton told one
of his shipmates 'that it was his wife's cross grainedness and ill
humours that forced him to goe to sea, because he could have noe
pleasure on shore'. Joseph Bagland was brought up as a clothmaker
in Gloucestershire, 'but could not fix to his business and had been
lewd in the country so he came to sea'.[5]

Criminal biographies provide further insights into the reasons
why youngsters went to sea. The motives were, as one might expect,
mostly very negative. Joseph Peacock, for instance, was the son 'of
parents in a pretty good way of life', but wasted their money and
patience by constantly playing truant at school, so 'his parents finding there was no hope of his doing well in London, resolved to send
him to sea'. Escaping authority was the motive of John Higgins, as
of many others who ran away from masters and parents. 'He had
done something that brought him in danger and so betook himself
to the sea. He says he was backwards and forwards, tumbling on the
ocean before the mast for about the space of eight years.' For Robert
Winroe, the sea was simply the last in a long line of failed occupations. 'He was a sort of an errand-boy, one while to a distiller, at
another time to a grocer, and then he got to be an understrapper at
a brew-house. But none of these pleased him long, his mind was
quite unsettled . . . And when he had tried all methods he could by
land, and none would doe, he betook himself to the sea.'[6]

The sea then provided a convenient dustbin for restless and often wild adolescents, as well as being a potential source of adventure or gain. However, such motivations whether positive or negative were probably unusual. Most sailors went to sea, in Ralph Davis's words, 'to do what father did'; in contemporary terms they were 'bred to the sea', just as other youngsters were 'bred to husbandry'.[7] They were born and brought up in maritime communities, the sons of sailors or fishermen, and from an early age it was understood that they would eventually go to sea in their turn. Only if they had not gone to sea would their behaviour have seemed odd and so have required some explanation.

This cannot be proved directly, since there is little information available on the parents of sailors, and all that can really be discovered is where sailors were born, information which was sometimes requested of people giving evidence in court. Analysis of the birthplaces of sailors shows, hardly surprisingly, that unless they were Londoners they were overwhelmingly drawn from the maritime counties. Well over 90 per cent of provincial sailors were born in maritime counties and the great majority of these within sight of the sea and ships, in port towns, coastal villages or on navigable rivers. It seems a reasonable assumption that most of their fathers were people of the sea.[8]

Evidence relating to the home port of sailors shows that many migrated from their region of birth, most going to London though other east coast ports also drew sizeable numbers of sailor migrants. The sailor's life was by its very nature one of movement, from ship to ship and from country to country, but one aspect of this mobile life for many was a move to London at some point in their career. These immigrants came from all over the British Isles and abroad, but some areas were particularly important as 'nurseries' of mariners for the rest of the country, such as the south-western counties of Dorset, Devon and Cornwall and the two eastern counties of Norfolk and Kent.[9]

Sailors were sometimes asked how long they had been 'using the seas' or when or at what age they first went to sea. Their answers show that some lads went to sea when they were very young indeed, such as Jack Cremer who began his 'rambling' career at sea when he was aged eight. However, such very young boys are by no means typical and simply catch the eye. The great majority of sailors first went to sea between the ages of twelve and sixteen, the same ages as were normal to start work in land-based occupations. And a substantial minority, mainly young men 'bred' to other trades, did not go to sea for the first time until they were in their twenties or even later.[10]

A majority of boys going to sea in their early teens would have had some schooling, since free or very inexpensive primary education was available throughout the country and most places were within a few miles of some petty, dame or parish school. This could range from a very good grounding in a country grammar school to little more than child-minding, but for most children destined for the sea it was probably very elementary, first reading and when this had been sufficiently mastered, writing and possibly basic arithmetic. The ability to sign a document is some indication of the result of such instruction and, in this respect, sailors were very much like other respectable working men.[11] Some two-thirds of ordinary foremastmen and over 90 per cent of men who held any type of office in a ship could sign their names. The English were among the most literate people in Europe and were becoming more so.

There was some difference in the literacy of common sailors born in different parts of the country. The Londoners came top, followed by the Scots and the sailors from the south-western counties, while the least literate were those born on the east coast but, overall, these results suggest that sailors were typical of the better-off working class. Some sailors no doubt came from very lowly homes but probably not very many, since at the lowest levels of society there was very little education and most men and nearly all women were totally illiterate.

The ability to read, write and calculate was not essential for a foremastman content to remain that way. It was, however, an increasing necessity for young sailors with any ambition, as is suggested by the high literacy figures for ships' officers. A boatswain, for instance, had to be able to check manifests, read bills of lading and 'give receipts for merchants' goods delivered aboard'.

Failure to do this satisfactorily led to the dismissal in Genoa of Robert Alwyn, boatswain of the *Elizabeth*, who 'wrote very indifferently, very slow, could not spell English'.[12] Ships' carpenters required calculating skills of a high order to do their work properly and they could nearly all read and write. Mates were increasingly required to keep logbooks whose sometimes tortured handwriting and spelling has both frustrated and fascinated this researcher. Navigation was crude, especially on small vessels, but certainly required numeracy, to calculate the ship's speed, the day's run and the latitude, blank pages in many logbooks being covered with the rough workings needed for these calculations.

Sailors were the greatest travellers of their day and many were linguists in addition to their other skills. Nicholas Lawrence was 'sent to sea at a very tender age as a cabin-boy and had no education [but], tho' he could never read a word in a book, he has been so much abroad as to be able to speak French, Spanish, Italian, Portuguese etc'. A foremastman on HMS *Newcastle* could 'understand Spanish and Italian and can speake as much of each as relates to buying and selling', while his shipmate Peter Breton could 'speake French and English and a little of Lingua Franca', the 'pidgin' of the Mediterranean. The Bicknell brothers who served on the privateer *Swallowe* were exceptional linguists who could both speak Latin, French, Dutch 'and a little broken Spanish and Portuguez'. Their captain, however, could only speak 'good West or Devonshire and this respondent was commonly his interpreter'.[13]

Specialist education in the skills necessary for officers in the merchant service was increasingly available in mathematical and 'writing' schools, often staffed by former ships' captains or by men with practical skills of a mathematical nature such as accountants. Most pupils were boys on the threshold of service at sea who would typically study for a few months or a year. William Dampier, for instance, was removed in 1673 'from the Latin [*ie* grammar] school to learn writing and arithmetick [and] soon after placed with a master of a ship at Weymouth', while Nathaniel Uring was sent to school in London for six months to be 'taught the first rudiments of navigation' before going on his first voyage. These schools taught mathematics, accounting and how to write in a good clear hand, as well as navigation, and they must have made an enormous difference in the general level of expertise in the merchant service.[14]

Schooling was important, but a sailor's real education began at sea, quite often but by no means always as an apprentice. The benefits of apprenticeship over other forms of entry into sea service were not overwhelming, as will be seen, and may well have accrued more to the master than to the apprentice. Some apprentices were hardly more than slave labour, since from 1705 masters could take on pauper apprentices who appeared 'to be fitly qualified both as to health and strength for that service'. This was cheap labour which could be selected or rejected at the master's whim, unpaid and bound for seven to nine years, and no doubt hundreds, probably thousands, of poor boys ended up at sea as a result of this legislation.[15]

Most apprentices were not paupers, but boys from different backgrounds were treated very differently. Some apprentices had fathers who had paid large premiums for their sons to be apprenticed as mariners. Such youngsters would expect rapid promotion once their terms had been completed and most would probably be masters or mates by their early or middle twenties. The normal run of apprentices had no such expectation and could hope for little more than a thorough grounding in seamanship. And such lads, whose fathers had paid modest premiums for their service, were themselves far more likely to receive reasonable instruction than the pauper apprentices who were treated as drudges fit only to do the worst duties of the ship.

Many apprenticeship indentures have survived and conditions varied considerably. Premiums demanded ranged from well over £100 for apprenticeship to a master of an East Indiaman, through £10 or £20 which was usual for apprentices to lesser masters in the eighteenth century, to nothing for those whose apprenticeship amounted to little more than several years of unpaid drudgery and little instruction except in such matters as how to haul on a rope or climb out to the yardarm.[16]

The actual training received might be very good if the master was a competent and conscientious instructor and the apprentice able and prepared to exert himself to get his rights or very bad if these conditions were not satisfied. The records of the Lord Mayor of London's Court include a few cases relating to youngsters dissatisfied with their apprenticeship to ships' officers which show the main causes of complaint. Some were the same as any other sailor's complaints, such as poor food or unfair punishments like the whippings administered to the apprentice Samuel White by the boatswain's mate 'who made him to cry and roare out in a very sadd manner'. More specifically, apprentices whose parents or friends had paid out large premiums thought they should live and mess with the officers and be treated as midshipmen and not be made to do menial duties, such 'slavish worke' being the lot only of those whose fathers had not paid much for their premium. And, finally, the apprentices in nearly all these cases complained that they had not received any or sufficient instruction. Captain John Ely of the *Coast Friggott*, for instance, not only 'did never teach or instruct [Gerrard Monger] in the art of navigation', but compounded his negligence by taking away for his own use the 'bookes and mapps touching navigation' given to the apprentice by his friends before he went to sea.[17]

The period of apprenticeship varied as much as the premium and the nature and quality of instruction received, from three to seven years with seven being marginally the commonest. Most masters promised some variation on the phrase 'to teach and instruct the art, science, mistery or trade of a marriner after the best manner he can', but few offered specifically to teach the 'art of navigation'. Most also promised what masters in land-based trades promised, to provide 'meat, drink, washing, lodging and apparel', though some masters crossed 'apparel' out and some included a promise to provide in addition 'due chastisement'. During the winter when many ships were laid up, some masters might get their apprentices to earn their keep ashore 'at tapstering or some other unseamanlike occupation'. Others simply washed their hands of their responsibility such as Robert Soares of Ipswich who promised to keep his apprentices 'in sicknesse as in health ... (except the winter seasons the time the shipp lye upp, then the said apprentice to find himselfe in sickness and in health and to be at his own hands till such time the ship goe to sea again)'.[18]

The work of an apprentice aboard ship earned wages from the owners, but these were actually paid to the apprentice's master. The apprentice himself got nothing except his keep, unless his indentures specified some annual payment for his service. These annual wages were quite common and were often on a sliding scale. George Atkinson of Gateshead, for instance, was to receive nothing for the first year, 20/- for the second, 30/- for the third 'and soe encreasing tenn shillings per annum till the end of the said terme [of seven years] which will be in all £13.10.0'.* Other apprentices got no wages, but received a present at the end of their term, two suits of clothes in the case of Charles Sadd of Ipswich, 'the one for Sabbath dayes and the other for working dayes'. And, at least according to their indentures, many apprentices received nothing at all for their service except their keep for a period of years and with luck some useful instruction.[19]

Overall, the sacrifice of wages and the uncertainty of instruction made apprenticeship to sea service a doubtful bargain in a trade open to entry in easier ways. Edward Barlow, who was apprenticed aged seventeen in 1659, makes the point in his usual forthright manner. 'If I had known then as much as I know since, and what it was to serve apprenticeship seven years at sea, I would have gone and learned as much in two or three voyages as a hired servant, as many do by the voyage or the year, and them that they go with giving them about £3 or £4 the year'.[20]

Most youngsters did in fact first go to sea 'as a hired servant' or as a 'boy'. The service of hired servants was similar to that of farm servants, hired by the year and maintained by their master either at home or at sea. 'Boys' were normally hired by the voyage and usually started by serving for no wages, as did Edward Witt of Weymouth who was aged fifteen when he gave evidence in 1692, by which time he had been working at sea for two and a half years. 'He has made ten or twelve voyages in the hoy (a coasting vessel) to the West Country but never . . . had any wages till this present voyage.'

---

* The old money, in pounds, shillings and pence, will be expressed either in words or in the form 17/6 for shillings and pence or £5.16.4 for pounds, shillings and pence. It is almost impossible to express these amounts in modern terms, so great have been the changes in relative values, but multiplying by 100 or 200 will give a very crude idea.

Once boys began to receive monthly wages these normally increased with each voyage, as in the case of William James of Poole who received nothing, 10/-, 12/-, 13/- and 14/- per month for successive voyages on a local coaster trading to London. Parents were often involved in the hiring of these youngsters. William Vineard was fourteen and lived with his mother in Stepney where he met Peter Bonneen, master of the *Betty*, who asked him 'whether he was willing to goe to sea and he answered yes. He . . . went with him to his mother's house and there hired him to goe to Ireland and agreed to allow him 13/- per month'. Boys were more vulnerable to dismissal and breaks in their training than apprentices or servants since they were only hired by the voyage, but even apprentices were sometimes not allowed to serve out their term. John Stocker, for instance, was apprentice to Thomas Chinnery, 'but displeasing his master the said Chinnery tore his indenture and turned him ashoare at New York'.[21]

Boys might be 'cabin boys' or 'common ship boys'. A cabin boy served the officers in the cabin and might have very menial employment, as did John Hollyday of the *Lucas* whose duties were described by the ship's surgeon. 'He was allwayes called Boy Hollyday and was employed by this deponent as a boy and about the buisnesse of a boy, in cleaneing the cabin, the knives, scrapeing of the trenchers, fetching of water and such like . . . a nimble, brisk boy.' Other boys were simply young sailors, learning on the job like 'Foster' who was the boy on the *Concord* of Poole. He was 'a very lusty boy of about fifteen or sixteen and tooke his trick or turne at helme and went aloft to help hand any sail according to his strength as well as any man'.[22]

Boys were presumably taught what to do by their shipmates and so gradually acquired sufficient competence to be described as 'a very pretty boy at his worke', as was William Stephens, the fourteen-year-old master's boy of the *Friends Adventure*, in 1691. Somehow or other boys certainly did learn to become competent sailors, with some assistance from a rope's end, and one can only hope that some of them were as well trained as the boys on Nantucket whalers in the late eighteenth century. 'At fourteen they are sent to sea, where in their leisure hours their companions teach them the art of navigation, which they have an opportunity of practising on the spot. They learn the great and useful art of working a ship in all the different situations which the sea and wind so often require; and surely there cannot be a better or more useful school of that kind in the world.'[23]

CHAPTER THREE

Conditions of Service

CHAPTER THREE

Conditions of Service

'I was hired at no certaine wages but
was to have what others had.'[1]

Hiring a crew and agreeing terms of service were normally fairly
straightforward, since both captains and sailors were well aware of
the current level of wages and the customs of the sea. Sailors might
apply in person aboard a ship or at the captain's home. Captains
could make the rounds of the alehouses and other places where
sailors lived, some so packed with men that they could supply the
crews of several ships as can be seen from listings of London's sailors
made in 1691. In most ports, there were also special places where
business connected with shipping was conducted, such as the
Exchange in London, and here captains could negotiate with
freighters or passengers as well as with potential members of their
crew, Jack Cremer, for instance, often went 'to 'Change to get a
berth'.[2]

There were also people called crimps who earned their living by
finding crews for ships, men like Robert Crispe of Shadwell who in
1704 described himself as 'a crimp provideinge mariners for masters
of ships . . . 'tis his business onely to bring the master and men
together. They make the agreement themselves'. In the nineteenth
century, crimps earned themselves a very bad reputation by getting
sailors heavily into debt and then forcing them to join a crew with
the threat of sending them to a debtors' prison. There is little evi-

dence of sailors being cheated by such people in our period though, and most sailors were free agents when they made their bargains with captains and not the debt-slaves of crimps.[3] Sailors were however likely to be in debt to other people ashore such as lodging-house keepers. These creditors kept a hold on their sailor debtors by making them take out a letter of attorney in their favour so that they had first claim on the sailors' wages, as did Anne Harrison of Stepney in 1705 in order to secure payment for what a sailor owed her for 'diet and lodging'. Some creditors went further and also insisted on a will made out in their favour. 'It is usual for people living in and about Shadwell who have money due to them from seafaring men', said Mary Ravenscroft in 1720, 'to procure them to make their wills in order to secure such debts'. These creditors, many of whom were women like these two examples, had considerable power over their sailor debtors which was sometimes abused. Interest rates could be very high, while some people made a business of forging sailors' wills and letters of attorney, a 'frequent practice' according to Daniel Defoe in 1728. 'When a ship or a fleet comes into harbour, they get a sight of the ship's musters and see who are dead, getting their names, and if possible a sight of their hand-writing, or the knowledge whether they were able to write or no.'[4]

In the late seventeenth century, the contract between sailor and captain was usually made verbally in the presence of witnesses and this was often a factor making for later disputes. From 1729 onwards, however, all ships had to have a document, known variously as the mariners' contract, portage bill or articles, which set out the wages and terms of service of every man in the crew who in turn signed or marked the contract to show that they agreed to the terms.[5] Few other men in the English labour force had such formal hiring practices and this change certainly made it much more difficult for captains and owners to cheat the sailors they hired.

Sailors were hired to serve on a specific voyage and believed that, if the voyage was changed for whatever reason, the contract was void and they could either negotiate for higher wages or leave the ship without forfeiting their wages as they would if they had deserted. Owners often denied the rights of sailors to negotiate in these cases, though it was felt that persuasion rather than dictation was the best policy, as can be seen from evidence given in 1659. 'When the master of a ship upon an opportunity of a good freight happens to alter his voyage, it is usuall for the master to perswade and invite his mariners thereunto but not to give them any rewards or more wages that they were first shipped at.' This is what the prudent master usually did, often sugaring the persuasion by agreeing to pay an advance on wages, as in the case of the *St John Baptist* whose captain was ordered in Lisbon to go to Newfoundland instead of the West Indies. This changed voyage was agreed 'upon att Lisbon by and between the master and the men . . . [and] all the company did there receive a months pay, they urging that Newfoundland was a cold countrey and that they should want cloathes'.[6]

For most sailors the pay they were to receive was of greater interest than the nature of the voyage. Payment took three main forms, by the share, by the voyage or by the month. Privateersmen usually got a share of prizes and this was often their only remuneration, the old contract of 'no purchase, no pay'. The other main group to receive payment in shares were fishermen. Those who worked in Newfoundland were paid monthly wages, but also 'it hath been a constant custom used beyond the memory of man to allow them one 5th or 6th part of the fish or every 5th or 6th fish they catch or the value thereof in money'.[7] When whaling revived after 1750, some members of crews received shares though most worked for monthly wages. In the mariners' contract of the *Britannia*, which set out in 1762 from Liverpool to 'Greenland or the Davis Straits for the whale fishery or other creatures in those seas', the captain, harpooners and a few others were to receive extra payment 'for each half gallon of neat oyl'.[8]

Payment by the voyage or the 'run' was the customary practice in coastal shipping and in other short-haul voyages, though sailors going to Norway were careful to ensure they got paid by the month if they sailed late in the season, lest they get frozen up and forced to spend the winter in Norway. It was also very common to hire sailors in the West Indies and the American colonies for the run back to England. Run wages were attractive for owners since they fixed an important element in costs, but they were a gamble for sailors as a witness from the Newcastle coal trade pointed out in 1692. He claimed to have made the round trip from London in as little as eighteen days and as long as nineteen weeks, though the average was about six weeks. However, since the typical rate for this voyage was roughly equal to six weeks at monthly pay, the sailors on colliers earned on average much the same as those in other trades.[9]

Sailors on every other route, including those who did the round trip to the American colonies, were normally paid monthly wages. These like everything else connected with the conditions of service of sailors were subject to various customs. Sailors bound from London in peacetime but not wartime, for instance, were paid 'river pay' at half their monthly pay rates until the ship had passed Gravesend when they entered into full pay, and other ports had similar customs. Delays could therefore be costly to the sailor whose ship lay idle in the river, while other ships on which he might have had a berth set out to sea.[10]

Sailors' pay was governed by the maxim that 'freight is the mother of wages', which meant in essence that no pay would be released until freight had been earned. River pay was an exception to this rule since it was paid before the ship had earned any freight. So was the custom of paying advances in certain trades. The most long established was the custom in East Indiamen that the sailors should receive in advance two months' wages which were paid to them ashore and were intended to help them settle their bills and provide support for their families. Each sailor was also expected to appoint an attorney, a wife or relation perhaps or very often a creditor, who would receive one month's wages for every six months served. Since a typical East India voyage lasted just under two years, the sailor and his attorney would receive between them five months' pay in advance and the balance when the return cargo had been delivered into the East India warehouses and 'freight shall be paid for the same'.[11]

Voyages on East Indiamen were exceptionally long and this is the main reason that such large advances were paid. The next longest voyage commonly engaged in by English seamen was the slave trade, the round trip from England to England via West

Africa and the plantations normally taking about a year. In the late seventeenth century, sailors on slavers were sometimes paid a month's wages in advance and in the eighteenth century this became standard practice. By the second half of the century, the advance had become two months' wages. Such generous treatment was not offered in any other Atlantic trade and suggests that the expansion of the slave trade had caused problems in securing sufficient sailors in what was well known to be a high-mortality trade.[12]

In most other trades sailors received nothing except their river pay until the ship had returned to England and unloaded. The main exception was in ships trading from port to port where the custom came into operation that sailors might discharge themselves if they so desired and should also be paid in the 'second delivery port'. This practice was commonest in the slave trade where the colonies to which the slaves were taken were regarded as a 'second delivery port' and in the Mediterranean where ships normally unloaded and loaded in several different ports, often starting with Cadiz, before eventually returning to England. Leghorn (Livorno), the entrepôt of the central Mediterranean, was the commonest 'second delivery port' and sailors were often paid there either part or all of the wages they had earned up to their arrival. Payment was made in local currency and one can sometimes detect captains trying to cheat the sailors on the exchange rate. The men of the *Happy Return*, for instance, who arrived in Leghorn in 1700 via Newfoundland and Cadiz, were offered wages but refused them because they were to be paid at five shillings to the dollar instead of the usual four shillings.[13]

Sailors rarely had rights to payment in the course of the voyage on other routes, though masters were usually prepared to lend money to their men or sell them on credit things such as clothes or liquor from the ship's stores. Indeed, this was an important part of a master's income since the loans earned him interest and the goods were sold at a considerable mark-up on their cost in England.

Rates of monthly pay varied according to age, rank and experience, but historians have calculated the wages of the typical foremastman throughout our period. These showed remarkable stability at around twenty-five shillings a month, except in wartime when they rose to fifty shillings a month or even more. When allowance is made for the value of the free food and 'lodging' that a sailor received aboard ship, these were good wages compared with those received by people of similar social origins working ashore. Sailors based in London earned much the same as tailors or weavers, once the free food is taken into consideration. Sailors from provincial ports, who received the same pay as their London shipmates, were relatively better off since wages for land-based jobs were much lower than in London. The trade of sailor was therefore an attractive economic proposition for a youngster growing up in Newcastle or Hull, one good reason why so many boys from these ports went to sea to make their living.[14]

Sailors may have been paid relatively well, but in order to earn these wages they had to incur major expenses fitting themselves out with suitable clothing and bedding at the beginning of voyages. Sailors normally bought these from specialist outfitters known as slop-shops and the inventory of one of these shops has survived, that of Joseph Haycock in London whose stock of clothes for sailors included jackets, breeches, shirts, stockings, gloves and caps, over a thousand items altogether.[15]

The clothes in Haycock's shop had the same generic names as those worn by other males, but sailors were as instantly recognizable by their dress as they were by their weather-beaten faces and rolling gait. Clothes made of ticking or canvas were unusual in other groups of society, but these materials were very common in sailors' clothes, a witness in 1667 saying that it was 'not usuall' for a man to sail to Sweden with 'under half a dozen canvis suites'. Cotton too was worn by sailors long before it was in common use generally as a clothing material, no doubt because it was relatively easy to wash. Many of the items were also very different in cut or appearance from those worn by men who did not use the seas. Jackets and breeches might be tarred for protection from the elements, shirts were often checked or striped, breeches loose and baggy and worn only to the knee rather like divided skirts, colourful neckcloths and handkerchiefs were knotted round a sailor's neck. Outerwear might be 'a whapping large watch-coat', a cloak or a military campaign coat around 1700,

a pea-jacket, dreadnought or fearnought later on, all of them thick
short coats of coarse woollen cloth for wear in inclement weather.
Headwear included the flat round cap called a Monmouth cap and
'mounteers', hunters' caps fitted with ear-flaps.[16]

Sailors were often fitted out with all this gear on credit and
details of this can sometimes be found in accounts attached to
probate inventories. These show how very expensive items were
when new which would later be valued at virtually nothing after
several months of wear and tear. John Hedley of the *Joseph and
Jacob* was fitted out at the expense of his brother Thomas in 1699.
His bedding, consisting of bed, rug, blankets, two pillows and two
pillow-cases cost £1.18.0. Clothing, such as shoes, shirts, caps,
woollen gloves, woollen and worsted stockings and a hat cost
£2.9.0 and this was by no means the complete cost of his outfit,
since it did not include such necessary items as jackets, breeches
and waistcoats. Sundries, such as books, razor, penknife, scissors,
thread, needles, paper, pens, ink and pewterware added another
£1.13.0 to Hedley's unpaid bill and finally, like most sailors, he took
to sea brandy and sugar to make punch, and cheese, pepper and
mustard to enhance his diet. Such outfitting costs were by no
means unusual and Edward Coxere was certainly not exaggerating
when he claimed that each voyage cost him £5 'for conveniences'.[17]

Debts incurred in fitting out would be paid later out of wages,
but the sailor's wages were very rarely the twenty-five shillings a
week he was meant to earn. All sailors paid sixpence a month to
Greenwich Hospital, an early form of contributory insurance
which was not very popular with merchant seamen since they
could only benefit if they later served in the Royal Navy.[18] The
Greenwich sixpences would be entered in ships' paybooks and
these often record other deductions such as purchases on credit
from the captain or purser of clothing, tobacco and, above all,
spirits. On top of this, many sailors had their wages reduced by
fines or charges for damages. The commonest fine was 'halfe a
dollar or 2/6 out of their wages for each and every day or night that
they lye ashoare without the leave or consent of their master' and
many paybooks record this fine, equal to about three days' pay for
each day's absence, being levied on some of the sailors.[19]

Anything which caught the eye of the captain or other officers might lead to deductions from a sailor's pay for damages, 'for a fowl chased over bord', 'for an hour glass he broke', 'to a new St. Georges ensign you wore out with sleeping in it' or, from a cooper's wages, 'six keggs you trim'd and all brandy lost'. Collective deductions were sometimes made for groups of sailors such as a whole watch, 'to seventh part two men slaves lost your watch', 'your proportion of the boat that was lost by carlisness'. Quite often the whole crew would be charged for damage to the cargo, even in cases where it was obvious that most of them were not to blame. Most sailors accepted deductions for damages clearly or even vaguely their fault, but got very angry when mulcted for those caused by storms, a leaking ship or poor packing ashore. Edward Barlow spoke for them all when he complained of these practices. 'They lay the fault on the poor seamen that sail the ships, and they must stand the damage . . . a thing the unreasonablest in England, and no other nation does the like.' Many cases relating to unfair deductions for damages were brought against captains and owners in the Admiralty Court and some were brought to a successful conclusion as Barlow noted with glee in the case of the *Queen Catherine* in 1663, 'only an angel [6/8] apiece that it cost us in law'.[20]

These, often petty, deductions were a constant source of grumbling and trouble on ships, though it should be noted that the great majority of sailors were only charged for their Greenwich sixpences and for things they had themselves requested, such as clothes and drink. Much more serious were the not infrequent cases when sailors did not get paid at all, most commonly when the ship was wrecked or captured. The law or custom was stated succinctly by a deponent in a Chancery case of 1700. 'It is the custom among merchants that the freight is the mother of wages amongst them, soe that this deponent conceives that when any shipp is sunke or lost before the same arrives at her unloaded port that in such case neither the master nor the marriners are intituled to any wages.' The rationale behind this harsh dictum was that all three parties, owners, freighters and crew should 'share in the common calamity'. It was held that 'if the mariners shall have their wages in these cases, they will not use their best endeavours nor hazard their lives to preserve the ship'. Sailors did not like this custom but had to accept it, while making sure that they did get paid what was actually due, such as wages earned outward-bound on a ship lost or captured on her way home.[21]

Loss of wages through capture or wreck was a calamity unique to sailors, but all workers commonly faced another problem, the reluctance or outright refusal of employers to pay what was due. In this respect, sailors had a great advantage over other workmen, who had to sue as individuals in the common law courts, for they had a court of their own. The High Court of Admiralty lost much of its jurisdiction in the seventeenth century,[22] but it retained a near monopoly right to try cases in which sailors sued for their wages. These suits had several interesting features. The mariners could 'join all in one suit', that is as a crew, so that the plaintiff often appears as one named sailor 'and company'. This meant that the rest of the sailors could go back to sea while the case was being heard. Indeed, even the named sailor often did not appear since crews could appoint a general attorney to act for all of them, 'two shillings in the pound out of what should be received' being a common commission. A second feature was that the action was usually *in rem*, that is 'against a thing' rather than a person or persons, in this case against the ship which stood as security for the payment of wages in a successful suit 'to the last plank'.[23] There were typically 100 or 200 of these cases brought by ships' crews against their captains or owners every year so they were not unusual. Many were settled out of court, but some went the whole way to a judgement that 'wages are due and ought to be payd', followed by appraisal and sale of the ship and payment of the men's wages out of the proceeds. In January 1752, for example, the Court ordered the inauspiciously named brig *Faithfull Bankrupt* to be sold at auction in order to pay the crew who had successfully sued for their wages. The brig was inventoried and valued and was eventually sold for £195, well below her appraisal value but sufficient to pay the men's wages.[24]

There were delaying tactics that owners could use and one often finds petitions by poor sailors against such unfair tricks.[25] However, the sailors were successful in the great majority of these cases and the existence of the High Court of Admiralty meant that they were far more likely to get their wages from intransigent owners in a reasonable time than were workers in other trades. They were also, as has been seen, paid wages which compared favourably with those current in occupations ashore, especially in the provincial ports where the great majority were born and bred. These were clear advantages of service at sea. On the other hand, sailors were faced with often arbitrary deductions at the master's whim and with the possibility of losing everything as a result of shipwreck or capture. The balance over the years would depend on the luck of the individual sailor, but good fortune was certainly not the lot of all as Barlow pointed out. 'Many times their ships are cast away and perhaps the men saved, and then they lose all they have, small and great; and many times they fall into enemies' hands, and then they lose all and suffer an imprisonment besides.'[26]

CHAPTER FOUR

Careers at Sea

Careers at Sea

'The principle articles required in a
common sailor to entitle him to full
wages are that he can steer, sound,
and manage the sails, by extending,
reefing and furling them as occasion
requires. When expert at these
exercises, his skill in all other matters
is taken for granted.'[1]

A career is perhaps not quite the word to describe the lives of
sailors, since they tended to progress from voyage to voyage with
little thought of a long-term future. For many, a career at sea was
in any case little more than a testing of the water, like the
humiliating experience of William Beck whose one and only
voyage was aboard the *Hopefull Indeavour* on a voyage to Sweden
in 1666. He only got as far as Newcastle before being dismissed
because he 'was so sick that he annoyed the whole ship's company'.
Other men overcame sea-sickness sufficiently to undergo a single
voyage in a privateer or an excursion as cook or steward on an East
Indiaman, an exciting adventure in the midst of a humdrum life
spent mostly ashore. Others combined occasional voyages to sea
with other occupations, such as working on the land or in the
inshore fishery, though 'seamen, even when short of work,
considered fishing demeaning'.[2] Even supposedly full-time sailors

passed much of their lives ashore in England, spending the money earned on the last voyage, seeking vainly for a ship, passing the winter season when many ships were laid up, 'refreshing' or 'recruiting' themselves after a long and arduous voyage.[3] Nevertheless, sooner or later, any real sailor would have to seek a ship again. In doing so, he would make choices, this ship or that ship, this voyage or that voyage, which enable some patterns of behaviour to be determined. Most sailors would also hope to make some progress up the hierarchy of the seafaring world.

The structure of a ship's crew favoured such progress, since the proportion of officers was quite high relative to the number of foremastmen and the foremastmen themselves were not all equal in terms of responsibility and pay.[4] The most basic crew structure was that of small coasters, which were normally sailed by just three people, master, man and boy, a simple hierarchy in which nobody was equal to anybody else. Most seagoing vessels and the larger coasters, such as colliers, had crews ranging from eight or nine to thirty or forty men. Small ships would have a master, mate, carpenter, cook, boy and four or five foremastmen of whom the less skilled would be described as 'ordinary', 'half seaman' or some similar epithet and the most experienced might be rated coxswain or quartermaster. Most ships with a crew of over ten would have a boatswain who acted as foreman over the crew and was responsible for the upkeep of the rigging. Roughly equal to boatswains were gunners, who were officers carried on most ships sailing west or south in the seventeenth century but less so as the seas became safer in later years. They were responsible for maintaining the guns and training sailors in their use, but this was not usually a full-time job so they also shared the boatswain's duties. Ships with crews of about fourteen or fifteen would normally have a second mate and those with crews of twenty-five or more a third mate. Vessels of this size would also be likely to carry mates for the carpenter, boatswain and gunner and a number of specialists who need not be sailors at all, such as one or more stewards, a sailmaker or cooper perhaps, a purser or a clerk for the captain. Most large ships also had a surgeon or doctor in the seventeenth century, but this became less common after 1700 when surgeons were increasingly replaced by a medical chest.

Most complex of all were the crews of East Indiamen. The *Havannah*, for instance, which set sail for China in 1771, had a crew of 106 men and boys of whom 56 were described in her pay book as 'seamen' with wages of 26 shillings a month. Below them were five servants. Just above them at 30 shillings a month were the fifth mate, a senior midshipman, five quartermasters, the ship's cook, two stewards and the mates of the cooper, gunner and boatswain. Higher still, at 40 shillings a month, were the fourth mate, the purser, the carpenter's mate and the sailmaker. And so one moves into the elite with wages of 50 shillings a month or more, the captain and the first three mates, the surgeon, boatswain, gunner, carpenter, caulker, cooper and the captain's personal cook.[5]

One important aspect of a career at sea was to move up these hierarchies, to become the man rather than the boy aboard a coasting hoy, to be rated foremastman proper instead of 'ordinary'. The ambitious would next want to be rated coxswain or quartermaster with a few shillings more a month or perhaps mate to the boatswain or gunner. And so at last would come the move from the forecastle to the cabins aft where the officers had their quarters. Offices such as boatswain, gunner or second mate were within the range of any competent sailor but further promotion was more difficult, since the most senior positions required more education and more influence than the generality of sailors possessed.

Chief mates had to be reasonably literate and sufficiently numerate to be competent at navigation, the sort of person who could take over command if the master should become seriously ill or die during the voyage. Captains needed the skills of a chief mate and many others, including man management and commercial ability. They also normally needed to have interest or business connections ashore, as did John Smart who 'is a master of a ship and . . . came to that imployment by freinds that knew him capable thereof'. Most also required access to the capital necessary for part-ownership of a ship. Edward Barlow had a great desire to be a master, seeing 'the way and the profit which they had, which none else in the ship had or could expect . . . and yet I knew a ship would cost a great deal of money, and I had very few friends or acquaintance which would stand my friends in helping me thereto'. Barlow was not alone in lacking 'friends' and money, so not many sailors could ever hope to become captains.[6]

What were the chances of at least some promotion? First of all, the great majority of 'boys' became 'men', usually in their late teens. The advance of boys up the pay scale from nothing to a progressively larger number of shillings per month has already been noted and sooner or later they would be deemed to be worth a man's wages. There was no formal procedure to this important step and it was usually simply agreed that a boy such as Edmond Thurkell, aged eighteen, was now fit for man's work since he 'was very able and strong of his age and . . . cou'd hand reef and steer and was extreamly usefull in the service of the ship'.[7]

There was considerable scope for advancement within the rank of foremastman, since the range of pay between the highest and lowest paid was often ten shillings and could be as much as twenty shillings a month. Such differentials reflect at the bottom the difference between 'ordinary' and 'able' seamen and, at the top, premiums paid to quartermasters or coxswains. Not many sailors remained 'ordinary' for ever so this second stage up the career ladder could normally be counted on, though obviously it would come earlier for the competent and nimble than for the clumsy and stupid such as Edmond Knapman of the *Temperance* whose incompetence on a voyage to Archangel so infuriated his officers.

> He was not an able seaman, or capable of takeing upon him the office of a foremast man or doeing his duty therein . . . He could not take his trick att the helme for he was often tryed, and knew not his compass, for being often asked how they winded he would answeare to a quite contrary pointe of the compass as the wind then blew . . . and in generall knew not the ropes or where to find the ropes he was bid to handle.[8]

There is not sufficient biographical information to measure exactly how many sailors were able to progress beyond the rank of foremastman and become officers in the course of their careers. Some depositions do however provide a brief outline of a sailor's career for several years before his appearance in court, so that one can observe, for instance, the progress of Humberston Clayton from when he was a master's servant at the age of fourteen through his promotion to foremastman and then at the age of twenty to 'quarteer', or quartermaster. Or, at a more exalted level, one can look at the six voyages made by Charles Newton to the East Indies, the first as an apprentice, the second as fourth mate, the third as third mate, the fourth as chief mate out and commander on the return voyage and the final two as commander.[9]

Such information shows that a sailor could become boatswain, mate or even master as young as nineteen, but that it was usually in the early twenties that promotion began for those in the fast stream, while for many it was not until their thirties that they were made boatswain or gunner. Captains are the only group for whom one can be more precise about the age of promotion since they were quite commonly asked how long they had been a master. The answers to such questions show that the great majority got their first command in their twenties and that over half were under twenty-five when they attained this peak of maritime ambition.[10]

Most sailors could not hope to become a master, but promotion to lower offices was a reasonable expectation if they remained in the sea service. Many men gave up the sea when still quite young, but those who hung around long enough were likely sooner or later to get at least some junior office in their ship. Sailors who hung around too long, however, might well be demoted again since one needed to be fit and strong enough to command respect to hold down such offices as boatswain or gunner. There were several elderly captains in the merchant service and quite a few elderly mates, but hardly any boatswains or gunners over the age of fifty. Many aged foremastmen had no doubt once been boatswains and some had been mates such as Peter Walker who when he gave evidence in 1668, aged 46, was serving as master's mate in the collier *George* of Newcastle. When called as a witness again in 1692, now aged 70, he was still maintaining 'himselfe and family by goeing to sea', still working on colliers but now only as a mariner.[11]

Promotion reflected competence and experience, but also loyalty since those who served in the same ship for several voyages were more likely to receive recognition than comparative strangers. Such loyalty cannot be measured in detail, since few records allow the crew of a ship to be analysed over several voyages, but it is possible to get some idea of continuity of service. Some muster rolls required captains to enter the last ship in which their men had served. A sample of these for Hull in the early 1770s shows that just over half of crews served at least two consecutive voyages in the same ship, the proportion being larger the smaller the crew.[12] Crew loyalty over a longer period can sometimes be discerned from ships' account books, such as that of the *Cadiz Merchant* which covers eight separate voyages between 1675 and 1683. This ship had a very varied experience during this period, two voyages within the North Sea, one to Cadiz, one to Lisbon via Norway, one to Smyrna and three to Jamaica and back. The ship was also idle for several months during some of the winters, so that crew loyalty was stretched by both the variety of the voyages and enforced unemployment. Analysis of the crew lists shows a mixture of high turnover and considerable continuity. In all, 189 crew places were filled for these eight voyages and 74 of these were taken by men who served only one voyage, while 33 men served more than once. All but six of the latter did so for consecutive voyages, two, three, four or five in a row before leaving the ship, providing continuity since at least a third of each crew had served on the preceding voyage and so could show the ropes to those unfamiliar with the ship. And, although experienced newcomers might be taken on for a voyage or two as mate or boatswain, there was also scope for promotion for those who served for a long time. Thomas Lee, for instance, who served all eight voyages, rose from foremastman to gunner's mate, while William Johnson, who missed only one voyage, was advanced first to boatswain's mate and then to boatswain.[13]

The snippets of biographical information in depositions suggest that such varied experience was typical. Some deponents stayed with the same ship or master for years on end. For instance, William Dye of Ipswich had sailed on the collier *Hopeful Seaventure* 'off and on for ten or eleaven years last past'. Other sailors shipped on a different vessel every time they went to sea. Sailors indeed were similar to servants in terms of their loyalty to particular masters or ships. Some, a minority, would stay with the same master for several years, men like Samuel Atkinson who said that 'where he likes the ship and the master he cares not where he goes'. Others might stay for two or three voyages but not much longer. And many changed ship every voyage, just as many footmen changed their master every few months, no doubt in the optimistic belief that the next ship or master would somehow be better or simply because they were the restless people that one expects sailors to be.[14]

Sailors were more likely to stay in the same trade for several years than in the same ship. This was especially true of masters, who gained very considerable advantages by serving continuously on the same routes. Familiarity would soon reduce the navigational dangers of a particular route, while constant trading to the same places enabled the master to gain a thorough knowledge of local customs and products and to build up a network of commercial contacts. So, although there were many masters desperate for a ship who would sail anywhere, the typical master was associated with a particular trade such as George Marlowes, a Yarmouth man who reckoned to have 'made more than a hundred voyages to Newcastle' and Thomas Collyer who 'hath used the voyage from this port of London to the Barbadoes for neare forty yeares'.[15]

Such consistency was reflected to a lesser extent in the careers of ordinary sailors, many of whom tended to spend much of their working lives in the same trade, such as Richard Murphy who had served in nine different slavers in the fourteen years before he gave evidence in 1683 and the black sailor Isaac George who had 'made eight or ten voyages between New England and London' before he was twenty-two. Such constancy often reflected the nature of the trade carried on from a sailor's home port, so that an east coast man might specialize in the coal trade and a west countryman in the Newfoundland fishery. But it might be simply the product of inertia and the ease of getting a berth in a trade in which one was known to the masters, though, occasionally, one can discover more pressing reasons for concentrating on a specific trade. Augustin Hanson was a Norwegian married to a London woman, so it is not too surprising to find that he specialized in the trade 'betweene London and Norway, being most of the winters in London and in the summers at sea and in Norway'.[16]

Contemporary observers believed there was some pattern to the choice of voyages by mariners over their life cycle, both young and old sailors tending to ship themselves in trades which would keep them away from home for comparatively short periods. It was a commonplace that the coastal trades, and especially the coal trade, were the 'nursery of seamen', while an observer in 1840 spelled out what he thought was the normal behaviour of more elderly sailors:

> It is the usual course of a mariner's life, that in his prime he is found sailing from ports mainly engaged in the foreign trade; as he advances in life he becomes less adventurous; and when he either settles with a family, or finds his strength decline, he fixes himself at some coasting port where the voyages are short, and he is more frequently at home.[17]

Careers at sea were not divorced from life ashore and one career decision to be made by sailors was if, who and when to marry. Sailors were mostly young and a majority at any one time probably bachelors, but marriage offered many practical benefits. Marriage and a home provided board and lodging, washing, making and mending and sex at much lower rates than demanded by professionals. A 'good wife' would also provide affection, bring up the sailor's children, work hard to support him and his family and prepare a haven to which he could in due course retire. Edward Barlow thought his marriage 'one of the best day's work as to my future happiness in this world, for I had met with a good wife ... And if I had sought all over England for one to make a wife, I could not have found one more agreeable and industrious; and it doth behove all seaman's wives to be the same, for no men under the sun run greater hazards and are under more incertainties than they do'.[18] Not all sailors were so happy with their wives, but overall mariners were not averse to marriage despite their wandering lives and in fact tended to marry at rather earlier ages than their shore-based contemporaries.[19]

One can then outline a 'typical' career for a sailor. He would first go to sea around the age of fourteen and would spend his first few years learning his business in the coasting trades. Then, in his late teens or early twenties, he would be likely to become more adventurous and seek to ship himself on longer voyages, to America, the East Indies or the Mediterranean. Richard Henry Dana noted that sailors acquired kudos from having made long voyages, 'an India or China voyage always is the thing', and in our period too a man might not be considered a 'real' sailor unless he had, like John Seagerts, 'been in all habitable maritime parts of the world'.[20] Such voyages might continue for the rest of a sailor's career but, as a man got older and had stronger ties with the shore as a result of marriage and children, he would be likely to revert to the short-haul and coasting trades of his youth. John Seagerts himself, who boasted of his knowledge of the maritime world, was sixty years old and serving as mate of a leaky collier when he made his deposition.

As a matter of fact there were not very many old sailors to make any sort of voyage.[21] This was partly because many sailors died young, as it could be a very dangerous and unhealthy occupation. The main reason, however, was early retirement. Sailors may have felt that they belonged to the sea, but most of them did so for only a comparatively short time. Most regarded service at sea as an occupation suited to a particular part of their life cycle and, if they survived, tended to move into other occupations in their thirties or forties, if not earlier. A sailor's work was hard and unremitting and it required levels of strength and fitness not commonly found in the middle-aged or elderly, despite such exceptions as the seventy-year-old John Marks of Shadwell who 'did not denye to doe any labour he was putt upon to doe and tho' old did doe as much as a young man would doe'. Most sailors were instead worn out by labour 'ten years before the rest of the laborious part of mankind', according to the naval physician Sir Gilbert Blane. 'A seaman, at the age of forty-five, if shown to a person not accustomed to be among them, would be taken by his looks to be fifty-five, or even on the borders of sixty.' To quote Barlow once again, 'he that is but a common seaman that goes to sea when he is past forty years of age, that man earns his living with more pain and sorrow than he that endures a hard imprisonment'.[22]

There was also much pain and sorrow for such men ashore, for it was not easy for a retired sailor to earn his living, especially a

common seaman with no savings and no skills save those needed to
sail a ship. These skills were however valuable in rigging and fitting
ships for other men to sail, work mainly done by active sailors
between ships or by retired men such as Robert Norman who after
a long career serving upon slave ships was helping to rig another
one when he gave evidence in 1696.[23] Former sailors could also use
some of their skills as shipkeepers or watchmen looking after ships
lying in the river. Others loaded and unloaded ships as porters or
lumpers, well-paid work but like work aboard ship too arduous for
those who were really elderly and decrepit.

The same was true of most other work available for men without
a trade, such as building work or general labouring. Fit men
between ships often did such work and so did many retired sailors,
but a building site was no place for the frail. There was also the
problem that such work was the resort not just of sailors or former
sailors but of any reasonably fit man out of a job, with the result
that it was poorly paid and often difficult to get. For the unfit or
elderly, alternatives were hard to find since there were few sedentary
occupations requiring no prior training though there were some,
such as tobacco-pipe making, the resort of Daniel Crosskeyes who
had to leave the seas in his early twenties, 'having lost one of his
leggs in service at Jamaica'. If all else failed, the former sailor would
have to look to charity, the parish or crime to keep himself alive.[24]

A sailor's career might therefore end in abject poverty and
misery, one reason why some men stayed on at sea into their sixties
and seventies despite the hardships and the taunts of their younger
shipmates. But other former sailors were more fortunate in their
search for work ashore. Many who were essentially landsmen
simply reverted to their original trade after a period of service at
sea, such as Thomas Parr, a Westminster poulterer whose sales of
chickens were no doubt enlivened by memories of his shipwreck in
Bengal while serving as cook's mate in an East Indiaman. The East
India Company also reserved some jobs ashore for former sailors,
such as John Hooper who retired in his early thirties after twelve
years' service and engaged as a pepper sifter in the Company's
warehouse. Other sailors started as apprentices to watermen,
alternating work on the Thames with service at sea until they

decided to settle down and spend the rest of their lives working on lighters or rowing passengers across the river. Ships' carpenters were also well placed to carry on their trade ashore, so it is no surprise to discover that after many years serving in slave ships Arthur Spalding was working 'at his trade in Sir Henry Johnson's yard at Blackwall' when he gave evidence aged fifty.[25]

Two groups of sailors stand out as being the most comfortable in retirement, those who had married a 'good wife', this often being the proximate cause of retirement, and those who had been able to make substantial savings from their lives at sea, which, as will be seen in the next chapter, was possible but difficult for common sailors and more than likely for officers. Such fortunate men might use their savings and their wives' experience and skills to establish some business catering for sailors, such as a slop-shop, an alehouse or lodging-house, such as George Roper, aged fifty-seven, who had 'used the seas for forty years . . . but now keeps a victualling house in Wapping which he hath done a year'. Others simply joined the common run of small businessmen serving the world at large as publicans, shopkeepers or whatever, like John Wilgoes, aged forty, who 'now keeps a brewhouse at Shadwell Dock'.[26] Best off of all were those former captains who used the savings, business knowledge and trading contacts acquired in a career at sea to become factors, merchants and shipowners, daily engaged in sending other men out to endure the dangers of the sea.

CHAPTER FIVE

Wealth and Possessions

CHAPTER FIVE

Wealth and Possessions

'Had I not been so thoughtless and negligent all my life I might have made a fortin and lived happy in my old age ... but I was always for a short life and a merry one.'[1]

Sailors are usually thought to be not only poor but also feckless people who would quickly blow what little money they had, such as 'Rambling Jack' Cremer quoted above, so a chapter on wealth and possessions might seem optimistic. And yet many sailors went to sea in pursuit of gain and some were very successful while a fairly large minority accumulated on a scale rarely equalled by people of similar origins ashore. Success was clearly more likely among those whose families could provide capital or 'interest' to accelerate promotion. It also depended on a rather unsailorlike collection of qualities such as sobriety, commercial instinct, willingness to save and, perhaps most of all, on good fortune.

Sailors were sometimes asked in court how much they were worth, 'their debts paid'. Such self-statements are unlikely to have been very accurate, but they do establish some parameters of sailor wealth. The majority of ordinary sailors said they were worth 'nothing', 'not much', 'little' or 'no more than their wages'. When a figure was given, this was typically £10 or less though a few admitted to a greater fortune including five who said they were worth

£100 or more, two of whom were over sixty and still active. The wealth of officers who gave a figure was from £10 to £300 with an average of just under £100 and a median of £50, levels of wealth roughly equivalent to those of a skilled artisan or middling shop-keeper in London.[2] This source suggests then that only a few common sailors were able to save anything out of their wages, but that the majority of officers, even quite lowly ones, could accumulate on a fairly regular basis.

More information can be obtained from the probate inventories of sailors backed where possible by their wills. The analysis here is based on the inventories of some 200 sailors. Many of these men died intestate, but the wills of about half the total sample have been found and these sometimes provide additional information. About a third of the wills were made, often verbally, on deathbeds at sea and these are the most valuable since they often list possessions which the dying sailor wanted distributed among his shipmates or carried home to loved ones ashore. Most of the other wills were made on the eve of departure on a voyage, many combining the will with a letter of administration in favour of either a wife or relative or a creditor such as a landlady or victualler.[3]

These sources rarely provide enough information to say exactly how much sailors were worth, but they do give a good idea of their assets and possessions. Most sailors were young men and a majority probably bachelors, so that not many had any assets ashore except perhaps a chest of clothes left with a relation or lodging-house keeper. When Aaron Houseman, for example, sailed for Jamaica, he left behind with a victualler some very fancy shoregoing clothes with silver buttons for his waistcoats, shirts and breeches and silver buckles for his breeches.[4] Such possessions ashore are unusual, how-ever, and the majority of common sailors had just two types of asset, their unpaid wages and the contents of their sea-chest.

Much the most important asset for most sailors was their arrears of wages, which sometimes included money due for more than one voyage, as in the case of James Ansley who was owed for service in the merchant ship *Canterbury* as well as three weeks' pay from HMS *Newcastle* 'in which ship he was cast away'.[5] The lump sum in unpaid wages due to sailors was obviously higher if they served on a ship engaged in a long voyage and it was often over £20 for those serving on East Indiamen. Few English workmen had assets worth more than £10 at any times in their lives so when a sailor stepped ashore with his wages after a long voyage, he was a wealthy man by the standards of the contemporary working class.

Unpaid wages might be the sailor's most valuable asset but they were of course unpaid and, as has been seen, might remain so for several months and occasionally for ever. His chest and clothes on the other hand were visible and present as well as being essential to his well-being and expensive to replace, a fact which deterred many a potential deserter since 'running' with one's chest though possible was difficult. The loss of these possessions in shipwreck or capture was a major disaster, as Barlow pointed out. 'The loss of a chest and clothes, though they be never so bad, are more to him than he can make good again in a twelvemonth time.'[6]

The complete contents of these seamen's chests are sometimes listed in inventories and other documents and these show that, although some sailors possessed very little of any value, most were well fitted out. Listings normally include adequate bedding such as hammocks, blankets, rugs, quilts, feather-beds, pillows and even sheets and pillow-slips. Most men had at least three complete out-fits of clothes, one probably 'best' for going ashore, like the 'cloth suite, shirt, shoes and stockings' left by Edward Smallbone to a messmate 'for looking after mee in my sicknesse'.[7] Typical clothes would include a cloak or other outerwear, jackets, breeches and trousers, waistcoats, shirts and drawers, cravats and neckcloths, stockings and shoes, woollen or leather gloves, handkerchiefs, hats and caps, flannel stomachers and perhaps a night-gown and night-cap. A surprising number of sailors wore a wig, all but one of four-teen mutineers whose descriptions in 1755 have survived, for instance, and these might have 'a paper of powder and a comb' to keep them in order. Finally, most sailors of any substance at all would have at least one gold ring and they often possessed a wide range of silver objects, such as Robert Ellis, cook on an East Indiaman who had 'a silver watch and chain and a cornelian set in silver, a silver snuff box, a silver tobacco box, a silver marrow spoon, a sett of plate buttons and a silver punch ladle'.[8]

Most sailors also had some tobacco or snuff, their own stock of drink, such as rum, arrack or brandy, and items to make their shipboard diet more palatable including sugar, cheese, bacon, pepper and mustard. Attention to their person and clothes required such items as soap and washballs, razors, penknives, scissors, thread and needles or a looking glass. Many also owned weapons such as swords, daggers, pistols or muskets. Leisure was occasionally reflected in games such as a 'set of tables' for backgammon, but more often in books, a bible or prayer book being commonest though 'reading bookes' can be found as well as seamanship manuals. And, finally, there was the chest itself. A provident and well-found sailor was thus very much self-equipped and it is no wonder that he should be very upset if some disaster of the sea resulted in the loss of his chest.

A good idea of the variety of sailors' possessions can be obtained from the following two extracts, one from the deathbed will of a foremastman who died in the East Indiaman *Amoy Merchant* in 1684, and the other an inventory from a court case of 1736.

THE WILL OF JOHN HUTCHINSON[9]

In the month of January the 19th day in the yeare of our Lord 1684 in the name of God Amen. I John Hutchinson being weake in body but firm in reason and memorie. Imprimis Item I give my soule to him from whence it came and before whome I hope it will appeare at the day of tryall. Item I give to John Gibson one bedd, two ruggs, two pillows, one blew wastcoate, one furr cap, two paire blew breeches; Item I give to William Sawyer one sad colloured coate, two wastcoates, one blew, the other coloured, one mounteer cap, one pillow; Item I give to Francis Norris one light coloured coate, one red wastcoate, one hat, all my thred and needles. Item I give to John Gibson one paire of bootes and that the rest of my things may bee equally divided amongst the three aforementioned excepting one campaign coate, one close bodyed coate, two paire breeches, one paire of drawers, two holland shirts, one paire white draw-ers, one paire new shoes English and one paire modderas [Madras?] all which I desire to be sold at mast. Item I give my chest to Christopher Hawson. Item I give to Francis Norris one paire woollen drawers white and red. Item I give to John Gibson my watch. Item I desire that John Gibson may carry home and give to my daughter my two paire silver buttons and to my sonn my Bible. Item I give all my tobacco to Christopher Hawson and John Gibson to be divided equally and that my gage [?] may bee sold at mast. This being my last will and testament as witnesse this my hand and seale.

INVENTORY OF THOMAS POWELL, FOREMASTMAN OF PEARL GALLEY, 1736[10]

Powell, a man of 21 from Bristol, was dismissed and put ashore in West Africa and 'had nothing upon him but a shirt, wastcoate, a cap, a hat, a pair of trousers, a pair of shoes and a pair of buckles'. He 'left on board the ship one gray coat, wastcoat and two pair of breeches, one pair of olave colour cloath breeches, one bed, blanket and pillow, two or three pillow cases, one Pee jacket, one thick flannel jacket, four shirts, some flanel wastcotes, two pair of flanel draws, four pair of stockings, two pair of woollen mittins, one pair of silver buttons, one gold ring, two new frocks, one half worn frock, one pair of thin canvass trowsers, one pair of blew and white striped cotton ditto, one pair of ticking breeches, one cotton cap, one woosted cap, one brown holland wastcote, a penknife, 4s 6d in money, one handkercher, one parrot, one calendar, two pair of compasses, two scales, one Atkinsons Epitome, one Card, a Book of Arithmetick, three pair of shoes, two razors, a pound of tobacco, a new Testament and one lock and key . . . all worth £10.

Many sailors and most officers had sources of income other than their wages. The most widespread was private trade, the sailor's own 'adventure' on the ship. This can be seen on a small scale in practically any trade. In 1660, for instance, Josias Burgis, a mariner on the ship *Commerce* loaded on his own account eight beaver hats in London and four and a half dozen of pickled oysters and about twenty pounds of tin in Falmouth which he sold in Genoa and Leghorn, reinvesting in oil, rice and anchovies to be sold in

England.[11] Such ventures might be small but they could be very profitable, trading arrack from Goa to Bombay at a profit of 'cent for cent', for instance, or selling raisins in London for 23/- a hundredweight which had cost just 11/- in Alicante.[12] Such enterprise was commonest in slave ships, East Indiamen, the tobacco trade and the trade in rum, this last trade being built into the contracts of mariners hired in the colonies, most of whom were paid so many pounds sterling for the run home and an equal number of gallons of rum. Many sailors who died in slave ships had a 'parcel of gold dust' or some 'elephants' teeth' listed in their inventories, as a result of bartering English goods in West Africa, while being paid half their wages after delivery of the slaves meant they were in a better position than most sailors to trade in the West Indies or the southern colonies of America. In 1719, for instance, a veteran of the slave trade to Virginia said that sailors were always paid there in the local currency 'and it is customary for the mariners to lay out their money in tobacco, whereby they generally make fifty or sixty per cent profitt'.[13]

Trading by common sailors was likely to be restricted by lack of money, a problem sometimes solved by bartering clothes for goods, especially when sailing from a cold to a warm climate. In 1691, for instance, John Bardon of the *Concord* sold some of his clothes in Newfoundland 'and therewith bought about three or four quintals of fish which he carryed to Avero [in Portugal] . . . and brought to England oranges and lemons'. Many sailors also traded with capital or a stock of goods provided by relatives or others in England, such as Isabella Pitt who in 1688 declared in court her interest in the estate of the sailor Robert Bundish. She had been his landlady in London and had

> . . . delivered to him . . . as a venture vizt. one silver hilted sworde and four other swords and a paire of pistolls and four hatts and a pillowe and a blanckett which he promised to carry with him to the East Indias and theire to dispose of them and to bring quilts for the use of her and her husband, [but] . . . neither shee nor her husband . . . ever received one penny in consideration of the above goods.[14]

The trade carried out by ordinary sailors was nearly always small scale and not very common, judging by probate inventories. Officers on the other hand nearly always engaged in private trade. Sometimes, this was just a small matter such as the 'small parcels' of currants lost by the mate and boatswain of the *Lady Frigott* when she was seized by a Genoese pirate or the 'dozen of bibles and some few things more' which Barlow traded from Holland to England and 'made some money of them'.[15] But often private trade was on a considerable scale and, assuming reasonable profits, must have provided an important part of an officer's income.

Masters of slave ships normally had the privilege of carrying freight-free two, three or more slaves, and mates and surgeons were usually allowed to carry at least one slave free. The effects of John Chapman, first mate of the *Daniel & Henery* of Exeter, who died in 1700, included '14 small elephants' teeth marked J.C. and one man and one girl slave branded J.C.'. Such privileges were condemned by some who claimed that the officers' slaves got special treatment and good food, were often trained on shipboard for a trade such as carpentry to enhance their value in the colonies and 'never die, since there are not ten masters in fifty who scruple to make good their own out of the cargo'.[16]

Similar privileges, often enabling an officer to invest several hundred pounds, were accorded in most other trades and it was rare for none of the sugar, tobacco, wine or whatever a ship was carrying not to include some belonging to the officers. Private trade by officers was however greatest in East Indiamen, whose privileges were very generous.[17] Inventory after inventory includes as outward private trade such items as woollen cloth and European clothing, watches and 'toys', wine, beer, tobacco and pieces of eight. Much of this was traded with Europeans resident in the east and returns were made in a wide variety of oriental goods, such low bulk but high value goods as silks and sashes, embroidered slippers, Indian prints, betel nuts and jars of mangoes, artificial flowers and diamonds, and also bulkier goods such as porcelain, lacquerware, tea, coffee, pepper and arrack. These goods were sometimes purchased by syndicates as can be seen from the will and inventory of Henry Lewis, surgeon of the *Resolution*, who bought 183 pounds of tea in partnership with three of his brother officers in 1686 and willed his share to his wife and eldest son, together with a 'tubb of China tea cupps'.[18]

Much of this trade was financed by loans or conducted in partnership with people ashore and many such business relationships appear in inventories, such as the £675 borrowed on bond from Governor Pitt of 'Pitt diamond' fame by Captain Dennis. Officers also often acted as commission agents for principals at home. John Waldo, surgeon of the *William and Mary*, for example, was consigned fourteen pieces of English broadcloth by two London merchants 'to be vended and invested in East India goods for their own particular interest and account'. The trading business of William Grantham, purser of the *Mary*, was more complex. He had his own private adventure worth £110 but also carried 3,720 pieces of eight [about £900] and £400 worth of assorted European goods for a syndicate of six Londoners, together with a variety of small adventures on behalf of seventeen other people, in gold, silver, 'tobacco and sweet powder', hats, 'three watches' and 'a box of toys'.[19]

Another source of income to ships' officers was provided by their servants and apprentices whose wages could mount up to sizeable sums, such as those of Rowland Jones, servant to Henry Lewis, surgeon of the *Resolution*, whose thirty months of unpaid wages at 18 shillings per month were listed as an asset in his master's inventory. But this was nothing compared with the money earned by the servants of another surgeon, William Hopkins, who died while serving on a hospital ship in 1692. He had five servants working under him on the same ship, all or part of whose wages accrued to his estate, a servant working for another surgeon on the same ship whose wages were split between the two masters and also an apprentice, Richard Gibson, who had been entered in HMS *Hampshire* as a surgeon's mate but 'was afterwards made chirurgeon of her'. Surgeon of a royal ship he may have been, but he was also an apprentice and Hopkins' widow was determined that 'whatever wages are due to the said Gibson shall be received by her'.[20]

Servants were not always a source of gain. They might run away and so not be due any wages, as did the two servants of William

Tice, boatswain of HMS *Reserve*, much to the chagrin of his widow, or, worse still, they might take advantage of their master's death to appropriate his goods as did Thomas Simkins, apprentice of Joseph Cole, trumpeter of the East Indiaman *Sampson*. Cole's widow declared that Simkins had 'possessed himselfe of and imbezelled' his master's clothes, bedding, private trade goods, bonds and notes 'due to her husband from persons on board the ship' and, not surprisingly, two trumpets.[21]

Sailors who were reasonably well off or married were also likely to have assets which had nothing to do with their ship. Ships' captains invested in the shares of other ships as well as being part-owner of their own. Officers with savings invested them not just in private trade or loans to shipmates but also in loans ashore, bills of exchange, 'tickets' representing the unpaid wages of other sailors or popular securities. For example, James Delgarno, mate of a slave ship, had South Sea Company stock worth £100 when he died in 1716.[22] Other sailors not only owned their own dwelling house in England but also possessed as a result of investment or inheritance other houses or real estate which provided them with a rental income. Such good fortune was not confined to officers. The three common sailors in the sample worth more than £100 were all well off because they owned houses or other property, rather than from their service at sea, the wealthiest being Charles Horsey whose main asset was a brewery in Weymouth run by his wife.[23]

The subject of houses brings us to the final set of sailors' assets, those contents of dwellings which are the main focus of other inventory studies. Only a minority of sailors had permanent dwellings ashore, but there are sufficient to get an idea of the range of homes occupied by the families of seafaring men. The homes of captains were naturally the best, substantial and well furnished with all the fashionable articles to be found in other middle-class houses of the period, such as clocks, chinaware, large numbers of pictures and books, silk and cotton bed hangings, looking glasses and tea tables, the contents of such houses often being worth £50 and sometimes much more.[24] Scattered among these possessions were objects proclaiming a connection with the sea, a few maps or a globe perhaps, 'two ships painted in frames', sea beds and sea chests, navigational instruments or a parrot in a gilded cage.[25]

The homes of common sailors were very different. There were only twelve of these in the sample and none had household goods worth £10, two or three pounds being typical. The families of most married foremastmen lived in one rented room, as did Elizabeth Westcoat whose husband died at sea in 1721. Her room in Shadwell was crammed with the paraphernalia of living, two beds, two tables, nine old chairs, a chest and clothes, cooking and eating equipment. And it was not devoid of decoration, since there were 'eleven small pictures', but most of these possessions were old and cheap and the whole lot was valued at just £1.5.6, one month's pay for a foremastman. The inventory also tells us how she earned her living, for she had 'a wheele and rises' and so was a silkwinder who prepared silk yarn for the Spitalfields weavers like so many other sailors' wives in east London.[26]

Overall, this probate material shows that it was difficult but not impossible for a common sailor to accumulate some savings from his wages and other earnings. The payment of several months' arrears of wages in a lump sum put him in a strong position compared to most workmen, though these large amounts of money were usually quickly dissipated in the repayment of debts, the expense of fitting out for the next voyage and the almost ritual shoregoing spree. Common sailors might of course be lucky or prudent, but one suspects that most of those able to enjoy some comfort in their lives owed this to the earning potential, prudence and good housekeeping of their wives. Most officers on the other hand were in a position to save money not only from their wages but also from their privileges in private trade and from such sundries as the wages earned for them by their servants. It is not possible to say exactly how much these men were worth but the impression one gets is that ships' carpenters, surgeons and mates could quite easily acquire the wealth and trappings of at least the lower middle classes, while a captain even in an unglamorous trade could expect to live very well indeed by the standards of the day.

CHAPTER SIX

Sailors at Work

CHAPTER SIX

Sailors at Work

'The discipline of the ship requires every man to be at work upon *something* when he is on deck, except at night and on Sundays. At all other times you will never see a man, on board a well-ordered vessel, standing idle on deck, sitting down, or leaning over the side. It is the officer's duty to keep every one at work, even if there is nothing to be done.'

Richard Henry Dana,
Two Years before the Mast[1]

Dana spent his two years before the mast in the 1830s, but the work done by sailors had changed little since the eighteenth century. Indeed, even by the late 1930s, work in sailing ships had changed remarkably little judging by Eric Newby's *The Last Grain Race*.[2] This work was hard and getting harder over time, as growing competition encouraged owners to employ smaller crews and strive for greater speed. It comprised a wide range of skills and a high degree of well-organized team work. It was often carried out under appalling weather conditions and it was never-ending. 'Duty' was the word used to describe a sailor's work and woe betide the man who neglected or 'denied his duty'.

There were no Danas or Newbys in our period to provide a detailed description of work at sea. Accounts of voyages and memoirs of life at sea take the work for granted and generally confine their attention to dramatic incidents, descriptions of the unusual and accounts of the exotic lands visited. Nor do depositions have much to say about work. The main source used has therefore been ships' logbooks.[3] These were usually kept by mates who were reasonably efficient in recording such routine matters as wind, weather, course and sail changes, but not so good at reporting how the 'people' had been employed. Lazy mates sometimes neglected to record such matters at all or confined themselves to reporting that the crew were 'variously employed' or engaged 'on the necessary duties of the ship'. There is, however, sufficient information in logbooks to enable one to get a good idea of the nature of the sailor's work.

This began on entry into the service of the ship, which might be on the eve of departure or several weeks earlier during the process of fitting out when the ship was little more than a bare hulk, topmasts and yards struck, sails unbent and stowed away and most of the rigging unrove.[4] Most ships had only a skeleton crew at this stage, such as the *Charming Sally* whose crew in the middle of the cold winter of 1775–76 comprised just the boatswain and the mate, whose logbook provides a nice vignette. The Thames was frozen from bank to bank, with people 'walking over the ice all day, a thoroughfare over the river', but the two men were snug on board, having got in 'coals for the ship's use' and sent a piece of beef ashore 'to be bak'd for dinner'.

Much of the labour employed during the early stages of a ship's preparation for the sea was hired on a daily basis, men such as carpenters, joiners, riggers, painters, caulkers and labourers. But gradually members of the actual crew would also come aboard, some old hands but also boys and landsmen to whom the chaos of a ship fitting out was a totally alien world. Ordered to do incomprehensible tasks in incomprehensible language, bullied and made the butt of age-old sailor jokes, they were usually miserable and often terrified, as no doubt 'the boy George' was when ordered by the mate of the *Charming Sally* to climb to the topmast with a bucket of tar and black the yards a hundred feet or so above the frozen Thames.[5]

Four main groups of tasks had to be undertaken before the ship was ready for sea, all requiring much hard work and skill and most of them difficult or impossible for a newcomer to undertake with any confidence. Nearly all ships required some major repairs after their previous voyage, a new mast or yards perhaps, holes in the hull to be mended, sometimes almost a complete rebuilding. And all ships required normal maintenance, a never-ending process through the life of a ship, as sides and bottom, decks and spars were scraped, caulked, tarred or painted, rigging overhauled, sails replaced, mended or cannibalized from other sails, and a hundred other necessary tasks undertaken. Then the ship had to be made ready for sea, yards and topmasts raised, rigging set up, sails bent, decks and hold cleared and the clutter stowed away, these activities being interrupted for such duties as 'clearing and cleaning the ship for the owners coming on board to dine'.[6]

Simultaneously, the sailors would be taking on board and stowing the food, fuel, water and stores necessary for the voyage. Barrel after barrel of salt pork and salt beef, biscuit and dried peas, would be taken on board and stowed away, sties, stalls and coops erected for live animals and fowls, water casks taken ashore, filled and hoisted in, candles, coal, firewood, beer, brooms and buckets, pots and pans and the myriad other things necessary for the independent floating world that was a ship would be hoisted in and carefully stowed.

Meanwhile, the main function of a merchant ship was of course to carry a cargo and most outward cargoes from England were composed of a heterogeneous assortment of goods which would have been trickling in throughout the process of fitting out. Bales of cloth and linen, boxes of herrings and shoes, pantiles and bricks, barrel staves and iron, furniture and carriages – these were the sort of things that English ships carried abroad, particularly to the West Indian and American colonies. Stowing any cargo required great physical exertion by the sailors and skill and forethought on the part of the mate and boatswain, as accessibility was weighed against the need to keep an even trim, while care was taken that the cargo would not shift once the ship inevitably began to pitch and roll. And some cargoes required special arrangements as did that of the *Swift*, which sailed from Newcastle to Maryland in 1773. This comprised inevitably coal, hard work but few problems for a Geordie crew, but also convicts and indentured servants for whom cabins and 'a necessary house' had to be constructed, while much of the crew's time was spent making bed sacks and filling them with straw.

Ships fitting out and loading normally gave their crews Sundays ashore but otherwise the work was continuous, a typical twelve-hour stint with breaks for meals with a crescendo in effort as sailing day approached. This would be heralded by such events as raising yards and topmasts, dismissal of the riggers, bending on of sails and the arrival of the last members of the crew. The *Swift* bent her mainsail on 24 November and next day 'got a pilot on board', but such signs of imminent departure did not mean an end of work as more barrels of beef and more casks of water were hoisted aboard, as further adjustments were made to the trim, and it was not in fact until 4 December that they weighed anchor and 'set sail out of Tinmouth Haven'.

Weighing anchor and getting under sail were major tasks requiring the attention of all hands, relaxation only being possible once the anchors were secured, all necessary sails set, yards braced correctly and the gear stowed away. Then, as evening approached, it was time to alter the organization of work to the time-old watch and watch system needed for the continuous work of sailing a ship at sea. Master and mate or the two mates if two were carried would divide the crew into the starboard and larboard watches, picking the men one by one according to their judgement of their qualities. 'Divided the ship's company and set the watch', noted the mate of the *Alexander* as she set sail from the Downs. Watches were four hours long, starting at eight in the evening through to four in the afternoon, when the two two-hour dog-watches ensured that the men worked different watches on alternate days. Those going on watch at 8pm would thus watch fourteen hours and those at midnight ten, though overall they would work longer since all hands were normally called at six in the morning to work all day with breaks for breakfast and dinner and, usually, some relaxation in the dog-watches. It was then an arduous timetable with not much time for sleep, the time below being itself subject to interruption if any emergency should demand that all hands be called on deck.

Work became harder over time as crew sizes fell so that, by the end of our period, the average crew on ships sailing overseas was only about eleven men, ranging from East Indiamen with ten times this average down to the eight, nine or ten men who sailed ships to the Baltic or the ports of western Europe. Such numbers include the captain who did not usually stand watch, being theoretically on duty all the time, and the carpenter and cook who were also not usually watch-keepers. So a watch on the average eleven-man ship would consist of just four men or, possibly, five if the carpenter and cook were enrolled in the watch system as they often were on small ships. At least one man would be at the helm, 'the work of the best man on board the ship', and another in the tops keeping lookout, leaving just two or three men to do everything else to keep the ship sailing on its course.

Some vessels, such as brigs and snows, had two masts and some such as the coasting hoys only one, but the typical merchant ship had three masts, each with two or three sails attached to horizontal yards (mainsail, topsail and often topgallant), a spritsail on the bowsprit, one or more jibs and a number of smaller sails such as staysails between the masts and studding or steering sails which extended the area of canvas on booms carried out beyond the yardarms. Any one of these sails might have to be bent (carried up and attached to the yards), raised or lowered, 'handed' (furled and made safe with gaskets), reefed or unreefed. Here, for instance, is the *Experiment* setting more sail as the weather improved on 16 April 1768. 'Out all reefs fore and main topsails, set the jibb and staysels, foretopmast stearing sail and lower ditto, spritsail and spritsail topsail.'

All this was done manually by sailors climbing the rigging and out along the yard where foot-ropes enabled them to stand and lean over to do their work, while the ship heeled and the masts heeled even further with the give of their hempen shrouds and

stays, the men hanging on 'by our eyelids up in the air . . . and
underneath us the raging of the sea, each wave ready to swallow the
ship and all up', as Barlow described some hazardous duty in a
storm off the coast of Genoa.[7] Work aloft might of course be done
in fine weather and daylight, but Sod's Law determined that it was
more likely to have to be done in driving rain and pitch darkness
as sail was rapidly reduced in the face of a storm. Logbooks are not
very graphic, normally providing just a brief record of fact in a
nautical shorthand, but sometimes they say enough to enable one
to imagine the scene as in this extract from the log of the schooner
Warren.

> Heavy thunder and lightning attended with heavy showers of
> rain . . . at 2 p.m. double reefe ye main top sail, at 11 p.m.
> handed ye main top sail and took two reefs in ye fore sail,
> fresh gales and a continual lightning to ye northward. At 2
> a.m. handed ye mainsail and gibb and layd to under a two reef
> foresail.[8]

Such work required agility, nimble fingers, a head for heights,
confidence in one's shipmates and the skill honed by experience
which enabled the sailor to find the right rope or the right eyehole
instinctively and quickly on the darkest of stormy nights. There
was plenty of work on deck as well, mainly of the heaving and
hauling variety as anchors were lowered or raised in coastal waters,
sails adjusted, ropes made fast, or the yards braced, that is pulled so
that they made a more acute angle to the mast. This was very heavy
work when men had to fight the wind in the sail without assistance
from winches. Such work may seem less dramatic than the
acrobatics high up on the yards, but it was potentially just as
dangerous in heavy weather as the sea poured in over the ship's side.
A slip from the yard could be fatal, but so could a slip on deck in a
heavy sea.

The number of changes to sails and adjustments to yards and
rigging required in any one watch varied enormously depending on
conditions. Often there were virtually none at all. In the *Charming
Sally*, for instance, bound for the West Indies, the men had little to
do to sail the ship once she had passed Madeira and picked up the

trade winds. Day after day, the logbook reads much as it did for 20 April 1776, 'wind NE these 24 hours, we have had a pleasant gale with a great swell from the northward, all sails sett'. Rather more work was needed to sail the *Alexander* crossing the north Atlantic in a convoy in 1761. On 29 May, a fairly typical day, there were the following sail changes: 'at 4 p.m. handed mainsail . . . 7 p.m. took a reef in each topsail . . . 9 p.m. handed foretopgallant sail . . . 10 p.m. handed maintopgallant sail . . . 2 a.m. set topgallant sails . . . 6 a.m. let the reefs out of the topsails and set all small sails'. All this work could be done by the men of one watch, except perhaps the heavy job of handing the mainsail, which may be why it was done at four in the afternoon when both watches would have been on deck. Crews did not thank masters and mates who called them out from their watch below without good cause.

What was good cause was a matter of opinion. Here is Edward Barlow having a good moan about the hard life of the poor sailor.

When we went to take our rest, we were not to lie still above four hours; and many times when it blew hard were not sure to lie one hour, yea, often we were called up before we had slept half an hour and forced to go up into the maintop or foretop to take in our topsails, half awake and half asleep, with one shoe on and the other off, not having time to put it on: always sleeping in our clothes for readiness; and in stormy weather when the ship rolled and tumbled as though some great millstone were rolling up one hill and down another, we had much ado to hold ourselves fast by the small ropes from falling by the board; and being gotten up into the tops, there we must haul and pull to make fast the sail, seeing nothing but air above us and water beneath us, and that so raging as though every wave would make a grave for us: and many times in nights so dark that we could not see one another, and blowing so hard that we could not hear one another speak, being close to one another.[9]

And so, through hard times and easy times, the ship sailed towards its destination 'by the Grace of God'. Navigation was primitive but usually effective, latitude determined when possible by a noon observation and longitude crudely calculated by dead reckoning, the ship's course plotted on a traverse board and her speed estimated by a regular heave of the log. Logbooks often record the miles covered in each day's run, but these were often wildly inaccurate given the crudeness of the estimating procedure, even in the absence of such behaviour as that of John Brown, mate of the *Glasgow*, who was 'very drunk . . . likewise deny'd his duty, could give noe account of the ship's way from 12 att noon till 8 att night and told me I might stick the logg board in my arse etc'.[10] When ships passed and 'spoke', they often asked each other what longitude they thought they were in, while fishing boats were quizzed on the same subject. The seas were not as busy in the eighteenth century as in later years, but they were already quite well populated, especially close to land, and such exchanges of information saved many a master from an embarrassing landfall.

Once a master thought he was near the land, he would reduce sail at night, put a good man to watch in the foretop and wait anxiously until he could find bottom with the long lead. Sailors had a very extensive collective knowledge of the appearance of islands, headlands and other aids to navigation, as well as a remarkable familiarity with the nature of the seabed in different parts of the world. 'Hove a cast of the led and struck soundings in 25 fathoms water . . . at 8 a.m. sawe the high land Sayaleon [Sierra Leone] eastward from us about 4 leagues'. 'Hove the line and struck the ground in about 70 fathom, fine white sand with black and brown specks . . . at 4 a.m. saw the island Scilly bearing NE about 3 or 4 leagues.'

Sailing the ship might seem to be the main task of a sailor at sea, but it was by no means the only one nor indeed the most time-consuming of his duties. In rough weather or in coastal waters, there might be little time to do anything else but 'hand, reef and steer' and other immediate duties necessary to keep the ship safe and on her course. But such conditions did not last for ever and once the ship had run into settled weather there were days on end requiring few sail changes and a minimal effort to keep the ship moving in the right direction. Now was the time for officers to ensure that every man was continually 'at work upon something

... even if there is nothing to do', though there nearly always was plenty to do on a wooden sailing ship.

Running repairs were the main priority after sailing the ship. No voyage of any length ever took place without some damage, often serious, to the ship or its equipment. 'Man at the helm broach'd the vessell to, carried away the maintopgallant mast', 'veary hey running sea, the ship broached too and splatt the foersail and foer staysail and carred away all the quarter bords and disabled the capstan'.[12] Sails blew out or were torn to pieces, masts and yards cracked or were carried overboard, blocks and tackle broke or jammed. Such incidents normally occurred in heavy weather and they required instant, often heroic, action as men ran aloft to clear away the debris and restore the ship to a modicum of stability. But this was only the beginning of the task, for hours of patient labour would then be needed to repair the damage, lowering and repairing or replacing a broken yard, patching a sail or cutting down an old sail to make a new one. Most ships carried just one carpenter, with no mate, and few ships except East Indiamen carried a sailmaker so that the men before the mast had to acquire these skills in addition to those required to sail the vessel.

Trouble at sea did not always come from above deck, since few ships were like the *Tenerife Merchant*, 'a very tight and stanch shipp, as tight as a cupp or can could bee', or the *Alexander* whose logbook reported her making only fifteen inches of water in three months. Most ships instead leaked on a more or less permanent basis, making pumping a regular and arduous task for the sailor. The *Ankerwyke*, for example, never made less than two inches of water an hour during her voyage to Bengal and back in 1775–76. Sometimes matters suddenly got worse with water rising rapidly, involving enormous difficulties in locating the damage in a packed ship. This might lead to a relieved entry in the logbook – 'leaking ... found holes and stopt them' – though matters were not always so happily resolved. The *Briton* had been leaking for months but, on her return from Jamaica, was found to be 'making water more than usual'. The leak was located but proved impossible to repair, so her crew were condemned to having 'one pump going every quarter of an hour' for the whole of her voyage back across the Atlantic.[13]

Disasters nearly always occurred on a voyage, but there were often weeks between them and this was the time for the normal, endless maintenance that was the main occupation of the sailor. Most days in the logbook of the *Alexander* start with the entry – '5 [or 6] in the morning up all hands and wash'd decks fore and aft' – and, although no other ship studied was kept quite so clean, this time-old occupation of sailors was the commonest way to start the day, often being the only work done on Sundays apart from sailing the ship. Jack Cremer recalled the boatswain's cry, calling all hands. 'Hoy! Wash decks. Pump, men! Buckets, scrubbers, and brooms.'[14] Sailors liked a clean ship and they also liked a dry one, so frequent attention was paid to the perennial problem of damp, drying sails and cables, bringing up bedding and bread to air in good weather, opening the hatches 'as usual to give air down', while the sailors took any opportunity to dry their own clothes.

Meanwhile, the job of maintenance went on, it being possible to do at sea nearly every task done in port. Rigging, blocks and cables were overhauled on a regular basis – 'hauling up anchor cables, cutting bad ends off and splicing the best ends together'. Sails were replaced, repaired or improved – 'unbent main topsail and bent new one, unbent staysail to repair', 'got the main foretopsail upon deck and began deepening him with an additional reef'. Every piece of accessible timber received attention, repairing, replacing, scraping, caulking, tarring, greasing and painting – 'blacking the mast heads', 'scraping the masts and greasing', 'got scrapers and screaped the ships bottom as far as we could reach and payd her sides with tar'. Attention was also paid to the trim of the ship, repacking and restowing cargo, replacing stores and water as they were consumed with casks of saltwater ballast, putting the guns down in the hold to 'stiffen the ship', adjusting the rake of the masts, trimming 'the salt in forehold more forward. N.B. since we trimmed the vessell more on an even keel comes up with and passes ships that got a head of us yesterday'. 'Commanded all my men into the greate cabben to bring her more by the sterne and in a small tyme I found her to gaine upon some of our fleet.'[15] Most tasks might be done at any stage in a voyage but some reflect the temperature, such as 'making awnings' as the ship approached the tropics, and some indicate a ship was nearing soundings, such as a sudden attention to the overhauling of the boats which had a vital part to play when the ship was in her delivery port.

When they could think of nothing else for the men to do or the weather was too poor for outside work, mates and boatswains had a range of time-consuming but comparatively gentle tasks for the sailors, many designed to produce the raw materials for other tasks or simply to use the free labour on board to make what could have been purchased for a few pence when fitting out. 'Drawing and knotting yarns', 'spinning spun yarn', 'making points and gaskets', 'making matts', 'picking oakham' (for caulking); when jobs such as these are the people's employment, one knows that life for once was fairly easy for the sailor.

All these tasks and many more were done by sailors on any long voyage, but there were some that were specific to particular trades. The crew of a slave ship approaching Africa, for instance, would be busy assisting the carpenter in preparing the slave rooms, making bulkheads and gratings, raising a platform to divide the slave quarters in two horizontally.[16] Preparations were also made against the dangers of attack, both from the slaves and from the free Africans ashore who had a disconcerting habit of 'cutting off' weakly defended slave ships, murdering the crew, looting the cargo and often carrying the slaves off to sell once again to another ship. The gunner would get the guns up out of the hold, mount them and check their effectiveness, while the small arms would be overhauled. The carpenter would make the roundhouse into a potential stronghold and build a 'barracada' behind which the crew could mass to cope with the common enough event of a slave uprising.

Once there were slaves on board, the crew had to engage in very unsailorlike work designed to guard the slaves and anticipate attempts at 'rebellion' and to keep as many alive as possible and so ensure a profitable voyage. So, on top of normal work, sailors acted as sentries and made frequent searches of the slave rooms – 'secured the after bulkhead of the men's room, for they had started almost every stantion', 'surprised two of them attempting to get off their irons, and upon further search in their rooms, upon information of three of the [slave] boys, found some knives, stones, shot etc. and a cold chisel'.

Cleanliness, food and exercise were seen to be the key factors in keeping slaves alive – 'serv'd the slaves with corn and beans at noon', 'the people buzy washing and danceing the slaves', 'scraping the slave rooms, smoking with tar, tobacco and brimstone for two hours, afterwards washed with vinegar'. Air and exercise on deck, washing and cleaning of rooms did something to reduce mortality, but only rarely were slavers' logbooks not punctuated with such entries as 'bury'd a boy slave No.25', that is the 25th to die. The final duties of the crew consisted in preparing the slaves for the critical eye of the planters and slave merchants in the delivery port – 'washed them all with fresh water', 'began yesterday to shave them all and this morning finished', 'imployed with taking care of the skin of the slaves', this last task involving covering up sores and ulcers and rubbing oil into the slaves' skins to improve their appearance.

Most ships spent much of their voyage, often several months, waiting in delivery ports for the return cargo to be assembled and loaded. This, of course, was not a period of rest and that normal maintenance which absorbed so much time at sea continued. The crew of the *Trecothick*, for instance, had little time to lean over the side and look at the view while they waited for a cargo of sugar at Jamaica. 'At sun rise had the decks and ships sides washed, employed two hands overhauling the rigging, two blacking the yards, mastheads, heels of the jibboom and bowsprit, others overhauling and scraping blocks, carpenter caulking the longboat.'[17] On top of such routine work, the opportunity was usually taken to do repairs or maintenance that could not be done at sea. Nearly every ship careened overseas, often several times, in order to scrape, caulk and tar or paint those parts of her hull normally under water, this often being the first job done on arrival. 'Came to an anchor in Nantucket road . . . this day in the afternoon creen'd ship and scrubb'd both sides.' Many ports had special careening places where a ship could be hauled down. Elsewhere, one made one's own arrangements as did the brig *Hooper* while loading tobacco in James River, Virginia – 'run the vessell on shore and cleaned one side . . . got under way and run down on shore and cleaned the other side'.[18]

Advantage was often taken of the abundant timber in America to survey masts and yards and to replace those in poor condition. Several weeks of the *Swift*'s stay in Maryland were dominated by the enormous task of replacing the mainmast. 'Unbent the sails, got down maintopmast rigging, maintop, mast and yards, got maintopmast and main boom up for shears in order to lift the main mast', an operation fraught with danger lest the mast should slip and plunge through the ship's bottom. Later we find the captain going 'over to the eastern shore to look for a main mast'. A suitable spar was chosen, towed up river to a wharf 'to work it', a new maintop being constructed at the same time. And then at last they were 'finishing the maintop and fitting him on the mast, heel'd the mast and tow'd him to the ship, took him in and stepped him', no doubt to great relief all round. Meanwhile, the old mast was not wasted (owners, please note). The bottom was converted into a bowsprit and the upper part split into stanchions for the hold.[19]

Repairs and maintenance did not of course interfere with unloading and loading and most of the crew of the *Swift* were in fact delivering coal during the drama of making and stepping her new mainmast. Unloading cargo was laborious work, bagging up goods loaded loose, such as salt or grain, shovelling coal into suitable containers, hoisting up barrels and bales, swinging them ashore on to a wharf or into boats or rafts made from the ship's spare spars. An empty or near-empty hold then had to be made ready for the next cargo. Maize and beans in the place of coal required 'cleaning and washing the hold, made us two fires to dry it'. Other cargoes required the construction of extra bulkheads or stanchions and the preparation of dunnage to pack the cargo in tight. An empty hold also provided an opportunity to deal with the perennial problem of rats, as on the *Alexander* anchored at New York.

Got every thing in readiness to smoke the ship, smok'd the ship and kept the hatches etc. close for about an hour and a half . . . [and two weeks later] . . . got everything in readiness for smoking the ship having still a great number of ratts aboard . . . at noon open'd the hatches and found several ratts stiffled.[20]

When one cargo was unloaded, it was time to load another. Sometimes this was waiting conveniently in warehouses or on a wharf, as in the Norwegian timber trade where loading was normally completed in a few days,[21] but more often it had to be assembled patiently over a period of several weeks or months. Slave ships took longest of all to make up their human cargo, with the ship anchored off the treacherous African coast and sometimes half the crew away in the boats carrying trading cargoes up and down the coast in their search for slaves. This was dangerous work. Boats capsized in the surf, while ashore there was the danger of being 'cut off' or taken hostage as a pawn in the arguments that arose in a business as dishonestly conducted, by black and white alike, as it was morally reprehensible. As the slaves slowly came aboard, one or two at a time, it was not a nice decision as to how many sailors could be risked out in the boats while the numbers to guard increased – 'having now twelve men slaves on board, began this day with chains and sentrys'. Mistakes could be hazardous as on the *Blakeney* lying half slaved off Cape Mount. 'About nine o'clock our men slaves, having broke down three stantions in their bulk head, some part of 'em got upon deck and rose on us, was oblidg'd to fire amongst 'em, kill'd two men and wounded three men and one boy more, 1/2 past 12 the punt came back and employ'd securing the bulkhead, the doctor imploy'd taking out the balls from the slaves.'[22]

Loading tobacco was not very dangerous, but it took almost as long as loading slaves. The *Experiment*, for instance, arrived at Yorktown on 12 October 1768 but did not even begin to load until January. And when she did, it was a long drawn-out business as the ship's boats went to pick up loads at lonely creeks and the local river boats called 'flats' brought hogsheads down to the ship's side. She spent a total of 130 days in Virginia, twice as long as the voyage across the Atlantic, and this was not an unusual experience. Local custom also required sailors to roll the half-ton hogsheads of tobacco from inland barns to the nearest navigable water, perhaps a few miles in the sweltering sun, work 'unfit for men' which caused Virginia to be thought 'one of the worst countries in the universe for sailors'.[23]

Sailors often got assistance from the shore, both for loading and unloading and maintenance work, though naturally owners liked this kept to a minimum. The *Alexander* had thirty men to help unload ordnance stores in Halifax, Nova Scotia, while most ships sailing to the southern colonies or the West Indies employed either slaves or free blacks on skilled work such as carpentry as well as general labouring. Local labour was also employed by East Indiamen, as in the *Ankerwyke* – 'came down from Calcutta four black caulkers and two carpenters to assist in forwarding the ships work'. Loading some cargoes was very skilled work requiring specialist assistance from the shore. The *Favourite*, for instance, loading cotton in Alexandretta, hired a stevedore and eight Greeks to 'steve' the ship, to compress the cotton and pack it in tightly, probably using a screw press.

Week after week, the work went on, punctuated only by the comparative rest of Sundays when duties were usually confined to washing the ship or there was 'no dutty required'. Sunday was also the day when leave was given, if given at all, as in the *Alexander* at Halifax. '5 a.m. up all hands and washed the ship, half the ships company on liberty went ashore to church, all came aboard in the evening.' The crew of the *Thomas and Betsey* in the Adriatic port of Ancona were not so pious, judging by these extracts from four successive Sundays. '17 March . . . clear warm weather . . . most all the sailors drunk . . . 24 March . . . wind variable, two or three men drunk . . . 31 March . . . all the men drunk . . . 7 April . . . clear pleasant weather . . . nothing more remarkable but all the men sober and on board.'[24]

As the hold slowly filled up, it was time to think of setting sail again, taking the boats down to the 'watering place', sending men to the woods to cut and stack firewood, receiving on board bullocks and sheep, slaughtering them, salting and packing the pieces in barrels. Yards and topmasts were raised again, sails bent, the pilot welcomed on board and anchors raised as the ship sailed off on its return voyage, another month or two of the watch and watch system, sleep deprivation, damp and the other discomforts of an ocean passage. And, storms permitting, the work of the ship continued, masts scraped once more, sails repaired yet again. Dana claimed that a ship was 'in her finest order at the end of the voyage' as she sailed proudly into her home port and most ships' logs show their officers certainly trying to achieve this. Nearly every ship, for example, was fresh painted on the way home if the weather permitted. This started on East Indiamen once they were clear of St Helena, the painting being done under the supervision of the gunner. Other ships carried no painting specialist but got painted all the same. Running out of paint was no problem as in the *Swift* making her way home from Spain in the summer of 1774. 'Hoisted out the boat and went on board a Dutch ship and got some yellow paint . . . excessive hot off Gibraltar'.[25]

It was then with fresh paint and patched sails that most ships approached the soundings at the mouth of the English Channel, no doubt welcoming the cry of 'ground 50 fathoms' and later the order to 'put the anchors on the gunnell'. Nearly home, but for many sailors, being 'safe in Liverpool Dock . . . thanks be to God for it' was not the end of their work. Custom varied from port to port and from trade to trade, but crews were very often not discharged until they had unloaded the ship. Sugar and tobacco, for instance, was normally unloaded by the sailors in the Thames unless they could provide (and pay) a substitute to do their work for them. In Liverpool, it was the custom in all trades that the 'mariners should also discharge the said ship' before they themselves were discharged.[26]

Weeks spent unloading in sight of home and the delights of the shore were understandably unpopular and it is not surprising that the vagaries of custom made unloading a potent source of dispute. In 1770, for instance, the captain of the *Sally* refused to pay his crew after they refused to unload a cargo of potatoes on the grounds that it was not customary, 'there being persons appointed solely for that purpose'. If the captain had wanted the crew to unload, he should have made an agreement to that effect before sailing, in which case wages should have been higher 'owing to the very great labour and fatigue'. One can only sympathize with the crew of the *Sally*.[27] Unloading potatoes must have been a 'very great labour and fatigue', but so was every other aspect of the sailor's work.

CHAPTER SEVEN

Life Aboard Ship

Life Aboard Ship

'I lyke the sea and the sea lyfe and the
company at sea, as well as any that
ever I lyved withal. The place is good
and healthfull to a willing mynde
. . . And though there be stormes
endured at sea, yet the end is
honorable and sweete and pleasing
to any that taketh the course.'[1]

Work dominated the sailor's life, but he also had to sleep and eat
and occasionally he even had time to enjoy himself. Sleeping
arrangements varied from ship to ship but, in general, there was a
strict distinction between the forecastle where common sailors had
their quarters and the steerage and cabins aft where officers and
their servants lived in some comfort and more space than the rest
of the crew. Lindsay described a forecastle in a ship of the 1830s and
conditions were not much different in our period.[2] The space in
which fourteen men lived was between decks in the bows, 21 feet
in width at its widest but tapering to a point and 20 feet long
amidships but much less at the sides. The only way in was through
a hatch which had to be closed in bad weather, thus condemning
the men to an airless and often completely black living space since
naked lights below decks were usually prohibited. The height of the
forecastle in Lindsay's ship was five feet from deck to beam and five

feet nine inches between the beams, while in smaller ships the height between decks could be as low as four feet six. This certainly sounds very cramped, though men were on average shorter than they are today. In 1755, for example, a description of fourteen mutineers gives their heights. The tallest was five feet six, half were under five feet and the average was four feet nine. None the less, forecastles were cramped spaces in which the men slept in hammocks slung from the beams, just a few inches apart, and the floor space was closely packed with sea-chests. Here sailors ate, slept and relaxed in their hours off duty, in 'a foulsome and suffocating abode', often soaking wet themselves and made wetter by a pervading dampness permeating the sides of the ship and by water pouring down the imperfectly closed hatchway. The smells of unwashed men, bad food and illicit smoking mingled with those of the bilges below and it is small wonder that such an environment attracted such unwelcome fellow-passengers as rats and lice. 'I buried Francis Forrest', recalled the naval chaplain Henry Teonge, 'as 'tis said eaten to death with lice'.[3]

Sailors welcomed fine weather when they could eat and also sleep on deck, in the boats, even in the tops high up in the mast. In 1737, Richard Walker of the *Dove* deposed where members of the crew were sleeping on the hot night in Leghorn when the captain was murdered in his cabin. He himself was asleep 'on the quarter deck over the cabin', another sailor 'a sleep on the hatches' while the mate eventually hanged for the crime 'was lying in the main sail upon the quarter deck'. Sleeping on deck could be dangerous, especially in West Africa where exposure to the fever-ridden night airs was thought to be close to suicidal while, at sea, a sudden heel or turning over in sleep might bring a precipitate end to a sailor's life as it did to that of Samuel Ware, cook's boy of the *Rochester*, as he lay asleep on the awning off the coast of Muscat. But for most it was a pleasant change from the gloom, smells and mosquitoes of the forecastle.[4]

Sailors enjoyed food even more than sleep and the wise captain knew that 'nothing grates upon seamen more than pinching their bellies'.[5] Many captains were not wise in this respect and complaints about food, usually its quantity rather than quality, are common in court cases. Stinting food was an obvious precaution on a slow passage, a necessity accepted by sailors whose complaints were usually because rationing was overdone or unnecessary in a particular instance. Captains and owners also had an incentive to pinch bellies as food was a major cost in running a ship, but such meanness is not often mentioned in court cases.

Standard rations consisted of salt beef and pork in cask, 'bread' in the form of ship's biscuit, flour, oatmeal, dried peas, butter, suet, cheese and the dried salted cod called stockfish. Sometimes, sailors had meat every day as in the *Favourite* sailing to Malaga in 1776 whose unimaginative weekly menu is in her logbook. On Monday, Wednesday and Friday, they had 'pork and peas' and on the other days 'beef and pudding'.[6] More often ships had a couple of meatless or 'banian' days on which the main component of the midday meal would be pease pudding or stockfish. The Swiss traveller César de Saussure described a weekly menu on an English man-of-war in the mid-1720s.

Each sailor eats one pound of boiled salted beef three days in the week for dinner, together with a pudding made of flour and suet. On two other days he eats boiled salted pork with a pudding of dried peas, and on the remaining two days pea soup and salt fish or bargow, which is a nasty mixture of gruel as thick as mortar.

De Saussure, who ate the same food, thought the sailors were 'well fed' and was particularly fond of the ship's biscuits, which were 'as large as a plate, white, and so hard that those sailors who have no teeth, or bad ones, must crush them or soften them with water. I found them, however, very much to my taste, and they reminded me of nuts'.[7] Typical rations on merchantmen were similar, a pound or rather more of meat and a pound of biscuit per head per day.

On ships of any size, food was eaten in messes of three to five sailors, one of whom would collect the meals for his messmates. Cooking was elementary, the cook's job often being simply described as 'boiling the kettle' though it went a little further than this. The cook's stores of the 100-ton *Welcome* in 1676, for instance, consisted of stew pan, frying-pan, spit, pot, tongs, brass ladle and flesh fork, twelve pewter spoons and twelve trenchers which, though simple enough, suggest frying and roasting as well as boiling.[8] A few sailors' recipes have survived such as 'crackerhash', a sea pie consisting of alternate layers of salt beef, peas and powdered ship's biscuit baked and eaten hot at noon and cold for supper. Janet Schaw drooled over

> . . . lobscouse . . . one of the most savoury dishes I ever eat. It is composed of salt beef hung by a string over the side of the ship, till rendered tolerably fresh, then cut in nice little pieces, and with potatoes, onions and pepper, is stewed for some time, with the addition of a proportion of water. This is my favourite dish; but scratch-platter, chouder, stir-about, and some others have all their own merits.[9]

This basic diet was supplemented with fresh food in port, while ships on long voyages eventually exhausted the provisions loaded in England and purchased local foodstuffs in their stead. Victualling can be traced in ships' account-books, the simplest being on colliers. Food, mostly fresh, was purchased up and down the east coast, but there was little variety. Just under 90 per cent by value of the food bought for two colliers consisted of beef, beer and loaf bread or biscuit. The remainder was made up of fresh fish, pork, pease, butter and such treats as 'cabages and turnups' or a 'calph's head and pluck'. Victualling was similar on the *Providence* trading from Ipswich to Norway, though with longer times at sea she carried 'biskett' rather than loaf bread, salt rather than fresh fish and cheese, which was not bought for the two colliers.[10]

The men of the *Viner Frigott* trading to the Mediterranean in the late 1670s started off with a similar diet, but once at Leghorn things began to change. 'Beveridge' (*ie* watered-down) wine replaced beer, olive oil replaced butter and the captain was good enough to buy 132 pounds of raisins 'for puddings for our men'. In Alexandria, where a long time was spent taking in cargo, food was bought fresh week by week and consisted mainly of mutton, beef, rice, beans, fresh bread – 756 loaves a week for about 32 men – and some luxuries for officers and guests such as blackberries, cream, pigeons and sherbet. 'Rusk' and 'maccaroons' (macaroni) as well as biscuit were purchased for 'sea store' when the ship set off back to Leghorn, while oxen were slaughtered and salted. In 1701 the *Upton Galley* was in Bengal where weekly rations were rice, oil, ghee, 'gram' (chick-peas), fresh bread, arrack, beef and large numbers of hogs kept on board in bamboo sties and tended by 'pariars' (*ie* untouchables) hired for the purpose.[11]

Both these ships also bought vegetables and fruit and consumption of these by sailors was probably higher than usually imagined with beneficial effects on the scurvy rate. Fresh vegetables, such as 'greens', onions, carrots and potatoes, were regularly bought by ships setting out across the Atlantic, often at the last moment in such places as Falmouth, southern Ireland or Fair Isle whose boatmen brought out 'the best cabbages in the world' according to Janet Schaw.[12] Ships in the West Indies or America bought yams, sweet potatoes, squashes, citrus fruits and other local products for the voyage home, while East Indiamen also took every opportunity to freshen up their men's diet in places such as the Cape Verde Islands.

Full use was also made of what was freely available in the sea, the air and on the land. Every ship carried fishing tackle, such as lines, nets and 'fish-giggs' or harpoons, and logbooks often mention the success or otherwise of attempts to harvest from the seas. The *Arabia*, for example, sailing through the south Atlantic in 1702 was so successful that fresh fish replaced salt rations for five weeks, 'to the great refreshment of our men'. Albacore, boneto, tunny and shark provided a welcome change of diet as indeed did an albatross or booby; Banks recalled the booby who 'made us a visit and slept his last sleep in the stomachs of some of our men'. Much could be acquired ashore as well, monkeys on the Mosquito Coast, an acquired taste since 'they looked so like young children broiled', penguins, goats and above all turtles, those on Ascension being so big that 'one of them will serve forty or fifty men'.[13] Many travellers' accounts read like fabulous cookbooks. 'The tail part of a young shark parboiled and fried with onions is pretty good eating', while albatrosses should be skinned and soaked overnight, parboiled and then stewed with 'very little water and when sufficiently tender serve them up with savoury sauce'. Others raved about 'a dish of flamingo's tongues', the pigs of the Nicobar Islands, 'exceedingly fine and sumptuous, being fattened on cocoanuts' or 'true dolphin . . . the whitest meate I have eaten and excellently well tasted. I do preferr it much beyond a salmon'.[14]

This emphasis on plenty and variety should not conceal the fact that much ship's food was inevitably of poor quality, salt beef rotting and stinking in the cask, rancid butter, sour beer and biscuit reduced to a mixture of dust and weevils being quite common complaints. And contrary winds or a cautious or mean captain might soon lead to rationing, 'only three or four ounces of beef in 24 hours whereas one pound of beef is the usual and customary allowance' as a sailor on the *Anne and Mary* complained in 1754. In no voyage studied did the food actually run out, but it could be a near thing. In 1769, the *Briton* was forced by contrary currents to change her route from Jamaica to Georgia so that the voyage took ten weeks instead of the usual four or five. On 13 November, the captain reduced the bread ration from its normal seven to five pounds per man per week and two weeks later to three pounds. By 14 December they had 'no eatables on board but beef' and were reduced to two quarts of water per man per day. Next day they broached the last barrel of beef and the last puncheon of water, but deliverance was at hand. On 18 December, the crew were 'employed fishing, catcht about a 100 black fish and whittings' and the next day 'our people in great spirits after eating the fresh fish'. And soon afterwards they anchored at Sunbury, Georgia, where a boat's crew had preceded them to buy 'some corn beef and potatoes which was a very pleasant sight to all hands'.[15]

Shortage of water was more often a serious problem and rationing was common in ships sailing to the tropics. Some captains kept a guard on the water-butts for this purpose, though there were other methods as on the *Swift*'s slow passage from Newcastle to Maryland in 1754. The captain 'allowed them no water to drink except what they could suck from the cask through a gun barrel which was fixed in the bung hole'.[16] Anything less than four pints of water a day per man was a serious deprivation in hot weather, two pints being described by Barlow as 'but a small quantity to poor men that eat dry biscuit and salt beef boiled in sea water and in a hot climate'. One man's hardship could however be another's gain as on the *Rochester*, also down to a quart of water a head. 'Our being so suddenly putt to allowance of water was very hard to bear to those who had noe other liquors insomuch that one of the men sold his wastecoate (being much athirst) for a quart bottle of water', a bad bargain since next day they sighted Madagascar and 'came off short allowance'. Rain was the other deliverer of ships in such a situation. 'We saved three butts of [rain] water for the publick and I believe as much in private in small casks, a great benefitt to us all who now were so well stockt that we could boil a little rice for breakfast if we had it of our own.'[17]

These private stocks of rice show that sailors did not rely entirely on their captain for food. Many took food aboard when joining the ship, cheese being the commonest item, and extra rations could be purchased or acquired by barter during the voyage. Barlow recalls bartering tobacco for lobsters off the coast of Norway, while sailors habitually bartered their clothes for food as well as for wine and women in the Mediterranean. Slavers and East Indiamen regularly visited Santiago in the Cape Verde Islands whose whole economy was devoted to bartering with sailors. Dampier wrote:

> When any ships are here the country people bring down their commodities to sell to the sea-men and passengers, viz. bullocks, hogs, goats, fowls, eggs, plantains, and cocoa-nuts, which they give in exchange for shirts, drawers, handkerchiefs, hats, wastecoats, breeches, or in a manner for any sort of cloth, especially linnen for woollen is not much esteemed there.[18]

Foodstuffs, especially cheese and bacon, were also sold to sailors and debited against their wages by captains and pursers, as were many other things such as bedding, clothes, tobacco and drink, either as ordered – 'to 30 gallons of brandy at different times' – or, retrospectively – 'to 6 dozen beer you drank and was catched with it'.[19] Some sailors were almost completely outfitted from the ship's stores, such as William Cotter of the snow *Lawson* who in six months bought a quilt, a wig and twenty items of clothing for a total of £7. Others committed themselves up to the hilt to purchase food and drink, a sailor on one of Jack Cremer's ships taking 'up almost all his wages in liquor and bacon'. So much did sailors indebt themselves that in 1773 the East India Company ruled that no one was to 'be furnished by the master or officers with money, liquor or provisions beyond the value of one third of what the wages of such seamen should amount to at that time'.[20]

The captain or purser would also pay and charge to a man's wages the bills he had run up willingly or unwillingly ashore. Thus, it was standard form to charge a recovered deserter for the posse who captured him as well as the expenses in the prison where he was left to cool his heels. Such costs could be high as could surgeons' fees ashore or 'the diet and lodging and attendance when you lay sick ashore'. Other expenses ashore included unpaid bar bills, 'to what you oad at ye signe of ye Fidell', payments to washerwomen and such comparatively unusual items as the whip-round held in 1691 'amongst all the English seamen in Smirna for the redemption of some English slaves'.[21]

Washerwomen were not available aboard, though one captain had his clothes washed by a black sailor 'to whom he gave a bottle of brandy every week'. For the rest, 'he that cannot be his own laundress is no sailor', as Ned Ward wrote, and most sailors did indeed wash their own clothes (in sea water) and this and making and mending them was a major call on their moments of leisure. Sailors were skilled at needlework as Janet Schaw observed of the crew of the *Jamaica Packet* at work on a sail. 'I never saw any thing so neat and handy as our Johns. Every man appeared with his clew of thread, his sail needle and his thimble . . . With this he works as cleverly as any sempstress with her needle.'[22]

Janet Schaw is one of the few writers to describe the delights as well as the horrors of a voyage at sea. She was as frightened as anybody in the midst of a storm, but she gloried in the return of good weather and noted its effect on the crew. 'How soon are our sorrows forgot; the sailors that were lately damning the Elements and grudging their duty now wonder how any man can be such a Lubber as to stay at land; and I find myself a little in the same way of thinking.' Even during the storm, the sailors could be good-humoured. 'And when the wind would permit us to hear them, we were serenaded with true love-garlands, and histories of faithful sailors and kind-hearted lasses.' And then after weeks of bad weather came the easy passage before the trade winds. 'What a relief to our poor sailors who will now have nothing to do, but dance, sing and make love to the [emigrant] lasses.' And a couple of pages later, 'I really think our present situation is most delightful. We play at cards and backgammon on deck; the sailors dance horn pipes and jigs from morning to night'.[23]

Sailors are traditionally portrayed as behaving in this way in their moments of leisure, skylarking in the rigging, telling stories, singing and dancing during the dog-watches, though such light-hearted behaviour rarely emerges from the sources used here. The first one knows of a small band on the slaver *Hannibal*, for instance, comes in the aftermath of a savage battle with a privateer in which 'our harper had his scull fractur'd by a small shot' and 'our bag-piper's leg was cut off a little below the knee'. Storytelling and songs were also a feature of this otherwise rather grim voyage, as can be seen from the captain's condemnation of those who treated their crews 'with cruelty or reproachful words, such as lubber etc., whereas they are such a sort of people that if . . . permitted their little forecastle jests and songs with freedom, they will run thro' fire and water for their commander'. The quantity and quality of music would no doubt be enhanced by the presence of some talented individual in the crew. Captain John Lemon in the Bilbao trade, for instance, 'blowed a good trumpet – as he had two, one brass, one silver –, gave grand entertainment, sung a good song, and a good moderate Bachus, always good nautered drunk or sober', while one of Dampier's ships had a man who 'had formerly learnt to dance in the musick-houses about Wapping', which turned out to be a useful social accomplishment in the East Indies.[24]

Gambling like music is a pastime on which the sources are remarkably silent. And yet one feels certain that Mr Crampton, third mate of the *Rochester*, was not exceptional in his love of cards nor in neglecting his duty in the process. 'To goe off from the deck to game for a watch I esteem worse than sleeping', wrote the purser. 'In this fleet there are severall who have ruined their fortunes by gameing and some of those are in our ship with whose feathers our gameing mate has equipt himself very gayly.'[25]

There is more evidence for sailors reading aboard ship than for either gambling or music, mainly in the form of books being listed in the contents of sea-chests. Most were devotional works such as a bible, prayer book or such pious works as *The Whole Duty of Man* or else books connected with navigation or seamanship. Other interests are illustrated in the inventory of Thomas Loveday whose library aboard an East Indiaman in 1664 contained books on astrology, astronomy, mathematics and medicine. One's suspicions that such serious works were not the only books read by sailors are confirmed by evidence relating to the voyage of the *Anne Hagboat*. The cook deposed that the row between the surgeon and the mate began because 'the mate and gunner reading or repeating in a paper or book some obscene verses . . . the surgeon offerred to take the same from him, saying it was not fitt to be reade among a parcell of boys and the ship's company and wondered they were not ashamed to read it'.[26]

Accounts of voyages say little about the minutiae of life at sea, but they all tend to report events which broke the tedium of a voyage. Some of these were tragic or threatening, the death and burial of a shipmate, a storm or the approach of a corsair. But most were fairly trivial and simply helped to pass the time. The wonders of the sea and nature provided much diversion – waterspouts and flaming volcanoes, the peak of Tenerife, 'accounted the highest land in the world', a floating island off the mouth of the Congo River. Animals and birds were another source of interest or wonder, 'saw the first swallow this summer', the first penguin, the first albatross, a shark or 'some fish of the whale kind called Grampus's . . . these sights being novelty's to many of us and gave us satisfactory divertion'.[27]

Animals and birds aboard ship provided further entertainment. Ships coming from the tropics often carried a menagerie on board, tigers, antelopes and other curiosities as presents for people in England, large numbers of monkeys, the men of the *Rochester* buying thirty when in the Cape Verde Islands and, of course, parrots, these exotic birds being the prized possession of many a sailor. Thomas Marshall excused his desertion in St Kitts in 1738 by claiming he had only gone ashore to search for his parrot, while the British consul in Lisbon related in 1724 that some wreckage was known to be from a ship from Brazil because of the parrots and monkeys washed ashore.[28]

Less exotically, most ships carried live fowls and animals as part of their food supply and a seasick or, even better, drunk hog could be guaranteed to provide amusement. Many ships also had a dog and at least one cat, an essential weapon in the war against rats as Captain Newton appreciated on the coast of Africa when he found that rats had been eating his spare set of sails, but 'can not get a cat upon any terms, and these we brought from England have been dead some time'. Henry Fielding recalled 'a most tragical incident' when a kitten fell into the sea. 'Sails were instantly slackened, and all hands, as the phrase is, employed to recover the poor animal.' Once close, the boatswain stripped off and 'leapt boldly into the water, and to my great astonishment, in a few minutes returned to the ship, bearing the motionless animal in his mouth'. The kitten revived, 'to the great disappointment of some of the sailors, who asserted that the drowning of a cat was the very surest way of raising a favourable wind'.[29]

This story serves to show that, contrary to popular belief, some sailors could swim, a skill often demonstrated in escape from shipwrecks. Many also swam for pleasure, though one tends to hear of it when it led to disaster, as in Barlow's account of sharks so fierce that 'in some places men, as they have been swimming for recreation, have had their legs bitten off and also have been quite carried away and never seen more'. However, a dip overboard did not have to end in disaster. John Nicol once saw a cask floating in the sea, off Cape Horn no less, and 'two men went down into the water and swam for it . . . to our agreeable surprize, it was full of excellent port wine'.[30]

Exercising the guns provided another break from routine, as did firing salutes at every possible opportunity. Ships saluted ports and forts as they came to anchor, merchants and owners when they came aboard, local dignitaries, passing men-of-war, anniversaries such as coronation day or the 'birth of Our Saviour' and on a host of other occasions. 'Had on board several jenteelmen and women, saluted them with ten guns'; 'came on board the Prince of Joanna whom we saluted with seven guns, soon after came on board the King whom we also saluted'; 'at 1 p.m. fired nine guns as did all the English ships lying here [Canton] in honour of the birth day of the Emperor of China's mother entering into her 80th year'. Barlow's crew were disappointed at Bergen in Norway when they 'saluted the castle with seven guns, but they answered us but with one again, which we took unkindly'. However, they made up for it a few days later. 'Our master making a feast on board and inviting some of the merchants of the town on board, they had a very good dinner, and drinking several healths, they were very merry and drunk so long that they were almost fuddled, for we fired near a hundred guns that day.'[31]

Some occasions were nearly always celebrated aboard ship, such as Christmas Day which was remembered if possible with traditional food such as plum pudding and enormous quantities of drink. Joseph Banks recalled Christmas Day in 1768 when he was with Captain Cook in the *Endeavour* off South America. 'All good Christians that is to say all hands get abominably drunk so that at night there was scarce a sober man in the ship, wind thank God very moderate or the lord knows what would have become of us.'[32] However, the occasions remembered most regularly were crossings of the line or rather lines.

The ceremony was designed to provide the older or more travelled members of the crew with large amounts of drink and, hopefully, some sadistic pleasure, while at the same time lining the captain's pocket. To maximize the potential fun, the same procedure was adopted when entering the 'Streight's Mouth', that is the Strait of Gibraltar, as well as when crossing both the Tropic of Cancer and the Equator. All those passing these lines for the first time had to pay a fine, usually a bottle of brandy and a pound of sugar, or else be ducked three times from the yardarm. Most sailors paid up, to the profit of the captain who supplied the drink. In the ship's book of the slaver *Suffolk*, for instance, we find that sixteen of the crew paid 'to brandy and sugar cross ye equinoctial' at 2/6 per head and a further three lads on their first trip to sea paid twice for 'crossing ye tropic and ye equinoctial'. All these bottles were 'merrily drunk by all the rest that had been there before, an old custom amongst seamen'.[33]

Some sailors were hardy enough to choose the option of ducking and some had no choice, as Joseph Banks related. 'Many of the men however chose to be duckd rather than give up four days allowance of wine which was the price fixd upon, and as for the boys they are always duckd of course.' Banks compounded for himself, his servants and his dogs 'by giving the duckers a certain quantity of brandy' and then enjoyed the 'diversion of the day', as man after man was tied to a wooden harness and dropped from the yardarm into the sea. 'Diverting it certainly was to see the different faces that were made on this occasion, some grinning and exulting in their hardiness whilst others were almost suffocated and came up ready enough to have compounded after the first or second duck, had such proceeding been allowable.' 'This is such fine sport to the seamen', wrote Captain John Newton to his wife, 'that they would rather lose some of their forfeiture (which is usually paid in brandy) than that every body should escape the ducking. And in many vessels, they single out some poor helpless boy or landsman, to be half drowned for the diversion of his shipmates'.[34]

Such sadistic pleasures should remind us that not all sailors were the jolly dancing 'Johns' portrayed by Janet Schaw. For the most part they were a rough lot given to arguing and fighting and contemptuous of those weaker or less skilled than themselves. Boys were regularly bullied and older men belittled or abused by 'being called "old dog" and "old rogue" and "son of a whore", and suchlike terms'. Most ships had at least one man who was the butt of his shipmates, the incompetent perhaps, a foreigner or even a sick man especially if his symptoms were as unpleasant as those of John Caton who was 'so nauseous and offensive that the mariners turned him out of his berth . . . and when he appeared on deck which was seldom he was the derision and makegame of the crew'.[35]

Sailors also liked a bit of fun, which often took the form of cruel, sadistic and sometimes fatal jokes. When the captain and the surgeon of the slaver *Plumper* came aboard and found the third mate asleep on watch, the captain said, 'we will have a bit of fun by

and by and immediately called for a glass of rum and a candle and
. . . poured the rum on the head of the said Matthew Bailey and
immediately put the candle to his hair which kindled into a flame'.
Joseph Bagland of the *Rochester* was 'a man too apt to joke on
people in their illness and not used to pytty them'. When he
himself fell sick, his shipmates 'resolved to affright him and finding
him asleep . . . tyed his leggs fast together and fixed a great stone to
him his leggs'. When he woke they said, 'wee thought a little while
agoe you had been dead so wee tyed that great stone to your feet to
sink you and were just agoeing to throw you overboard and had
done it now if you had not cryed out'. According to the purser, the
shock of this practical joke was too much for Bagland who went
into a decline and was literally 'frightened to death'.[36]

Running like a refrain through this description of life aboard
ship is drink, huge quantities of it, which was at once the main
solace of sailors and their greatest curse. One can only agree with
Philip Dickenson that it was 'a common failing among mariners to
drink more than they ought and to be disguised with liquor when
they can get it'. They usually could get it, a 'drink-water voyage'
only lasting till the liquor stock could be replenished. Ships in
home and European waters supplied their men with beer and,
when this ran out, with wine in the Mediterranean, rum in West
Africa, the West Indies and America and arrack in the Indian
Ocean, a pint of spirits a head a day being the normal allowance
according to Barlow. Extra drink was also provided as reward for
hard or unpleasant tasks, 'drink to our crew heaveing out ballast',
'a barrel of wine for our men that workt hard', while Nathaniel
Uring recalled the virtues of alcohol in keeping the men pumping
when his ship was sinking off the Azores. 'We plied the people well
with wine and brandy which made them work very heartily, so that
the water increased but little upon us.'[37]

Most sailors also brought brandy aboard when they joined ship
and, as has been seen, could buy spirits on credit when at sea.
Indeed, so keen were some captains on their profits from this
source that they might victimize sailors who did not buy drink
from the ship. 'He who is the best customer for the Captain's arack
at this rack price shall have the best place in the Captain's favour,

but he shall keep that favour no longer than he continues to be a good customer.'[38] More drink was acquired in foreign ports, in Goa perhaps where in 1744 the sailors of the *Onslow* bartered their shirts and blankets for arrack, which 'is in very great plenty and more cheap than common Geneva', or in Spain where Barlow records sailors buying clothes on credit from the purser to sell at a loss ashore 'and this they will do many times for a cup of good drink'. And if all other sources should run out, some sailors were in the fortunate position of being able to drink the cargo, as did the men of the *America* returning home from Malaga in 1691. 'There was a hole made through the forecastle . . . and great quantityes of wine were drunck out thereby.'[39]

Sailors would drink anything, but much the most popular tipple was punch. The ingredients were sugar – a lump 'the size of your fist' – water, lime juice and brandy in home waters, rum in the colonies or best of all arrack, 'arrack punch much our friend' as Francis Rogers noted on his way home from Bombay. This was distilled from rice wine or ideally from 'toddy' or palm wine, as Dampier explained. 'None is so much esteemed for making punch as this sort, made of toddy, or the sap of the coco-nut tree . . . but it must have a dash of brandy to hearten it, because this arack is not strong enough to make good punch of it self.' The sailor's bowl of punch kept him happy and occasionally made him 'fudled', to use a favourite expression, but it also had a therapeutic side-effect. Regular consumption of lime juice in punch probably reduced the impact of scurvy, though not as much as if lemon juice had been used as it was in the Royal Navy's grog from the 1790s with very beneficial results.[40]

Drunkenness, as opposed to merely convivial drinking, was a major source of disharmony, leading to arguments, fights and occasionally homicide as well as being the single most important cause of indiscipline. A drunken sailor was far more likely than a sober one to refuse his duty, strike an officer or say what was better left unsaid. The worst time was when a ship arrived in port after a voyage, logbook after logbook presenting a picture of apparent harmony until the men return from their first run ashore.[41] Such drunkenness might last until the ship set sail again, as in the *Swift* heading for Bayonne after a binge in San Sebastian.

Light airs and clear, made all clear for seas, with the assistance
of two boats tow'd out of St Sebastians, mate excessive drunk,
Robert Taylor seaman drunk also and hauling in wrong
braces, oblig'd to order him below no sooner below than a
sleep. At 5 cook went out to bring in the jibb guy but being
much in liquor the spritsail yard top'd and he was near being
drowned. At 7 mate tumbled down after hatch way and cutt
his brow being much in liquor.[42]

Hangovers and hard work normally solved such problems after
a few days at sea, the normal ration of alcohol and occasional bowl
of punch not seriously incommoding the ship's passage. In some
ships, however, drunkenness was common at sea as well as in port
with obvious consequences for the ship's safety, to say nothing of
that of the men running aloft after imbibing too much punch. The
worst case found was in the *Rochester* whose crew almost invariably
got drunk on Saturday night, even when running through heavy
seas in the southern Indian Ocean, 'the poor men being drunk all
night continue still mad and unfitt for their buisness which though
of dangerous consequences in this place is yett very common'. The
captain seemed powerless to control his crew.

According to our old illawdable custom the men began to be
drunk yesterday [Saturday again] so that Mr Crampton the
mate on deck complained to the captain that the men were so
drunk that he had not men enough in his watch to brace the
yards, so the captain ordered that when the men of one watch
were too drunk to doe their buisness that all hands should be
called up, they continue still in their drunken pickle.

Such behaviour was clearly dangerous, but worst of all was a
drunken captain, which was not all that uncommon. Edward
Coxere recalled serving under one during a bad storm in the
English Channel. The captain was incapable of commanding the
ship, but 'a fortunate sea, as I may call it, hove him and the bottle
to leeward and broke it to pieces. So then for want of brandy our
master was kept sober, so that we had some help of him, for he was
able enough when sober'.[43]

There is not much evidence of other vices aboard ship, except swearing, which by all accounts was only too common. Sex or the lack of it caused few problems aboard except frustration, as illustrated in two 1770s logbooks of American brigs. One is dedicated to 'Hannah Masters the Beauty of the World Boston garl . . . the flower and glory of women and brighte as angles' and includes a poem about the writer's love for this young lady. The other, kept by a sex-mad mate from Newburyport, has the name 'Maria Boas of Bilbao' written at frequent intervals in the margins and contains a number of sketches of naked women and of sailors in various states of undress, including one of a man about to penetrate someone from behind, the gender of his partner being rather ambiguous.[44]

Some sailors, mainly captains, combated such frustration by taking their wives to sea with them, though this was not common. Captain John Crowther bound to Virginia in 1700 went so far as to buy a woman from an emigrant ship with whom he was in company. He 'did buy and take from aboard the said ship *Lyon* and did bring aboard the . . . *Preston* an English woman whose name was Isabella Smith and gave sugar, rum and lyme juice for her but to what value or whose goods the same were knows not'.[45] Most women on merchantmen were however passengers, either willingly or as slaves or convicts. Their presence was clearly a temptation to sex-starved men and sometimes led to trouble, since not all sailors were prepared to 'make love to the lasses' simply by dancing and singing to them like the 'honest Johns' on Janet Schaw's emigrant ship. Captain John Newton recorded his displeasure when 'William Cooney seduced a woman slave down into the room and lay with her brutelike in view of the whole quarter deck, for which I put him in irons'. At least some of his distaste can be put down to fear that Cooney's attentions might lower the slave's value. 'If anything happens to the woman I shall impute it to him, for she was big with child. Her number is 83.' It was not only slaves who were at risk, if one can believe the deposition of Elizabeth Hughes who travelled from New York to England in 1748 as the maidservant of Joseph Scott, owner of the *Tryton Snow*. When the captain tried to rape her, she 'called out to Mr Scott for help but to

no purpose, he saying it was the business of every body on board to
oblige the Captain'. She went on to claim that, later in the voyage,
the captain did succeed in raping her, his example being followed
by every other member of the crew. The sailors admitted that
'people lay with her' but, not surprisingly, claimed that 'she was
willing'.[46]

Elizabeth Hughes' evidence, though very detailed, sounds a bit
far-fetched and her case did not come to court. However, it would
be strange if women in her position did not attract the attention of
sailors. Nevertheless, most mariners seem to have been able to
manage without women without any great difficulty. Most voyages
were not all that long between ports, where there were always
plenty of women to satisfy their lust. In Leghorn, for example,
there were 'many kind-hearted courtesans and brothel-houses,
where many a man empties his pockets of moneys in keeping
company with them, and here are some English men and women
who live here which keep the trade going. . . There are such English
men and women in most places of any great trade'. In Calicut 'you
may have a black hore for a small matter, for as you walk up and
down they will ask you whether you have any mind to it or no'.
And if a sailor on an East Indiaman could not wait till Calicut there
was always the Cape Verde Islands where the women were 'very
loose in their behaviour and easily led away by the sailors'.[47]

The advent of gay liberation has attracted attention to
homosexuality in the all or nearly all male world of ships. Research
by naval historians has however shown that such relations, though
not unknown, were rare at sea.[48] Sodomy was disapproved of in
English culture and was a capital offence, while the crowded
conditions of shipboard life made it difficult to conceal
homosexual relations from other members of the crew. The
research for this book tends to confirm these findings, just three
references to sodomy having been discovered. Two of these relate to
ships in the service of the Dutch East India Company whose cruel
punishment for those caught in the act was a byword in a cruel age,
the partners being tied back to back and thrown alive into the sea.
This was duly reported, as was the fact that in both cases the older
man was said to be Italian, the effeminate stereotype of the

period.[49] The one case discovered in English records is interesting since it illustrates the reaction of the crew to such behaviour. The case concerns Robert Gregory, aged eighteen, who was sodomized in his sleep by Joseph Lewis, a foremastman on the *Portland* in 1754. Gregory complained to the carpenter and the mate and they informed the captain, who 'called the crew together to consult what to do with the said Joseph Lewis and they all agreed that he should be confined and he was therefore put under close confinement'. Lewis himself resorted to the commonest excuse of sailors in trouble. 'I never did it but once and then I was drunk and did not know what I did.'[50]

'But alas! falling into the seafaring life, which of all the lives is the most destitute of the fear of God, though His terrors are always before them.'[51] Robinson Crusoe's view of the religious convictions of sailors was a common one, but not all sailors were 'destitute of the fear of God'. Many, indeed most, listings of possessions include works of devotion such as bibles and prayer-books, though they may of course have been read only *in extremis*, as when the dying John Fraser asked a messmate 'to read over severall chapters in the Bible to him'. Most sailors' wills are as unhelpful in assessing their faith as those of landsmen of the same period. Many were totally secular in nature and those that do include a spiritual introduction tend to follow the usual formulae found in other wills, though they occasionally give some insight into belief. Charles Wood, surgeon of the *Rochester*, was 'penitent and sory from the bottome of my heart for my sinns past' and, unusually for a sailor, left £10 for 'the poor of the parish where I was borne'. Robert McCenny, in his deathbed will of 1713, demonstrated a certain pluralism in his belief when he committed his 'body and soul to the Gods above'.[52]

The crew of the collier *Conclusion* were questioned about their church attendance in a court case of 1677. William Kingmead, a Scotsman, was a presbyterian who had 'heard the common prayer about twenty times within this twelvemonth last, going most times to meetings and sometimes to common prayer'. Christopher Blackett was 'a son of the Church of England, and when he is att home hee frequents his parish church to heare divine service and sermons . . . and for that hee was most at sea he hath not heard the common prayer above twelve times within these twelve months'. There is no reason to suppose this crew unusual amongst sailors and their range of answers were much the same as those given by non-sailor witnesses asked similar questions in the church courts. Fewer sailors than landsmen had ever received the sacrament of 'the Lord's Supper' but this could be explained by their being so much at sea or, in the case of William Hersee, by his 'not thinking himselfe sufficiently qualifyed for the reception of so sacred a mistery'. Both groups seem to have gone to church or meeting fairly often when they could, though this was obviously harder for sailors, even those more often in port such as the crews of colliers.[53]

Even in their own element sailors were not quite as irreligious as landsmen claimed. Most masters respected the Sabbath if possible, judging by logbooks, 'being Sabath day our captain was not willing to saile', 'being Sunday we rested from our labours'. Persistent blasphemers were disapproved of, such as Captain Luke Grove who 'sometimes will prophane God's name' and was known as the 'God Damne me Captain' in the Caribbean. And there was certainly some formal religious observance, even though virtually no merchant ship carried a chaplain. The East India Company even went so far as to rate all their ships in the middle decades of the eighteenth century at 499 tons, since ships over that size, which most were, had to carry a chaplain. But this does not mean that there was no religion aboard East Indiamen. Most logbooks and journals of East Indiamen record prayers and the occasional sermon, though by no means on every Sunday.[54]

No other logbooks studied report religious services aboard, but silence does not mean that there were none. Edward Coxere, referring to the 1650s and 1660s, wrote that 'our manner at sea of devotion is before night all the seamen with the master to read a prayer and sing a psalm'. The slaver John Newton referred to his regular service for his crew only on the Sunday that he failed to hold it, 'for the first and, I hope, the last time of the voyage'. Henry Fielding recorded a Sunday off Cornwall during his voyage to Lisbon.

Nothing remarkable past this day, except the captain's devotion, who . . . summoned all hands to prayers, which were read by a common sailor upon deck, with more devout force and address than they are commonly read by a country curate, and received with more decency and attention by the sailors than are usually preserved in city congregations.

Religion aboard could also lead to strife, as shown by the case brought to court by the widow of John Rogers, carpenter of the *Delight* sailing to China in 1684. The captain 'became displeased with John Rogers because hee did not use to come to prayers, the captaine using the presbiterian way and John Rogers using to pray by the booke of Common Prayer'. Displeasure turned to grudge and ended with a savage beating at the capstan from which it was claimed Rogers died, crying out on his deathbed, 'You presbiterian rogue you have killed me'.[55]

Such scattered evidence suggests that religious observance was not unusual on merchant ships, though regular prayers may well have been commoner in the seventeenth than in the eighteenth century. Much no doubt rested on the piety or otherwise of the captain or on the presence aboard of a clergyman passenger or a man such as the purser John Pyke who conducted the services held on the *Rochester*. And when he did, he often faced competition from other forms of entertainment, as in this description of a Sunday at anchor in St Helena.

At 10 this morning I read prayers on board with those who were sober enough to come . . . Our people according to their accustomed way of getting drunk on a Saturday for a preparation to be madd on a Sunday have so enraged themselves that, at most not above three of the foremast men on board being sober, they are almost all gott together by the eares.[56]

Sailors were better known for superstitions than for religion and these can come as a surprise in the usually straightforward sources used for this book. In 1762, the logbook of the *Alexander* goes on for months and months prosaically recording the work of the ship and then, during severe weather on the way from New York to Barbados, suddenly reports 'a man and a horse near one another was seen near the ship by which we may be convinced of a great deal of mischief and loss happening this day'. In 1684, Edward Man of the *Neptune*, in an attempt to explain his incompetence in bringing the ship to Milford Haven instead of London, told the court he had been bewitched by the ship's cat and that it was 'the Divell had brought them thither'.[57]

Witchcraft could explain many things that happened at sea, such as calms or storms or contrary winds, and was often attributed to people with good reason to feel malevolence against the ship, such as the landladies of Bergen whose bills were not paid by some men on Barlow's ship got their revenge by causing it to run aground on the Goodwin Sands. Sailors were also troubled by premonitions of death, by hobgoblins, fairies and bullbaggers, the ghosts of dead shipmates, pursers transmigrated into albatrosses and such spectres of the deep as sea dragons or 'Pongo, a terrible monster, half tiger and half shark'.[58] But most sailors' superstitions relate to the behaviour of birds, fishes and marine animals or phenomena in the sea or sky which might help them to predict the weather – rings about the sun or moon, comets, shooting stars and St Elmo's fire, 'thousands of flamingoes' or 'porpoises in herds on both sides of the ship'.[59] Correct interpretation of such signs and portents might help the sailor counteract the perils of the sea which are considered in the next chapter.

CHAPTER EIGHT

The Perils of the Sea

The Peace of the Sea

The Perils of the Sea

'Bold were the Men who on the
  Ocean first
Spread their new Sails, when
  Shipwreck was the worst.
More danger now from Man alone
  we find
Than from the Rocks, the Billows,
  or the Wind.'[1]

Edmund Waller's lines pinpoint the most dramatic perils of the sea, shipwreck and capture, one or both of which most sailors were likely to experience in their careers. About one in every twenty or thirty ships was wrecked each year, while the chances of capture in wartime were greater and even in so-called peacetime no sailor could feel safe from predators until the 1730s, by which time a concerted effort by navies and governments had largely eliminated the long-standing problem of piracy.

Systematic registration of shipwrecks does not begin until the nineteenth century, but some idea of numbers and the pattern of shipwrecks can be obtained from the shipping newspaper *Lloyd's List*, which regularly reported marine casualties from the 1740s. The coverage of English shipwrecks is quite good but not complete. However, a very good idea of the likelihood of ships wrecking in our period can be obtained from specialist studies of, for instance, ships lost by the Dutch and English East India Companies and also from official Board of Trade figures for the early nineteenth century. A pattern emerges from this material so that, ignoring extremes, it can be said with some confidence that in our period between 3 and 5 per cent of any population of ships was likely to be wrecked every year.[2]

Just over a thousand wrecks or losses of ships were reported in *Lloyd's List* during 1770–75.[3] These reports are rarely very detailed, often giving just the name of ship and master, the place and a single word such as 'lost', but it is still possible in most cases to get some idea of the nature of the wreck from these terse descriptions. A total of 112 of the losses, slightly more than one in ten, occurred in the open sea, 63 of these being described as overset or foundered and lost at sea. There were also ten ships sunk after collisions, five sunk or abandoned as a result of being leaky, four abandoned following fires, six Greenland whalers 'lost in the ice' and one slaver blown up off the African coast, no doubt as a result of smoking or the careless use of naked lights below decks. Finally, there were twenty-three ships which simply vanished, such as the *Mary*, which sailed from Jamaica on 26 July 1769 for Dublin and was reported nine months later as 'never heard of'.[4] One can only speculate that these too foundered or were 'overset in a violent gale' or possibly were consumed by fire, that most terrifying of all experiences at sea in a wooden ship. Most ships, however, were lost as a result of hitting reefs, rocks or the coast so that the great majority were lost close to land or actually on the coast, the entrances into bays and ports and passages through narrow channels being the most dangerous parts of voyages. Most of these ships were simply described as 'lost' or 'entirely lost', though such phrases as 'cast away', 'drove from anchors and lost', 'on rocks and in pieces' provide a little colour to these sad reports.

An anonymous author in 1867 thought that about half of all wrecks were attributable 'in nearly equal proportions to unseaworthiness, or other defects in the ship or equipment, and to the neglect or incompetence of the captain or crew', while the other half were mainly caused by 'stress of weather', though this too was often aggravated by the poor condition of the ship or by incompetence and drunkenness. A similar enquiry held one or two centuries earlier would probably have come to similar conclusions. Stress of weather could wreck any ship, but so could drunkenness, ignorance, inattention and the existence of such floating coffins as the *Lindsey*, which, coming home from Jamaica in 1698, 'sunck downe in the sea . . . and was wholly lost. She was old and crazy and not fitt to goe to sea'.[5]

Shipwreck was usually uncomfortable and frightening, but otherwise the only constant factor for the sailor was loss of wages and usually personal possessions, though these were often given a high priority in terms of salvage, as in the wreck of the East Indiaman *Huntingdon* in 1774 when the captain ensured that as many as possible of the seamen's chests were got ashore. Loss of wages always seemed harsh to men who suffered shipwreck, but attempts to sue for wages after shipwreck were rarely successful, unless the cargo was saved, even though it might reasonably be argued that the ship was lost through 'noe fault of the mariners but the said extraordinary winds and the will of God'.[6]

This argument was made by Joseph Bond, boatswain of the *Anne*, which in the winter of 1658 was 'forced upon the coast of France and there bilged and shee and her lading lost . . . The winds were very high . . . and the seas were mighty boysterous insomuch that they beate over the deck of the said ship with such a force that the company on the deck could scarce stand upon their leggs'. Frightening though this experience must have been, no one was killed or drowned in the wreck of the *Anne*. Nor was anyone lost in the wreck of the *Huntingdon* when she struck uncharted rocks off the island of Joanna, even though she was 'so fast on the rocks that the tide flowed and ebb'd regularly in and out of her'.[7]

These two examples show that, dramatic as shipwreck often was, it did not necessarily result in loss of life or even serious injury to the sailors. Exact figures on the mortality of sailors in shipwrecks cannot be obtained for this period but, using what information there is in *Lloyd's List* and extrapolating from early nineteenth-century Board of Trade material, one might hazard a very rough guess that there was some loss of life in about a quarter of wrecks and that all hands or nearly all hands lost their lives in about half of these.[8]

Such relatively low mortality may seem surprising, but shipwreck was not necessarily as dramatic an event as it is usually
portrayed. Many ships were lost quite gently, drifting slowly but
inexorably towards a lee shore until at last they ran aground and, in
the contemporary expression, 'bilged' or 'bulged' before slowly
breaking up with each successive tide. Others were driven ashore
more dramatically, but still not so violently that the crew could not
jump out and wade or swim to safety. Many ships struck rocks
which ripped holes in their bottoms but such damage rarely caused
the immediate sinking of the ship, even ten minutes being
sufficient for the crew to save themselves in the boats, while a
longer period of grace would enable them to save any valuable or
easily portable items in the cargo, together with provisions, drink
and canvas to provide sustenance and protection from the
elements.

Sailors, like most people, had a strong sense of self-preservation,
but they also had skills which made preservation more likely. Faced
with disaster, they would quickly lighten the ship by throwing the
guns and some of the cargo overboard and cutting down one or
more of the masts, this being standard practice and often sufficient
to save a ship. If such emergency procedures failed, they could
nurse a sinking ship and lay it ashore in the safest place. They could
handle small boats in the roughest of seas and, if necessary, navigate
them for hundreds or even thousands of miles to safety. Many
sailors could swim and might be able not just to save themselves
but also get ashore with a line to provide a passage to safety for their
shipmates. And, if the worst came to the worst and they found
themselves cast away on an alien and desolate shore with their ship
in pieces, they were used to hardship and short commons and had
the skills to build themselves another vessel or a raft out of the
wreckage, as did the crew of the *Nonsuch* who arrived safely on a
raft in Havana after having been 'totally lost' on the Colorados reef.
The men of the *Little William*, after being wrecked on the barren
coast of south-east Africa, rebuilt and enlarged their longboat with
timbers from the wreck and arrived a month later at a port in
Madagascar, 'by God's great mercy saving all our lives'.[9]

But not all shipwreck stories have such a happy ending. Among the many entries in *Lloyd's List* reporting 'all the crew saved' or 'taken up' by another ship, there are many others which report the loss of all or most of those on board such as the *Cranbrook*, a large three-decker on her way to Jamaica in 1775 which 'drove ashore and was utterly lost' with all hands on the Goodwin Sands, or the *Jolly Bacchus* returning home from Jamaica in 1772, which was 'totally lost off Dungeness and all the crew except the captain's slave', an unusual experience for a slave who, lying below in chains, was usually the first to die in a shipwreck as in the *Expedition*, which foundered at sea thirty-five leagues off Senegal, a disaster which drowned all 110 slaves on board but none of the crew.[10]

Foundering at sea or being 'overset' was one of the major causes of heavy loss of life, especially if one assumes that this was the fate of most of the ships 'never heard of'. Even in calm weather in harbour, being overset could lead to heavy mortality. Barlow tells of a ship loading sugar in Jamaica which, 'being a little top-heavy, would not bear herself very well; and all the men running over on one side to do some work, she was fallen over and overset and sunk down to rights, and about ten or a dozen men drownded, and all the sugar lost'. When such accidents happened in a gale a long way from shore, with the boats smashed to bits or washed overboard by heavy seas and sometimes the ship completely capsized, there was little survivors could do but search the horizons for another ship. Such saviours often did appear and many men from foundered ships were 'taken up', sometimes at the last gasp as was the case of the three survivors of the *Fanny* lost in a storm at sea in 1775. They 'went up in the foretop, being the only place of refuge, where they were nine days without the least subsistence' until they were fortunately sighted and taken aboard a ship headed for Barbados. But many other immediate survivors of such disasters searched in vain and were later reported 'all dead'.[11]

When sufficient evidence is provided, the reasons for high mortality on ships wrecking on or near the coast are what one would expect. The violence of the weather was obviously one factor, so that there was an even greater concentration of high mortality shipwrecks in the winter months than of shipwrecks as a whole.[12] Remoteness from the coast was also a factor, since the crew had less chance of getting ashore. For those who were wrecked on the coast, a sandy beach was obviously more hospitable than a wall of cliffs, as the men of the *Benbow* discovered in 1703. 'The Captain and forty men of the company were lost and drowned and fell downe from the clift, and was knocked on the head, two perished for want of help upon the clifts, soe that but six of the company were saved.' But it was the violence of the shipwreck itself which was most important. The quicker the ship broke up, the more likely there would be heavy loss of life. Many ships were described as having 'struck rocks and gone to pieces' or 'ashore and beat to pieces' and most of these had many drowned and killed, as did ships which broke in half. One such ship was the *Margaret* of Poole, which 'struck against one of the Scilly rocks and split in half; all the crew perished except two, who were driven upon the rock, and remained there three days before they could get assistance'.[13]

Finally, it should be noted that at no time was discipline more necessary aboard ship than in the aftermath of shipwreck and at no time was it harder to impose. After Captain Cook's *Endeavour* ran aground on the Great Barrier Reef, Joseph Banks confided to his journal his surprise at the good behaviour of the crew, who 'exerted [their] utmost for the preservation of the ship, contrary to what I have universally heard to be the behaviour of sea men who commonly as soon as a ship is in a desperate situation begin to plunder and refuse all command'. Banks was right; seamen often did loot and especially drown their fears in drink when a ship wrecked, as Nathaniel Uring discovered when he was wrecked off the coast of Honduras. 'When our people found the ship upon the rocks, they soon broke open the casks of liquor in the hold, and many of them got drunk ... such unthinking, ungovernable monsters are sailors, when once from under command.' Such behaviour was understandable but hardly conducive to the safety of the crew.[14]

Shipwreck was a fairly constant danger to those who used the seas. There might be more wrecks one year and fewer the next, depending on good fortune and the vagaries of great storms, which could throw twenty or thirty ships at a time on a coast with colossal damage, the worst incidence in the early 1770s being the great storm in September 1775 which wrecked 'above a hundred fishing shallops on the north-west coast of Newfoundland' and drowned five hundred men of all nations.[15] There were generally more wrecks in wartime than peacetime, as ships were forced to sail in dangerous seasons or were run aground by their crews in an attempt to escape pursuers. But, sometimes more and sometimes less, there were always plenty of shipwrecks, plenty of danger 'from the rocks, the billows and the wind', as perusal of any winter issue of *Lloyd's List* will confirm.

The danger from 'Man', however, which Waller thought even greater than from shipwreck, decreased over our period and was worst during the first seventy or eighty years when the seas were roamed by an alarmingly large number of predators whose only function was to seize or destroy merchant ships. These were of three main types, privateers fitted out in time of war, pirates, and the semi-piratical Barbary corsairs who sailed from bases in Algiers, Tunis, Tripoli and Morocco, especially Sallee (Salé), to prey on Christian shipping. These Moslem corsairs were the most feared of all since they enslaved those they captured and, although ransom was possible for the fortunate or wealthy, the fate of most poor sailors was enslavement for life. Some suffered as galley-slaves, though the English like the French and Dutch were usually 'people exempt from the oar because they are too feeble'; some worked as labourers in chain gangs; but many were employed as sailors on the corsair ships themselves, under supervision by armed guards as they did their jobs and chained together in fours as the ship closed for action. 'Not a sailor goes to sea in a merchant ship', wrote Defoe in 1725, 'but he feels some secret tremor that it may one time or other be his lot to be taken by the Turks'.[16]

Defoe was guilty of exaggeration since, by the 1720s, the danger from Moslem corsairs was largely a thing of the past, for the English at least, though a wise sailor would still keep his eyes open, especially when sailing anywhere near Morocco. The danger was at its peak just before our period. David Hebb has estimated that from 1622 to 1642 over 300 English ships and around 7,000 English subjects were captured by the Barbary corsairs, an average of some fifteen ships and 350 men (and occasionally women and children) a year.[17] Numbers are not known after 1642, but may have remained high for another ten or twenty years, since, although the corsairs were past their peak, they were still able to fit out a hundred or so ships between them in the 1650s and 1660s and some of these had as many as twenty or thirty guns and 200 or 300 men.

References to capture by corsairs are common in the early years of our period. Edward Coxere described the passage through the Strait of Gibraltar in the late 1650s as 'running the gauntlet', with some justification since he was captured by the Spaniards in 1656 and the corsairs of Tunis in 1658. His book has a good description of his life as a slave in this corsair city from which he was ransomed by the English fleet after five months. Edward Barlow wrote of Algiers in the 1660s as 'one of the greatest enemies of all Christian nations in the whole world, it being a place of pirates, having many ships which rove up and down in the sea making prizes of all they can take, and making slaves of many a poor Christian, bringing them into their markets and selling them to one another like so many sheep'. In 1668, his ship was in Algiers and he was able to contribute to the release of some of these sheep. 'A speech was made in our ship to desire from every man in all the ships five shillings . . . [to be] given as a free gift towards the ransome of so many poor men in slavery. So every man gave his consent freely, and thus there were twelve or fourteen redeemed from slavery.'[18]

The fact that Coxere was redeemed after only five months' captivity and Barlow's ship could enter Algiers without fear of capture suggests that matters were rather different than they had been in the heyday of the corsairs, as was indeed the case. The danger to English (and French) ships and sailors was gradually reduced from the 1630s onwards as a result of direct action by navies who from time to time sent expeditions to the different corsair ports 'to teach the pirates a lesson'. These expeditions were never totally successful, usually involving little more than a token bombardment and the sinking of a few corsair ships, but they spoiled the corsair business and nearly always resulted in a treaty which released most of the captives of the attacking nation and also included a guarantee of protection from attack and capture for some years into the future.[19]

Protection was ensured by the system of Mediterranean passes which were usually honoured by those corsairs at peace with England, though, given the nature of corsairs, such protection could never be absolute. In 1668, for instance, in a not uncommon incident, the ketch *Ruby* was captured by an Algerian man-of-war off Cape St Vincent. When the crew complained 'that they were of London and that at that time and for a long time before . . . there was peace between his Majesty of England and Algier', the corsair captain simply changed course for 'Sally which was a place then in enmity with England' and the crew were 'carryed to the market place there to be sold as slaves'. Such incidents became less common as the English and French and, to a lesser extent, the Dutch wore down the Barbary corsairs, forcing them to reduce the size of their fleets and concentrate their attention on the shipping of other, weaker, nations. No attempt was made, however, to destroy the corsairs completely since they were useful in reducing competition. 'It is not in our interest that all the Barbary corsairs be destroyed', wrote a French official in 1729, 'since then we would be on a par with all the Italians and the peoples of the North Sea'.[20]

In 1695, the outgoing English consul in Algiers took home with him forty-five British captives, all that then remained in Tripoli, Tunis and Algiers, 'except one that refused his liberty'. His successor, Robert Cole, reported that the only British brought in during his time were sailors working on ships of nations with whom Algiers was still at war and he could usually get these men released on the spurious grounds that they were really passengers and so not liable to enslavement.[21]

While the danger from Algiers dwindled to almost nothing, the Moroccans and the Sallee rovers, in particular, remained a threat, although they rarely set out more than eight or ten ships each year compared with the forty or fifty of their prime. John Morgan of Rotherhithe, when asked in 1722 how he had passed the last seven years, replied that he had spent six of them as a slave in Tangier. Sallee rovers were still taking the occasional English ship in the 1720s and 1730s, though their principal prey were Portuguese and Spanish, and as late as 1746 the British consul in Lisbon reported ninety English captives in Barbary 'of whom nineteen are turned

Moors for want of subsistence'. Most were in Morocco, which remained a law unto itself, a place where shipwrecked sailors were routinely enslaved, as were the crew of the privateer *Inspector* when she 'sprang a leak in a brisk gale' and was grounded in Tangier Bay in 1747. Worst of all perhaps was the strange fate of Edward Andrews, mate of the *Negroes Merchant*, which foundered in 1713 some two hundred leagues east of Newfoundland. The crew of eighteen and one woman passenger escaped in the boat, which took 48 days to approach the coast of Portugal, by which time only the captain and Andrews were still alive, 'the rest having fed on one another'. And then, in sight of a merciful release from their appalling experience, these two last men were captured by a Moroccan cruiser. The captain soon died, but Andrews was sent into the interior as a slave.[22]

As Moslem piracy waned from the 1660s, European piracy entered its so-called 'Golden Age'. First on the scene were the buccaneers in the West Indies, men of all nations but mainly English and French who operated from bases in Jamaica and Tortuga. They were at their peak in the 1660s when there were usually over 1,000 men and twice that for special exploits such as Henry Morgan's raid on Panama. However, these rovers posed little threat to English sailors, who were more likely to be among their number than to be captured by them, since the buccaneers concentrated on raids by sea and land on the Spanish. Some turned to indiscriminate piracy after 1670 when the Treaty of Madrid led to a half-hearted attempt to suppress the buccaneers, but the danger to English shipping was small, despite such incidents as the capture off Hispaniola in January 1683 of the slaver *Thomas and William* by pirates who carried off twenty-five slaves and some £3,000 in gold dust.[23]

European piracy moved into a new phase from the 1680s when the bolder spirits began to move out of the Caribbean, some across the isthmus and into the Pacific and others by way of West Africa to the Indian Ocean. Here Madagascar and the island of Sainte Marie off its north-east coast became places where ''tis the common report of the world that the pyrates doe resort to . . . and bring their riches thither'. These 'pyrates, sea rovers and blades of fortune' were supplied with arms, liquor and other necessities by ships from the American colonies who also marketed their booty and arranged for their repatriation by contracting 'to carry them as passengers and put them ashore between the Capes of Virginia and the east end of Long Island for 100 pieces of eight each'. No one seems to have counted these deep-sea marauders of the late seventeenth century but there were plenty of them, some operating from their bases in the Indian Ocean and others leading a wandering life as they looted their way from one side of the Atlantic to the other. These pirates were less discriminating than the buccaneers but still retained a certain 'residual loyalty' and did not often attack English ships, except when short of drink or provisions.[24]

There was a lull during the latter years of the War of the Spanish Succession, but peace ushered in the most devastating explosion of deep-sea piracy ever known, a period of anarchy at sea which fortunately for sailors was short. Marcus Rediker has estimated pirate numbers at 1,500 to 2,500 men in twenty or thirty well-armed ships from 1716 to 1722 and then a rapid decline to a mere handful by 1730.[25] These pirates operated in a similar way to their predecessors of the 1690s, some from bases in Madagascar, West Africa and the Bahamas, some roaming for years with only brief sprees ashore as they marauded and captured ships almost at will from the Caribbean to the Indian Ocean and almost everywhere else. Residual loyalty had now vanished and many English ships were captured and looted, though just how many is not certain. This time, however, the pirates had overstayed their welcome and their numbers and savagery brought about a concerted campaign to eliminate them. Some were brought in on the promise of pardon, some betrayed ashore, but most were captured in action by ships of the Royal Navy and later brought to trial and sentenced to hang, not just three or four at a time as a warning to the rest as once had been the case, but ten, twenty, even fifty at a time. It was, as Robert Ritchie has said, 'an extermination campaign' which saw at least 400 and possibly as many as 600 pirates hanged between 1716 and 1726, after which date there were few left and little incentive for new men to 'go upon the account'.[26]

The threat first from Barbary corsairs and then pirates was

sufficient to put fear into any sailor's breast, but the chances of capture were minimal compared with the risk from privateers in the wars between the European states. The Barbary corsairs took 300 English ships in their heyday between 1622 and 1642, a number which can be compared with the 360 English merchantmen taken by the Dutch in the four years of the Second Dutch War and the similar number taken in the Third Dutch War. Even these Dutch successes pale into insignificance compared with the great period of French privateering between 1695 and 1713 when nearly 10,000 ships were captured, between a half and three-quarters of them English. The Barbary corsairs were taking fifteen English ships a year in the 1620s and 1630s, the Dutch around a hundred a year in 1664–67 and 1670–72, while in the War of the Spanish Succession the French captured over six hundred ships a year of which four hundred or more were English. Things were never to be so bad again during our period, despite the eruption between 1716 and 1726 of the pirates, one of whom, Bartholomew Roberts, is said to have taken four hundred ships of all nations during his short and very violent career. The French privateers were back at work in 1744, but they had only taken some 1,600 ships by the end of the war in 1748, somewhat down on their average during the wars around 1700. And their take in the Seven Years' War was even lower, just 1,121 ships captured from the English, though even this works out at some ten times the annual average of the Barbary corsairs at their peak. Capture by a French privateer was hardly the same devastating experience as capture by a pirate or corsair, but it was certainly far more common.[27]

Whether capture was by corsair, pirate or privateer, the experience was likely to be similar. It was in what happened after capture that the difference lay. All predators relied on speed, guile and superior strength and they used similar tactics, lurking behind islands or headlands, flying false flags, luring their prey into a false sense of security, which sometimes enabled a ship to be captured by simply coming alongside and boarding as apparent friends. But usually the men in a threatened ship would realize their situation sooner or later and then the captain had to decide, often in consultation with his crew, whether to run, stand and fight or, most common, stand and surrender at once since the odds were usually hopelessly against the merchant ship. Privateers were often specially built for speed but, even if only converted merchantmen, they could normally outsail their prey since they were likely to be fresh out of port, unencumbered with cargo, clean-bottomed and well-fitted and with very large crews who could change sails and handle the ship far faster than the minimal crews of merchantmen. A privateer, then, would normally catch his prey, unless as often happened it was deliberately run ashore, but the chase might be long and exciting like that of the *Berkeley Galley*, which was chased 'from the dawning of the morning untill twas about eight of the clock in the evening' when she was finally taken by the *Victory* of St Malo.[28]

Once cornered, few merchantmen fought, not surprisingly given their disparity in arms and men with the majority of privateers and corsairs. Owners and merchants naturally thought that too few ships put up any defence, an accusation difficult to prove one way or another, though those accused of cowardice were quick to find witnesses to defend them, like Joseph English who said that Captain Hobman of the *Swan* was 'a very stout and resolute fellow and a man of very great courage [who] would not any wayes be induced to betray a ship or ladeing'. If they had any chance at all, the men certainly had an incentive to fight since capture would mean loss of wages and their chests and often loss of liberty. To make this incentive stronger, the practice of men insuring their wages against the event of capture was made illegal, though one still finds the occasional case such as the crew of the *Richard and Mary* who in 1692 refused to sail from Cadiz to Barcelona 'unless their wages thither were insured'.[29]

A ship prepared to fight might scare off her aggressor as did the *Rochester* when threatened by a French privateer in 1703. 'When she (as we concluded) was ready to board us wee all unanimously agreed to fight her and sounding our trumpetts wee beat our kettle drum and gave her challenge, but she shewed noe colours and made noe answer but fell astern.' Others fought and won. The *St John Baptist* in February 1694 destroyed a privateer flying the flag of the exiled King James II, only to be captured later in the voyage after another fight with a privateer from Toulon. Such fights could be violent indeed, like 'the very gallant defence' of the *Panther* off Portofino in 1719 in which nearly half of both crews were killed or wounded before the English ship was boarded and taken. However, such epic contests were the exception. Most who fought did not last long and most ships did not fight, such as the slaver *Eagle* when faced with a pirate in 1697. 'He cam up with us, and fiered a gun att us, soe we stroke our ensign and boare down under his lee, we nott being abell to withstand hime.'[30]

Capture was not necessarily the end of the story, since recapture by a friendly ship was by no means uncommon, such successes being rewarded by salvage payments on a sliding scale depending on the time the captured ship had been in enemy hands. John Bromley illustrated the wheel of fortune in the privateering game by quoting a letter written to a London merchant in 1706. 'Dear Uncle . . . 'tis ill news of poor Captain King . . . who has been four times taken and retaken about six leagues from Lisbon.' Bromley said that such an experience 'was not unusual' and the records of the Admiralty Court show that he was right. Less common, but even more dramatic, was the recapture of a ship by the captured sailors themselves, usually as a result of the inattention of the prize crew as in the case of the *Eagle* of Yarmouth, which was retaken in 1696 by two English sailors and a boy who overpowered the seven-man French prize crew and brought the ship and her cargo of currants into Bideford amidst much jubilation.[31]

Nathaniel Uring thought it very hard when captured in 1697 'to be plunder'd of all my new cloaths and other necessaries . . . After being strip'd of most of my wearing apparel I was sent on board the privateer, where I was plundered of what little things I had left'. Torture of those who might know the whereabouts of concealed treasure was another possibility to be faced by captives. 'It is, and ever was usuall and common amongst privateers of all nations upon takeing of their enemies, where they suspect any hidden treasure to be aboard, to use some torture or other', deposed Bartholomew Biggs as he looked back on a privateering career covering fifty years. The commonest torture was to place lighted matches between the bound fingers of the victim, but there were many others such as screwing fingers in a vice or 'woolding', the buccaneers' favourite, in which a rope was tightened round the victim's head till his eyes popped out.[32]

Such unpleasantness aside, the fate of captured sailors depended on the nature of their captor. Capture by a pirate might involve no more than giving up food, drink and equipment and then continuing with the voyage. But, if the pirate was short of hands, capture could well lead to the terrible choice of joining the pirate crew, a career decision made willingly by many hundreds or even thousands of unhappy or adventurous sailors and unwillingly by many others who were forced or claimed to have been forced to change their allegiance. Capture by a Barbary corsair, by contrast, involved no choices. It was almost bound to lead to the slave market, unless by some miracle the ship was recaptured, as was the *Owner's Imployment*, taken by a Sallee man-of-war in 1685, but then 'about a day before the full of the fifth moon ... met with an English vessel under English colours called the Venice Merchant [and] was surprized, seized and taken and brought into the River of Thames'.[33]

Sailors captured by privateers faced very different conditions depending on whether their ship was ransomed at sea or taken into an enemy port. Authorities in both England and France disapproved of ransom since it could give rise to collusion between captor and captive and in any case bypassed the procedure of Admiralty Courts. Ransom was however very common and accounted for around one-third of all captures by privateers during our period. The normal procedure was for the two captains to negotiate a figure for the ransom, usually 'no more than a third part of the intrinsect value of ship and goodes'. Two men, usually officers, would then be taken to France as hostages for the payment of this sum, while the captured ship was free to continue her voyage with a pass to protect her from recapture by another privateer, the *Charming Nancy* in 1760, for instance, having a pass which allowed her 'sixty days grace'. Owners were sometimes slow to pay or refused to pay, in which case the ransomers, as the hostages were often called, might have to endure a lengthy and unpleasant captivity like Thomas Williams, boatswain of the *Dover Merchant* in 1705, whose wife claimed that he 'lyes naked and almost eaten up with vermine amongst all sorts of malefactors in a gaole at Marseilles in France'. However, most owners were honourable and most ransomers treated well, being paid full wages while in France and having an allowance of half a crown a day for their maintenance, sufficient to live well according to evidence given in 1706.

An English man may live and maintaine himselfe in all things necessary and convenient in St Malo, Dunquerque and Calais for the said rate of 2/6 a day . . . There is a sort of ordinary [restaurant] att St Malo for hostages in the castle of the town, where they have two meales a day, vizt dinners and suppers, and usually wine at each meale to the quantity of an English pint each meale.[34]

Such good living was not the fate of that majority of captive English sailors whose ships had been taken into enemy ports. Some were simply dumped ashore to save the cost of feeding them, but most ended up in prisons in the privateering ports. Here, like their French counterparts in England, they were fed at government expense but hardly in the luxury accorded to ransomers, since the allowance in both countries was only about fivepence a day per head and the gaolers cheated the sailors of even that, 'two ounces of stinking cheese and a little bread' being the daily ration in Dunkirk in 1703 according to one complainant. Overcrowding and disease were other problems, though really bad treatment could be checked by the threat of retaliation, as in February 1703 when the Comte de Mornay declared that 'unless the French prisoners in England are better treated, retaliatory treatment will be dealt out to the English prisoners in France'. Captivity did not usually last for very long, since both France and England were always desperately short of sailors for their navies and even fivepence a day soon added up to large sums when there were thousands of prisoners involved. Exchange was normally organized on a 'man for man and quality for quality' basis and, throughout the wars, there was a shuttle service between, say, Dover and Calais or Plymouth and St Malo taking boatloads of French prisoners back to France and bringing home an equal number of Englishmen. How long the average captive sailor spent in a French or Dutch prison is not certain, but where time was mentioned it was usually a few months but not much longer before most sailors returned to face once more the perils of the sea.[35]

CHAPTER NINE

Mortality and Medicine

CHAPTER NINE

Mortality and Medicine

'And when he is dead [they] sew him
up in an old blanket or piece of old
canvas, and tie to his feet two or
three cannon bullets, and so to heave
him overboard, wishing his poor soul
at rest . . . and there he has a grave
many times wide and big enough,
being made meat for the fishes of the
sea.'[1]

'Les Enfans Perdus or the Forlorn Hope of the World' was how
Daniel Defoe described sailors. 'They are fellows that bid defiance
to terror, and maintain a constant war with the elements; who, by
the magick of their art, trade in the very confines of death, and are
always posted within shot, as I may say, of the grave.' 'Sea-men',
wrote John Flavel, 'are as it were a third sort of persons, to be
numbered neither with the living nor the dead: their lives hanging
continually in suspense before them'.[2] Such literary emphasis on
the risks and high mortality of seafaring was commonplace while
maritime records, such as logbooks, confirm the propinquity of
death for sailors, who literally spent their lives one slip away from
a watery grave. Logbooks also demonstrate how devastating
sickness aboard ship could be, but just how high was mortality?

A good idea of mortality rates at the end of the period can be obtained from muster rolls, which listed the crews of ships at the beginning of voyages and then noted who had died in the course of the voyage. Such information is likely to be accurate since a sailor's pay stopped on the day of his death. Similar information can be found in the paybooks of East Indiamen, which have survived in large numbers. Analysis of the experience of some six hundred voyages in the early 1770s, of East Indiamen and of ships sailing out of Liverpool, Bristol and Hull, shows that the chances of dying depended, as did so many other things at sea, on where a sailor sailed to.[3]

Well under one per cent of sailors died on any voyage in European waters or on voyages to the northern American colonies or to the Arctic to hunt whales. Indeed, the life expectancy of sailors on these routes was marginally better than that of young men working ashore in the ports from which they sailed. Sailors were fit young men, the sea was bracing and there was no reason for them to die in these waters unless by accident or in a shipwreck. Life expectancy for those who sailed to the southern American colonies or the West Indies was not so good, with some two or three per cent of crews dying on average in the course of a voyage. But these were still low figures compared with the two trades in which sailors really were likely to die. On average, one in ten of those who sailed on East Indiamen died or were killed or drowned in the course of their long voyages and an astonishing one in four or five of those who crewed the slave ships. When allowance is made for the time that the sailors were at risk, crew mortality on slave ships was roughly equal to the infant mortality rate in eighteenth-century London, an appalling rate of mortality for young adults.[4] Such findings provide strong support for the views of abolitionists such as John Newton and Thomas Clarkson that the slave trade, far from being a nursery for seamen as its supporters claimed, was in fact their grave.

Muster rolls normally distinguish those who were killed or drowned from those who died of disease. So, if some allowance is made for those who lost their lives in shipwrecks, one can summarize very roughly by saying that, out of every thousand English sailors who went to sea, about five would die in an accident each year, another ten would die in shipwrecks and some forty-five would die of disease, this last figure being very unevenly distributed among the sailors in the different trades.

A total of 150 sailors were reported drowned or killed in the sample of musters and paybooks, of whom 86 were serving on East Indiamen and 34 on slave ships. This concentration is not too surprising, since these ships sailed in dangerous waters and their voyages were longer than those of the other trades examined. What is perhaps surprising is that, of the 2,500 sailors in whalers, only two men were reported lost by accident, one killed and one drowned. Daniel Defoe called whaling 'the most nice, difficult, and dangerous' trade in the world and everything about it certainly seems to have been incredibly dangerous. Hunting was carried out in the floating ice in the seas off the west coast of Spitsbergen or in the Davis Strait, areas with extremely low sea and air temperatures. Once located, the prey was chased in six- or seven-man rowing boats and harpooned by hand. The Greenland whale is not an aggressive creature, but such close-quarter action meant that many boats were smashed to bits by the whale's tail, while the paying out of up to 1,000 yards of line as the whale dived deep or took refuge under the ice could cause horrific accidents if a man got caught in a loop of the line. Once the whale had finally been killed, the huge dead weight was towed back to the whaling ship and flensed by men wearing spurs to stop them slipping off the whale's back. Descriptions of whaling are full of men falling into the icy water or leaping from ice floe to ice floe or even on to the backs of live whales. Despite these dangers, low mortality is confirmed by William Scoresby who published a fascinating account of the whale fishery in 1820. 'Fatal accidents do not so frequently occur as a general view of the bold and hazardous operations connected with the capture of whales would lead us to expect.'[5]

Logbooks and journals, especially those of East Indiamen, provide plentiful evidence of the nature of accidents suffered by sailors in other trades. 'A great sea from the south-west which has made us roll and labour a great deal', records the logbook of the East Indiaman *Ankerwyke* for 19 May 1771. 'At 9.30 p.m. James Taylor seaman fell overboard out of the main shrouds and was drowned, the sea running so high it was impossible to get a boat out with safety.' Barlow wrote in 1697:

> The ship *Charles* came to an accident, losing four of her seamen for being on the main topsail yard about to reef and shorten sail, the weather brace broke; and the yard flying away at once and the sail filling, struck four of the men off the yard; two falling in the sea, were drowned, and two falling into the ship, were killed by the fall.

Some men were lucky and were washed back aboard by the sea or managed to grab a rope to save themselves as they fell. Two men from the *Caernarvon* were saved in 1720, one by being 'took up with the boat hook as he was sinking' and the other 'they throed a roap to him and was hauld in'.[6] Others were picked up by the boats which captains nearly always launched if possible. But the time it took to heave to and get a boat out meant that such manoeuvres, though good for morale, were rarely successful. Most men who fell into the sea were lost forever.

Being killed or drowned as a result of a fall from the yards or shrouds was by far the most common fatal accident, but there were many others. Men were washed overboard or slipped over the side of the ship when working, such as James Batty who, 'in going over the quarter to clear the log line, fell overboard and was drowned'. Loose tackle could pose great dangers as it did for James Nye who 'in swaying up the gaff was unfortunately knocked overboard by it and was drowned'. John Neil was killed when 'the bitts of our windlass gave way which occasioned one of the handspikes to strike [him] over the temples'.[7]

Danger did not end when a ship came to anchor, since plying to and from the shore in small boats could be extremely hazardous, especially through the surf which guarded the coasts of West Africa, though this was by no means the only dangerous place. 'Michael Cooper seaman, being unfortunately overset in a sampan, was drowned', records the logbook of the *Calcutta* as she lay in Whampoa loading tea in 1771. Indeed, nowhere was really safe for a sailor and even the most elementary functions of human life could prove fatal. 'Our cook, named William Cox, in the night rises out of his sleep and goes into the ship's head and either slips or falls overboard and was drownded: he was drunk and was not missed till the next day at nine in the morning.'8

Such accidents could have a traumatic effect on the dead man's shipmates, as Dana recalled.

When a man falls overboard at sea and is lost, there is a suddenness in the event, and a difficulty in realising it, which give to it an air of awful mystery . . . The man is near you – at your side – you hear his voice, and in an instant he is gone, and nothing but a vacancy shows his loss. Then, too, at sea, – to use a homely but expressive phrase – you *miss* a man so much . . . There is always an empty berth in the forecastle, and one man wanting when the small night watch is mustered. There is one less to take the wheel, and one less to lay out with you upon the yard.9

Death by disease was not usually so dramatic as accidental death but it could be equally traumatic as one's messmates dropped dead one after the other, sometimes with alarming speed. 'I never see men dye so soudainely in my life', wrote one captain in 1652 as his crew rapidly dwindled. This was on a slave ship in the Gambia River and, as has been seen, it was in this trade that mortality from disease was much the worst. This was at its highest when the ships lay on the African coast and muster rolls confirm the speed of death as sailor after sailor is marked 'dead' within the passage of a few days. The mortality of sailors, but not of slaves, normally declined dramatically once the ship set out to sea for the 'middle passage'.10

Mortality in West Africa was said to be worse for those on their first voyage than for 'seasoned' sailors, worse for heavy drinkers than the abstemious, worse for those who went up the rivers than for those who remained at sea off the coast, worse in the rainy season between May and October but, whatever the conditions, few European visitors to the area escaped without at least a bout of fever and a very large number died. The chief killers were dysentery or the 'bloody flux' and 'that low, malignant fever of the remitting kind' or malaria, but there were a host of other diseases which could kill Europeans or permanently disable them, such as river blindness whose sightless victims were a focus for pity in the slaving ports of western Europe.[11]

Voyages to the East Indies had also been notorious for high crew mortality from the very beginnings of the Portuguese adventure in Asia. It was nothing unusual for Portuguese ships to lose between a third and a half of their crews on the way out and a rather lower proportion on the way home when the ships were less crowded. Dutch historians, too, are familiar with Van der Woude's concept of the 'East Indian leak', the haemorrhage of Dutch manpower which saw about a million sailors, soldiers and artisans leave Holland for the 'fatal shores' of the East Indies between 1602 and 1795 of whom only about one-third returned. For the 1770s, Professor Jaap Bruijn and his colleagues estimate mortality among voyagers on Dutch East Indiamen to have been 15 per cent for those sailing out to Asia and nearly 6 per cent on homebound voyages. Such figures are not strictly comparable with ours since they relate to passengers as well as crew but, for all that, they are surprisingly high compared with the figure of just under 10 per cent for the whole round trip in English ships of the same period. This disparity in mortality between English and Dutch ships was long-established if we can accept the views of Edward Barlow who wrote in the 1670s that fewer men died on English than on Dutch East Indiamen. He thought this was because 'English ships commonly make shorter passages and are better provided with provisions', practically the only time in his *Journal* when he comments favourably on the food in English ships.[12]

Dutch rates of mortality had shown a marked increase in the course of the eighteenth century and Bruijn suggests that this may have been because of greater overcrowding or deterioration in the physical quality of crews, as the Dutch found it increasingly difficult to find men to sail in their ships. Support for this assessment is provided by the very high mortality on the first leg of Dutch voyages, from the Netherlands to Cape Town. This was 6 per cent in the 1760s and nearly 12 per cent in the 1770s, higher than the English average for the complete round trip. This part of the voyage took on average just over four months and so can be compared with mortality on English ships in the first four months of their voyage, which was only just over 1 per cent. Such figures certainly imply that English sailors were much healthier and fitter when they first came aboard than were the Dutch.[13]

A major killer in early voyages to the east was scurvy and this remained a problem, despite a general knowledge that fresh fruit and vegetables could help to prevent or cure the disease and that citrus juice was particularly effective. It took about six weeks on salted and sometimes rotting shipboard rations before scurvy made its appearance, so it was mainly on East Indiamen with their very long passages between ports that the disease had really serious effects. A slow passage on the way home was the worst scenario as in the *Devonshire* in 1773, which had thirty-two men on the doctor's list with scurvy and dropsy by the time they saw the Lizard, 'and those that stand the deck so weakly as to be incapable of very little duty'.[14]

Ship fever or typhus was another disease likely to attack crowded ships on long journeys and this was certainly a factor in mortality on East Indiamen, though probably not as much so as in the ships of the Royal Navy. It is however clear from the dates of death recorded in the pay ledgers that most disease in East Indiamen was picked up from the shore just as it was in West Africa. Dysentery was once again a major killer, as was malaria and a variety of unspecified fevers such as the notorious Batavia fever. James Lind in his 'Diseases in the East Indies' provided a league table of unhealthiness in the four English presidencies in the east. Heading the list was Bencoolen on the west coast of Sumatra, 'the most sickly and fatal', followed by Bengal, Bombay and lastly Madras, which 'is esteemed the most healthy government belonging to the English'. The two voyages in our sample which terminated in Bencoolen certainly provide support for Lind since they had the worst mortality of all, with about a third of the crew dying in each case. Calcutta and Bombay are also confirmed as fairly deadly places, while the lowest mortality occurred on ships sailing to China.[15]

Africa and Asia were notorious as killers of white men, but so were the West Indies and it might seem surprising that mortality on ships sailing there was relatively low. English sailors certainly believed the West Indies to be unhealthy, at least by comparison with the Mediterranean, and sometimes refused to go there for that reason.[16] Such a belief had plentiful foundation since Caribbean diseases included malaria, yellow fever, dysentery, dropsy, leprosy, yaws and hookworm – a horrendous list – and the dangers of the area for the unseasoned, both black and white, have been well documented. Historians have estimated that between 12 and 15 per cent of all white emigrants to the West Indies died within their first year in the area. Sir Gilbert Blane, physician to the West Indies fleet in 1780–81, recorded the death of 1,577 men from the fleet in one calendar year, 'nearly every seventh man', of whom just 59 died in battle or from wounds.[17]

There are two factors which probably account for the relatively low mortality of sailors on merchant ships voyaging to the West Indies. A fairly high proportion of crews had made the voyage before and so were 'seasoned', an important factor in coping with tropical climates. Merchant seamen also did not spend as long in the West Indies as did emigrants or seamen in the Royal Navy, unless they were discharged or deserted in the islands and so vanish from observation. Length of time at risk was a major factor in the mortality rates of all ships sailing to the tropics, but especially for those sailing to the West Indies. The mortality rate on ships taking more than eight months to sail to the West Indies and back, a good indication that they had spent a long time in the area, was four times as high as on those which returned in a shorter time.

Sailors were not completely helpless in the face of disease. Captains were aware of the therapeutic benefits of fresh provisions, especially fruit and vegetables, and records of such purchases often say they were specifically 'for the sick'. Sailors were also aware of the benefits of cleanliness in helping to prevent disease and were enthusiastic about fumigation of cramped living quarters, especially on slave and emigrant ships. The medicine of the day could do little to combat shipboard disease, but there were some encouraging innovations. Jesuit's bark or cinchona, from which quinine was later isolated, had proved valuable as both a preventative and a cure for malaria (the bark could 'be made extremely palatable, by infusing it in spirits, especially if a little orange-peel be added'), while laudanum had been shown to be effective in the treatment of dysentery.[18]

Nevertheless, most journals and logbooks show that the people aboard were fairly fatalistic once a ship had become 'sickly'. What could be done would be done and the sick were often cared for very tenderly by their messmates, but there was an overall feeling of helplessness in the face of disease. 'The distemper which my men as well as the blacks die of', wrote Captain Phillips, 'was the white flux which was so violent and inveterate that no medicine would in the least check it; so that when any of our men were seiz'd with it, we esteem'd him a dead man, as he generally proved'. The reaction of most surgeons to sick sailors was simply to bleed them or to do nothing on the grounds that 'two-thirds had such bad constitutions that no physician could save them, and the rest such good ones that all the physicians in the world could not kill them'. Such surgeons were likely to write a man off once he had caught the prevailing disease, so one can appreciate the pleasure with which the captain of the slaver *Glory* noted an occasion when his surgeon was proved wrong. 'This night our doctor gave the white man up to death' but, on the following day, 'the white man better so hope he will deceive our knowing doctor'.[19]

The best medical attention available was on East Indiamen. The East India Company had created a marine medical service in the early seventeenth century and in 1664 established hospitals at Madras, Bombay and Calcutta, while medical services were also provided at Bencoolen, China and St Helena. All the ships carried surgeons and surgeons' mates and these were generally of higher quality than those serving in other merchant ships who were normally regarded as very lowly members of their profession. Despite this, surgeons on East Indiamen were no more effective than anyone else in combating sickness once it had gripped a ship. Indeed, it is clear from logbooks that the only real cure for such epidemics was to get the sick men ashore and it is astonishing how rapid and effective such 'refreshment' was. A few days or weeks ashore at St Helena or the Cape or even in the hospitals in India and an East Indiaman's sick list dwindled to virtually nothing, St Helena being described as 'one of the most healthful places in the world, and our sailors . . . when carried ashore here, recover to a miracle, rarely any dying though never so ill when brought ashore'.[20]

In the middle of the seventeenth century, most large ships going any distance carried a surgeon but such a supernumerary was increasingly seen as an unnecessary expense. By the eighteenth century, surgeons were usually only employed on East Indiamen, on ships with large numbers of passengers, privateers, slavers and occasionally whalers. This reduction in medical cover does not seem to have increased mortality, which if anything probably declined, a fact which may reflect the quality of the surgical services provided. Very few comments on the quality of surgeons survive, though the regret expressed when surgeons died, as they often did on slave ships, suggests that sailors thought they were at least better off with a surgeon than without one. Even so, most sailors probably shared the low opinion of sea surgeons expressed by Barlow:

And the surgeons and doctors of physic in ships many times are very careless of a poor man in his sickness, their common phrase being to come to him and take him by the hand when they hear that he hath been sick two or three days, thinking that is soon enough, and feeling his pulses when he is half dead, asking when he was at stool, and how he feels himself, and how he has slept, and then giving him some of their medicines upon the point of a knife, which doeth as much good to him as a blow upon the pate with a stick. And when he is dead they did not think that he had been so bad as he was, nor so near his end.[21]

Surgeons were better at dealing with wounds and injuries than with disease, as one might expect from their name and the nature of their training. A healthy sailor might feel some confidence that a surgeon would repair him if he broke his leg or suffered a gunshot wound but, if he became sick, he was very much in the hands of fate as indeed were his contemporaries ashore.

By the eighteenth century, most English mariners sailed on ships without surgeons and relied for medical attention, if they got any at all, on the ship's medical chest or 'Docter Box'. Such equipment was not required by law until the nineteenth century but was quite common in our period, complete chests being put up in sea ports by apothecaries who also provided instructions for the use of their contents.[22] Doctors and surgeons also wrote manuals for the use of those at sea, though most were unintelligible to a layman, at least until N. D. Falck's *Seaman's Medical Instructor* of 1774. This was produced specifically 'for ships that carry no surgeon' and was written in sensible clear language, complete with a useful 'anatomical and physiological description of the human body'. The medical content of manuals obviously reflected the preoccupations of medicine ashore with its emphasis on blistering, purging, sweating and enemas and above all bleeding. 'Begin with phlebotomy', advises Aubrey in *The Sea-Surgeon* of 1729. 'There is, perhaps, not a greater remedy in medicine than bleeding', writes Falck, though some writers thought it was going too far to bleed 'almost all the men, as is often done in the merchant's service when first they come into a warm latitude, by way of prevention'. Sailors believed in bleeding no less than physicians and might resort to self-help. 'I found my fever to increase, and my head so distempered that I could scarcely stand', wrote Dampier. 'Therefore I whetted and sharpened my penknife in order to let my self blood; but I could not, for my knife was too blunt.'[23]

The medicine chest was normally administered by the captain, unless one of his crew was known to have healing skills. He would have a look at the box and discover that bottle number eight, balsam drops, for instance, was 'a good medicine in a bad cold or burning fever' or he might carefully follow the instructions in Falck regarding the setting of a bone or the extraction of a tooth. 'Set the patient steady on a chair or chest and if he is a coward, let somebody hold his hands, but a man of spirit will not want this officiousness.'[24] Such treatment was clearly necessary in an emergency and might or might not have been successful, but most sailors no doubt preferred to wait if possible until they could get attention from a qualified doctor or surgeon on another ship or ashore. 'To a docktor, man who fell off ye mast', records the account book of the *India Merchant* in 1729. 'Four rubles . . . to Mr Miller chirurgione aboard his Zarish [Czarist] Magisties ship the

Sampson for curing of my thoum', acknowledged George Drummond who had borrowed the money from his captain in Reval. 'Got a doctor from the shore who says the mate is a dying, left a bottle for him to take every hour a spoonfull of', reported the logbook of the *Swift* at Bayonne in 1774.[25]

Manuals of maritime law stated that 'if a mariner falls sick during a voyage, or is hurt in the performance of his duty, he is to be cured at the expence of the ship', so long as his sickness did not arise from 'the pursuit of his own private concerns', by which they meant venereal disease or injuries sustained in drunken brawls.[26] Some ship's accounts show such responsibilities to the sick being honoured – 'to a dockter to look after men', 'to looking after sick men ashore'. Many captains, however, simply charged such expenses against the men's wages. Captain Burnside of the *Lyon* of Dublin, for example, deducted money from the wages of many men in his crew for such things as 'paid to doctor when you were sick', 'your diat and lodging and attendance when sick ashore', 'to the Doctor of Deale Castle for blistering you'.[27]

Since most of this medical attention was ineffective, he also deducted from wages the cost of the funerals of those men who were buried ashore. Sailors' wills normally included some such phrase as 'my body I commit to the earth or sea as it shall please God to order', but they fervently hoped that God would so order things that they might be buried ashore rather than be committed to the deep, for which most sailors had a superstitious aversion. And, since sickness often struck in port, many sailors were indeed buried ashore all over the globe, at some expense to their heirs. Typical expenditure for those dying on the *Lyon* was fifteen shillings for a coffin, thirty shillings for funeral charges and between six and ten shillings for 'liquors for his funerall', the equivalent of about two months' wages. The cost of a senior officer's funeral was much greater. The funeral of Captain Dennis of the East Indiaman *Nathaniel* cost £23.12.0, to which was added another £12 for interest at 50 per cent, while Captain Alexander Reid was buried in Bengal at a cost of 207 rupees (about £26) plus another 42 rupees to settle 'Captain Harnatt's bill for firing guns'.[28]

Burials at sea were cheaper, indeed often almost costless, but they displayed the same disparity in ceremony between those of common sailors and senior officers. The men were typically sewn up in a piece of canvas or often their own hammock weighted with shot and, after a short prayer, tipped into the sea, their passing sometimes being accompanied by the raising of the skull and crossbones or by a 'tolling of the bell' or both. This short ceremony might be followed by some 'liquors' in memory of the deceased, especially if he had provided the wherewithal as did Charles Wood, surgeon of the *Rochester*, in his deathbed will. 'I doe likewise will that the ship's company shall have tenn gallons of brandy and the officers two dozen bottles of wine.' Most dead men were buried very soon after their decease and some were despatched with no ceremony at all, like those who died on the slaver *Florida* in 1714. 'We conceal the death of the sailours from the negroes by throwing them overboard in the night, lest it might give them a temptation to rise upon us.'[29]

The funerals of senior officers, by contrast, were rather more dramatic. When Captain Newton buried his mate in 1751, he flew the colours at half-mast and 'fired fourteen minute guns', while no ceremony at all is recorded in his journal for the burials of the ordinary sailors who died upon his ship. Captain Phillips of the *Hannibal* went to even greater lengths when his younger brother died off the African coast.

Our pinnace being hoisted out, he was lower'd into her [in a coffin], and myself, my doctor and purser went in her to bury him, the colours of our own ship and the *East India Merchant* being lower'd half-mast down, our trumpets and drums sounding as is customary upon such melancholy occasions. We row'd the corpse about quarter of a mile from the ship to seaward; and the prayers of the church being read, I help'd to commit his body to the deep, which was the last office lay in my power to do for my dear brother. The *Hannibal* fired sixteen guns at half minute distance of time, which was the number of years he had liv'd in this uncertain world; and the *East India Merchant* fir'd ten guns. He was buried in twenty-five fathom water.

Hierarchical distinctions were thus maintained in death, even if sailor and officer were both destined to be 'meat for the fishes of the sea'.[30] How they were maintained in life will be the subject of the next chapter.

CHAPTER TEN

Discipline and Punishment

CHAPTER TEN

Discipline and Punishment

'By the Common Law, the master has authority over all the mariners on board . . . and it is their duty to obey his commands in all lawful matters relating to the navigation of the ship and the preservation of good order . . . In case of disobedience or disorderly conduct, he may lawfully correct them in a reasonable manner; his authority in this respect being analogous to that of a parent over his child, or of a master over his apprentice or scholar.'[1]

Discipline aboard ships tends to arouse images of brutal arbitrary punishments, the boatswain with a rope's end 'starting' the last man to the yards, the lash eating out chunks of flesh from the bare back of a spreadeagled sailor, the ultimate horrors of keelhauling or the noose dropping from the yardarm. No one doubts such things could happen to sailors; the problem is to determine their frequency and to assess the degree of punishment on a 'typical' merchant ship not commanded by a sadist.

The most detailed studies on discipline have been done by historians of the Royal Navy whose work shows an increase in both strictness and the severity of punishment over time. Bernard Capp summed up discipline in the 1650s as 'brisk paternalism' and thought it was normally no worse than in contemporary merchantmen, an equivalence not made by any historian of a later period. J. D. Davies found the severity of punishments, measured by the number of lashes ordered in courts martial, increasing in the Restoration period but rarely exceeding a hundred lashes. Daniel Baugh wrote that 'the putative severity of naval discipline' in the 1740s was not dwelt on by contemporaries and was inclined to play down the harshness of the naval code. Nicholas Rodger, too, took an optimistic view of naval discipline in the Seven Years' War, though the punishments ordered by courts martial were far harsher than in the seventeenth century, 100 to 300 lashes being standard for desertion and 200 to 500 for theft.[2]

John D. Byrn, whose focus was the Leeward Islands station between 1784 and 1812, considered not just punishments awarded by courts martial but also summary punishments recorded in logbooks. By this period, the system of 'collective terror' he describes was draconian indeed though he insists on its basic fairness. Fair or not, the punishments ordered could be horrendous, especially that of flogging round the fleet with from 50 up to 500 lashes. The ubiquity of the lash is shown by the 7,429 summary punishments he collected, 6,776 of which were 'flogging at the gangway' with more than the legal maximum of twelve lashes ordered in over a third of cases. On average, there were between three and four floggings a month on each of the ships in his sample, though over 90 per cent of crews never felt the lash. Nor was this all. Logbooks say nothing about 'starting', the arbitrary use of a rope's end or other weapons by boatswains and other junior officers.[3]

The degree of punishment is far harder to determine on merchant ships, since not many logbooks survive and the sailors were not subject to courts martial. The only two historians to address this problem both felt conditions deteriorated in our period. 'Life on board ship was carried on amid a discipline which grew harsher with the passage of time', wrote Ralph Davis, though he provided little evidence to support this assertion. The same could not be said of Marcus Rediker who piles example on example in his description of discipline in the first half of the eighteenth century. The picture he paints is one of extreme brutality in which sailors are cowed into obedience by beatings which 'were vicious almost beyond belief'. Men were beaten with cats, ropes, canes, even 'an elephant's dry'd pizle'. They were punched, kicked, head-butted, terrorized with knives and guns, threatened with mutilation or loaded down with weights until blood gushed out of their nose and mouth. It is a powerful picture of the use of absolute authority and brute force at sea but, as Rediker accepts, his examples are 'extreme cases, and in fact are preserved among admiralty records because they represented transgressions of both custom and law'.[4]

Sailors bringing these 'extreme cases' and witnesses in their support no doubt exaggerated to make their point. Nevertheless, they were unlikely to exaggerate so much as to make their claims ridiculous. They hoped to be believed and sometimes were, a fact which makes it probable that there were indeed such monstrous officers at sea. At one end of the spectrum of discipline in the merchant service then there stood the brutal physical authority of captains and other officers whose behaviour resembles that of bullying gangster chiefs rather than capitalists imposing a protofactory discipline as Rediker would have us believe.[5]

If such cruelty was the extreme, what was the norm of discipline in the merchant service? England had no general code of maritime law, relying instead on continental ordinances, some very ancient,[6] the 'custom of the sea' and the occasional words of wisdom from judges in the Admiralty Court, such as Sir Thomas Salisbury who gave judgment in favour of an ill-treated sailor in 1766. 'I shall always endeavour to discourage obstinacy and disobedience in the mariner and to prevent cruelty and tyranny in the captain, whose behaviour on this occasion appears wantonness and violence.' Such an attitude was typical of judges in both the High Court of Admiralty and the colonial vice-admiralty courts, though it throws no light on just what such words as obstinacy, disobedience, cruelty and tyranny actually meant.[7]

Everything connected with discipline at sea was shrouded in vagueness and subject to different interpretations by captains, sailors and judges. No one doubted, however, that the 'master has

authority over all the mariners on board . . . and it is their duty to
obey his commands in all lawful matters relating to the navigation
of the ship and the preservation of good order . . . Such an
authority is absolutely necessary to the safety of the ship, and of the
lives of the persons on board'. No one seems to have doubted
either, not even the sailors, that 'in case of disobedience or
disorderly conduct, [the master] may lawfully correct [the
mariners] in a reasonable manner'. However, everyone agreed there
were limits to such correction which if exceeded were grounds for
a suit at law, a possibility which made masters 'very careful in the
exercise' of their power. This was still true in 1860 when Captain
Sproule gave evidence to the Select Committee on Merchant
Shipping. 'I know very well that a master can flog a man, but it is
a very dangerous thing to do.' The danger lay in the absence of any
clear definition, since all that commentators were prepared to say
was that correction must be 'moderate' and should only be given
for 'sufficient cause'.[8]

Some partial answers to this problem of definition can be found
in the evidence in court cases brought by sailors. These were of two
main types. A man might bring an action for his wages on the
grounds that he had been unfairly turned out of the ship or forced
to desert as a result of harsh treatment which had become unbear-
able or was so savage that he feared for his life. More directly, sailors
who thought they had been treated brutally or unfairly brought
actions against officers for damages. This was a worrying possibility as Edward Barlow found when mate of the *Sampson* in 1694.
The widow of one of the sailors claimed he had died as a result of
a beating by Barlow and threatened to prosecute him. Barlow
admitted to his journal that he had given the man several blows
with a cane for dereliction of duty, but was certain this was not the
cause of his death. He saw the threatened action as 'a conspiracy to
get money', but thought it wise to compound with the widow's
lawyer, to whom he gave £50 to avoid trial.[9]

When an action for damages went further than this, the first
stage was for the plaintiff to get a warrant issued for the arrest of
the alleged offender, who would normally be released on bail in the
sum of the damages claimed and potential expenses, £100–£150

being a typical sum. Sampling of the warrant books shows that there were some eight to ten arrests in cases of damages a year, not many but sufficient to show that this was a path sailors were prepared to take if sufficiently aggrieved.[10]

That such actions were often a bluff or part of a bargaining process by the sailor is shown by the fact that of 35 arrests for damages made in the years 1733–36, twelve never even made it into court and most of the rest were abandoned or dismissed after a relatively short time. Sometimes the plaintiff failed to produce his libel stating the grievance, often because he was unable to raise bail to cover expenses if he lost, sometimes he instructed his proctor to discontinue the case or it was stated that the case had been 'agreed'. On other occasions, the cause was dismissed by the court for various technical reasons. And at least two cases ended with the death of the plaintiff, in the case of Marchant v. Yates after over three years of rambling through the procedures of the court.[11]

Such long delays were common and contrasted with the fairly rapid completion of wage cases. However, sailors were sometimes prepared to see the process out and some cases did go the full distance to judgment and sentence. Andrew Anderson, the man who claimed to have been beaten with an 'elephant's dry'd pizle', failed to prove his case and had to pay expenses of forty shillings to the defendant, William Blinstone. Timothy Terrill was also unsuccessful against Gabriel Ingo, former mate of his ship, though on this occasion expenses were not awarded to the defendant, suggesting that the court did not think him totally innocent. Cortis v. Hart ended in a somewhat pyrrhic victory for the plaintiff, Gouche Cortis, cook of the *Mermaid*, who was awarded his expenses but only one mark, 'to wit, thirteen shillings and four pence', for the 'blows and other ill usage' he had received from Thomas Hart. Nathan Drew by contrast was completely successful against Eustace Hardwick, master of the *Pearl Galley*. His 'cruel usage' was proved and the court awarded him his expenses, back wages and £40 in damages against his captain.[12] Such success was rare, but that it could happen at all explains why many defendants were prepared to compound with their accusers either before or during a case. It is a reasonable assumption that the court was normally suspicious of a sailor's claims and that the procedure, expenses and burden of proof required tended to act in the defendants' favour. Nevertheless, the case of Nathan Drew and others shows that the court was not totally biased against a sailor suing his captain or mate.

No reasons are given for the decisions in these cases and it would be hazardous to assess reasons from the depositions and other evidence. However, depositions do provide clues to what was considered reasonable discipline and punishment. Witnesses were clearly coached by lawyers and one can assume they nearly always exaggerated. Nevertheless, there is some middle ground in what both officers and men were prepared to accept.

First of all, in theory at least, only the captain had the legal power to punish, although he could give permission to other officers to correct a man and, if he was ashore or sick, his power devolved to the chief mate. A drubbing by the mate was however seen to be illegal if the captain was aboard and fit, as can be seen from evidence given for both parties in Cortis v. Hart. 'No mate has a power to beat a cook of the ship he belongs to or any foremast man on board such ship', claimed James Dowie and many other witnesses. Such might be the law but reality was rather different. 'Some times for the sake of keeping peace on board the ship they are compell'd to do it.'[13]

The treatment of boys was different from that of men. Just as a master ashore was entitled to chastise his own servant, so he could on board ship, though it was 'not usual for officers of ships to command each other's servants or for the boatswain to correct the servant of any officer without his leave and approbation'. The unfortunate common ship boys with no master might however be corrected by any officer, as was John Clarke who 'sometimes for giving ill language was corrected by the respondent [a midshipman], the boatswain and other officers'.[14]

Cases brought by sailors against officers were characterized by a legal ritual of character assassination designed to set the scene. The officer would be described as hot-tempered and violent, a man who had beaten many unspecified sailors in the course of the voyage. Bartholomew Biggs, boatswain of the *Arcania Merchant*, was 'very abusive to the mariners . . . and upon very small matter did fight with and strike them and was very hasty and cholerick and given to much drink'. The mate of the *Mermaid* was 'a person of a quarrelsom temper and of a cruel and barbarous behaviour [who] quarreled with and beat and abused several of the mariners'. The sailors, needless to say, claimed they were well behaved, obedient and considerate. The men of the *Edward*, for instance, whose captain was described in 1669 as 'a frantic or mad person', were 'soe diligent and willing to please him that they cutt off theire shoe heels because they would offend or disturb him'.[15]

Witnesses for the accused were quick to respond. The sailor plaintiff would be described as insolent and disobedient throughout the voyage, 'a person of a morose temper' who abused the officers and was often drunk and incapable of doing his duty. Timothy Terrill, for instance, 'within the time of the said voyage several times insulted and abused [many of the officers and crew] with ill language and was frequently drunk and at such times neglected and refused to perform his duty and would not let others of the company worke at theire duty without abusing and interrupting them'. Witnesses for the sailors did their best to deny such allegations, though the charge of drunkenness was sometimes so notorious that it could hardly be denied. Walter Deniston was forced to admit that Andrew Anderson 'was at some times fudled but not oftner than the rest of the ship's company . . . a quiet man and does not know that he was ever disobedient'.[16]

Moving on from general abuse, it was necessary to show there were no grounds for punishment in the particular instance that was the focus of the case. This was normally done by simply stating that the beating or other punishment was inflicted 'without any reasonable or just cause or provocation', a formula which appears repeatedly. However, sailors were often more specific about the lack of due cause. Punishment was seen as unfair if it was for refusal to obey what was thought an unreasonable order, such as being ordered to load ballast in clean shoregoing clothes or perform a trivial task during one's watch below. Incompetence was reasonable grounds for punishment if it should endanger the ship, but it was certainly unfair to punish a sick man who was unable to hold the ship on its course. Sailors also felt they had a right to complain and thought it wrong to be punished for doing so, like John Baker who was beaten 'for saying that the provisions the captain allowed his men were not fitting for dogs'. It was also unfair to victimize a man for a reason unconnected with his duty. Philip Williams, for instance, was reportedly beaten simply because he was Welsh. Captain Scott 'did in an insulting passionate manner say that his owners on his last voyage were Welchmen and that he loved a Welch man with all his heart and . . . told him that he would drub him every halfe hour, and the morrow would make a catt of nine tailes and whip or have him whipped from ship to ship'.[17]

Williams may have suffered for his Welshness, but he was also accused of embezzling butter and this brings us to what was seen as due cause for punishment. Theft certainly was and so was refusal to obey an order or do one's duty. Disobedience was closely followed by abuse of the officers, the two offences often going together as in the case of Daniel Yorkson who was not only disobedient but also swore at the mate, calling him 'old rogue, old dog and old sun of a bitch and drunken old swab'. 'Being disguised by strong liquor' could be grounds for punishment, although drunkenness was normally condoned except when it led to other things, such as 'breeding a great disturbance on board the ship and (as was then said) for endeavouring to have killed another of the company with an axe'. Being drunk or asleep on watch was always a serious crime, especially when acting as sentry 'at the barricado door between the negroes and the ship's company'.[18]

The custom of the sea allowed for a wide range of punishments, from gagging with an iron bar for insolence or blasphemy to running the gauntlet for theft. However, the two main types of punishment employed were confinement in irons and beating, the former often preceding the latter. Confinement in the bilboes, a long iron bar with shackles fastened to the deck, was seen by some sailors as cruel and unlawful and protest sometimes took the form of throwing the instrument overboard. In most cases, however, the point at issue was the length of time a man was confined, which ranged from a few hours to several weeks, and sometimes where he was confined; leaving a man in irons on the open deck in bad weather would be considered cruel, for instance, especially if he was sick.

What constituted a 'moderate' beating is fairly clear from the evidence. The use of the cat-o'-nine-tails was not very common on merchant ships, though certainly not unknown, especially in East Indiamen. The weapons normally used were a rope's end or a cane, though anything at hand might be used on occasion. Witnesses for an aggrieved sailor would emphasize the size or cruel nature of the weapons used. 'Immoderate' weapons included such things as a rope with a knot 'of the circumference of seven inches at least', 'a rope almost two inches thick', 'a billet of wood the thickness of a man's wrist', a 'cane which was large' or was 'knobbed', a rattan 'slitt . . . in four parts'. Witnesses for the accused officer, if they admitted the beating at all, emphasized the gentleness of the instrument, 'with a small bamboo cane and not with a knobbed stick which could not possibly doe him any damage', 'two or three blows with a small rope about an inch and a quarter and not more round which cou'd not nor did any ways hurt or injure'.[19]

The number of strokes was also important. Witnesses for officers rarely admitted to more than half a dozen, while witnesses for the plaintiff stressed the large number of strokes, '31 blows on the bare back', '40 or 50 blowes with a cane', '67 blows with a cat and nine tails . . . very severe and unreasonable'. They also stressed that the beating was not just on the back, which was seen as legitimate, but also on the head and about the face. It was also important to show that serious damage had been done to the man, blood gushing out, loss of sight, multiple contusions and, in some cases, death. Surgeons were usually loyal to the accused officer and would minimize or deny the damage done and, if a sailor died, would normally attribute his death to some other cause.

It was finally valuable to stress that the damage done was such that the victim was unable to do his duty, since it was lawful to correct by blows only 'soe as they doe not maime them, or hurt them soe as to make them uncapable of doeing theire business'. Thomas Hance, second mate of the *Friendship*, claimed in 1736 to have been severely beaten over the head by the master and 'ever since such beating [he has] been troubled with a dizyness in his head and cou'd not goe aloft without danger'. Other sailors claimed that their injuries kept them below for several days or weeks so that they could not do the duty of the ship. John Fox, for instance, who claimed to have been kicked and brutally beaten with 'a peece of a date tree', was so badly bruised and swollen that he 'kept his bed for about five days and was very ill and indisposed in his body and was lett blood for the same by the doctor of the shipp'. Masters and officers refuted such claims. Hugh Crawford, master of the *Mermaid*, said the cook was so far from being disabled as a result of a beating that he 'did his duty better in the homeward than he did in the outward voyage'.[20]

These cases provide some evidence as to what sailors thought was due cause for punishment and what they meant by 'moderate correction'. They do not however give any idea of the frequency of punishment, since by their very nature they reflect the unusual. The only sources which can be used to determine the pattern of punishment on a 'normal' voyage are ships' logbooks. These, however, never report such casual punishments as 'starting' and there is no guarantee that they record every formal punishment either. Nevertheless, logbooks do provide some counterpoint to the picture of maritime violence revealed in court cases.

East Indiamen provide much the largest number of surviving logbooks and these record formal punishments. Long voyages and large crews were the most likely environment for trouble and East Indiamen were often thought to impose harsh discipline, so these logbooks provide a reasonable yardstick for an assessment of punishment on merchant ships. Punishment was supposed to be carried out formally, with the offender 'called to answer for himself' before a 'consultation' of officers. 'If they ordered the delinquent any punishment they wrote the reason therefor and appointed how many blows he should have for his offence to which all the principal officers subscribed their hands.'[21]

The only formal record of such consultations discovered was in a book kept on the *London* in 1664–65. Just two cases are reported, one relating to a sailor found guilty of theft and the other a man accused of a crime unlikely to be easily forgiven by superstitious sailors. Three witnesses deposed that he had advised them to leave the ship at Surat, since 'neither ye ship nor any in her should goe home . . . and moreover saide that he had seen that which he would not see againe for a thousand pounds'. He was found guilty of 'wicked and malicious words . . . tending to divination or witchcraft and discouragement of men in the ship' and was punished severely, receiving ten strokes on two of the Company's ships in the roadstead and five on the third, before being 'turned ashore'.[22]

Records of consultations can also sometimes be found in logbooks, but only rarely in detail. One such case occurred in 1723, when the *Duke of York* was on short allowance of water in the south Atlantic and four men were accused of tapping the captain's water and drinking it. On 1 July, 'the trial of Edward Farren before the captain and officers' took place. The joiner and six sailors gave evidence against him and 'after examination wee found him guilty which he did not deny himself . . . so he was condemned by the officers and ship's company and had thirty lashes'. The other three men 'was found as aiders and abetters and received ten lashes each . . . and was ordered to be their own executioners, each man giving the other ten lashes which they did'.[23]

Such detail is unusual and all that logbooks normally record is the offence and the punishment. Searching the logbooks of East Indiamen is slow work, so the analysis below is based on a small sample of twelve voyages in the 1720s, 1760s and 1770s.[24] In all, these voyages produced exactly fifty punishments, most commonly twelve or sometimes more lashes at the gangway, though some offenders were confined in irons, demoted from office or made to run the gauntlet. Two voyages recorded no formal punishments at all, while on others the gap between punishments was often very long, sometimes more than a year.

Overall, if the logbooks recorded all the punishments, there was absolutely no comparison between the level of punishment on an East Indiaman and on Royal Navy ships as analysed by Byrn. Even on the smaller of his ships with less than twenty guns which were more akin to East Indiamen in size of crew, there were nearly two floggings per month.[25] In the East Indiamen, by contrast, there were just 37 floggings recorded during a total of twenty years, just

under two floggings per year. This is a very small sample which may
be atypical but, even on the *Ankerwyke* in 1770–72, which had the
greatest number of punishments, only eight men were flogged in a
voyage of just under twenty months.

Five of these men were recaptured deserters who received twelve
lashes apiece, bar one man who for the additional crime of
throwing the bilboes overboard received twenty-four. Not many
deserters were recaptured but those who were on the other ships do
not appear to have been flogged. Some were placed in irons and
some handed over to Royal Navy ships, as were three men from the
Lord North in 1771 who 'ran away with the yawl on board a Dutch
ship' and were recovered a couple of months later, placed in irons
and finally 'entered on board H.M.S. *Northumberland*'. This was a
convenient method of getting rid of trouble-makers which was
employed in other trades as well as in East Indiamen.[26]

Theft was one of the commonest causes of punishment, eight
men being flogged for this offence and six ordered to run the
gauntlet, one suffering this punishment 'a second time having
being detected in severall shifts'. Running the gauntlet involved
proceeding once, twice or more times, through a double line of
one's shipmates, each of whom was provided with a small piece of
rope called a 'knitle', and was normally reserved for those who stole
from their shipmates. Those who stole from the ship were usually
flogged, like John Ewens who received two dozen lashes 'for
stealing the provision' or John Grimes who suffered a very severe
thirty-six lashes while the *Calcutta* was in China 'for carrying the
ship's shott into the hoppo [customs] boat to sell, and for
drunkenness and neglect of duty'.[27]

Other crimes punished by flogging were striking or 'collaring' an
officer, abuse to an officer, refusing duty or neglect of duty, insolence and such 'mutinous' behaviour as drawing a knife or making
'mutinous expressions' while other men were being punished.
Mutiny itself was common enough in some form or other, men on
two of the twelve voyages being punished for this crime. When the
Godfrey was anchored in the Downs on her return from Bombay in
December 1772, 'there was a mutiny of the ship's company in
which the Captain and several of the officers were collard'. Eight

ringleaders were turned out of the ship and replaced by men from Deal, while two were placed in irons, presumably to face punishment in London though in fact one was released 'upon his asking pardon of the captain' and the other escaped at Woolwich. Fifty years earlier, the crew of the *Duke of York* refused to work and went ashore in Bombay without permission because they objected to the mate replacing the captain, who had died at sea. The Governor of Bombay ordered two companies of soldiers to 'take them up' and later punished two of the men as an example to the rest in the East India Company's version of flogging round the fleet. 'Two of our seamen whippd alongside by order of the Governor and Councell, likewise aboard the other ships receiving five lashes each', which presumably means five lashes alongside each ship.[28]

The only other merchant ships whose surviving logbooks report floggings were slavers. In his journals of three slaving voyages between 1750 and 1754, Captain John Newton ordered six floggings, three for theft, two for drunkenness, fighting ashore and losing the punt, and one for behaving 'very mutinously in my absence, daring the officers and refusing his duty'. This last offender was the carpenter and Newton noted that 'the barricado not being built I could not afford to put him in irons' and so 'gave him two dozen stripes', a punishment which achieved its aims since the barricado was built and there was no more trouble from the carpenter.[29]

Confinement in irons was quite a common punishment. It had the immediate effect of immobilising a drunken or abusive man until he quietened down and sometimes an hour or two's confinement was enough to restore harmony aboard ship. For the more intransigent, the discomfort and humiliation of confinement provided the stage for a piece of theatre in which the man was eventually released on the promise of future good behaviour. In October 1750, for instance, Captain Newton returned from a visit to another ship and

> ... the officers and all the ship's company to a man complained that the boatswain had behaved very turbulently, and used them ill, to the hindrance of the ship's business.

Having passed by several of the like offences before, I thought it most proper to put him in irons, *in terrorem*, being apprehensive he might occasion disturbance.

Three days later, he 'dismissed the boatswain from his confinement, upon his submission and promise of amendment', and had no more trouble from him. Confinement in irons might also be the prelude to the offender being handed over to some other authority. Four trouble-makers on Newton's *Duke of Argyle* were confined in irons and a week or so later handed over to the tender mercies of HMS *Surprize*, 'and received four men in exchange'.[30]

Logbooks make it clear that most indiscipline on board merchant ships, other than slavers and East Indiamen, occurred in port. Apparent harmony regularly broke down after the first run ashore or when liquor from the shore was brought aboard. Captains had a variety of means of dealing with the fighting, abuse or 'mutinous' behaviour likely to follow. The simplest was just to have the man or men taken below, and if necessary restrained, until they slept it off. Worse cases could be dealt with by confinement in irons for a few hours or days and, possibly, the transfer of the offender to the civil authority or a convenient Royal Navy ship. Other men could be demoted, discharged or encouraged to desert. In none of the logbooks examined, however, was a formal flogging ordered for such indiscipline, though it is clear from court cases that informal violence was common enough.

Logbooks, then, give a very different picture from that presented in court cases, a picture mainly of harmony and very little formal punishment. Since one would hardly expect either a logbook or a witness in court to tell the whole truth, one can only conclude that the reality must lie somewhere between the two extremes. It seems clear that formal flogging was fairly unusual in merchant ships, even in East Indiamen, which were the only ones which flogged with any regularity at all, such public punishments being seen as 'a mark of shame and a great disgrace to the person whipd and are not inflicted upon any but such as offend in a very high manner'.[31] Merchant captains preferred instead the informal and less shameful 'drubbing' with fists, rattan or rope's end.

Authority aboard ship might sometimes rest in the nobility of a captain who only had to speak and look to be obeyed. Other captains no doubt got along by treating their crews in a free and easy way and hoping they would give no trouble. But, usually, authority rested ultimately on the threat of violence, the sort of casual violence that does not get into logbooks. Jack Cremer illustrates two approaches to discipline in his description of his service as mate of the *Bansted Galley*. The captain had no discipline over the crew and so, 'to get them in order I begun with fighting and beating them one after the other; which when my captain found out, he said that to live easy and have a full belly was the best way for him'.[32] Cremer may have been more brutal and aggressive than most officers, but his attitude towards discipline was probably commoner than that of his captain.

Such violence needed to be inflicted with moderation, however, since there were a number of ways sailors could retaliate. They could go to court as has been seen; they could mutiny as will be seen in the next chapter; or they could bide their time until an opportunity occurred to take vengeance. The crew of Cremer's ship swore 'that one time or other they would remember me' and such threats to deal with unpleasant officers were commonplace. The crew of the *Peace* were heard to say that if they met the captain ashore 'they would do him a good turn for being so cross to them in the said voyage', while John Soule, boatswain of the *Preston*, 'challenged the master to fight him att the next Christian shore they came to and threatened to post him for a coward if he would not fight with him'.[33]

Captains were rarely totally isolated when faced by indiscipline or worse. They nearly always had the loyal support of some or all of their officers and, judging by those prepared to give evidence in the captain's favour, by considerable numbers of their crew. Captain James Lowry of the *Molly* was distinctly unusual in this respect. He was tried in 1752 for the murder of a sailor who had died after a savage beating and not a single member of his crew gave evidence in his support. He was found guilty and sentenced to be hanged.[34] In port, where problems of discipline most often came to the boil, masters had many other allies – the Royal Navy, masters and officers of other merchant ships, British consuls, colonial magistrates, civil officers of the East India Company and a whole range of foreign authorities from African kings to European magistrates. Application to any of these powers could quickly bring 'a guard of seapoys' or 'a file of musquetters' to whisk an offender away to prison ashore.[35]

Captain Phillips thought it was 'the greatest prudence, as well as interest, of a commander . . . to gain his men's good-will and affections by being humane to them'.[36] This was clearly true and it seems probable that on the silent majority of ships which provide no evidence of punishment or problems of discipline, this was the most effective way of managing a crew. But, where there *was* trouble, it was good policy to involve both the offender and the crew as a whole in resolving the problem. As has been seen, one major purpose of confinement was to bring an offender to an acknowledgment of his offence and a promise 'to behave better from after'. And it was not just in East Indiamen that the whole crew were made party to a punishment, even to the extent of each man playing a part in inflicting it as in running the gauntlet. If logbooks can be believed, most ships had just one or two trouble-makers whose names appear in a crescendo of annoyance on the part of the writer of the log. No doubt, such men often annoyed their shipmates as well as their officers and it was not difficult to find sailors to bear witness against them and to collude in their punishment.

Carrying the crew to a semblance of collective decision-making might often be a piece of theatre, but it was effective theatre in many situations other than the decision to punish a man disrupting the harmony of the ship. It was advisable, as has been seen, to get the agreement of the crew to a change in the originally contracted voyage. Collective endorsement was also prudent in situations when a decision was likely to lead the crew into potential danger. When the *Rochester* was faced by what appeared to be a powerful privateer in 1704, 'one Edward Smith midshipman on behalfe of divers of the ships company proposed that if the Captain would promise to take care of the wounded and disabled men that they would all stand out to the last, which being considered on was intended to be done'. When William Dampier was in danger in the southern Indian Ocean, he 'called all our men to consult about our safety, and desired every man, from the highest to the lowest, freely to give his real opinion and advice what to do in this dangerous juncture'.[37]

Captains might also get the crew's agreement before calling off a search for a man lost overboard, as in *Two Years before the Mast* where the captain 'called all hands aft, and asked them if they were satisfied that everything had been done to save the man, and if they thought there was any use in remaining there longer. The crew all said that it was in vain, for the man did not know how to swim, and was very heavily dressed'. Similarly, when a decision was made in 1682 to spend no more time waiting for the longboat and six men of the *Francis* who had been sent to search for a harbour, it was noted in the logbook that 'councell thought good rather to make the best of our way on our voyage then to strive in vain'. Reducing rations was likely to cause trouble so, once again, it was sensible to get the crew to accept the necessity. When the *Thomas and Betsey* was short of food in 1776, the captain got the ship's company to survey what was left and then made an inventory in the logbook which was signed by two sailors on behalf of their shipmates.[38]

These and similar incidents may often have been stage-managed, but they show that discipline and the running of a ship was not necessarily a matter of confrontation where the captain or captain and officers were always in direct opposition to the forecastle men. Indeed one of the commoner and more disruptive divisions on board ship was not between the captain and crew, but between the captain and chief or only mate. This was a difficult relationship since the mate, though clearly inferior in rank, was often the older man who would have or think that he had a greater knowledge of seamanship. He took over command when the captain was ashore or sick and was also the captain's normal successor if he died, all situations likely to lead to problems. In smaller ships, the two watches were commanded by the captain and mate whose rivalry, criticism and jealousy of each other is often only too evident from depositions. Anthony Ford, for instance, was hired as mate on a voyage to Newfoundland in 1670:

He behaved himself very crossly and obstinately towards [Daniel] Watson the master, and frequently slighted him and jeered at the orders and commands of the said master and did often affront him with contemptuous words . . . deriding him and laughing at him behind his back as if the said Watson did not understand his office.[39]

Such confrontation often led to serious trouble, as it did in this instance, which ended with Watson beating and abusing Ford and leaving him ashore in Newfoundland. 'Boatswaine', he was heard to say, 'I charge you upon the perill of your wages not to lett Anthony Ford on board the ship, and if he offers to come knocke him downe with a hand spike for God damne mee hee shall not come on board againe'. These cases of hostility between captain and mate often led to a serious breakdown in the management of the ship since the sailors were likely to be divided in their loyalties between the two men.[40]

Examples of the strains of this relationship run like a refrain through the latter part of Edward Barlow's *Journal*. When he was hired as chief mate of the *Delight*, he was wary from the beginning about his captain John Smith since he 'had none of the clearest report for his civil and his honest carriage towards his men and his servants'. This reputation proved accurate. 'We could give him no content, and one morning above the rest, having some business wherein some differences arose between him and me, and some few words passing, he abused me very much.' A quarrel led to a scuffle and eventually the captain claimed that Barlow had attempted to strike him and turned him ashore in Sumatra. Very much the same happened again on Barlow's last voyage to China when he discovered too late that his captain was 'a young high-flown, conceited, proud, imperious, base and perfidious sort of a man . . . a young seaman and had been but three voyages . . . and [most demeaning of all] a former milliner of small wares'. Antagonism between the two men began to come to a head during an argument over seamanship in the Indian Ocean. 'As though I could not tell how to hand sails, having used the seas six times the time he had.' Matters did not improve and Barlow was put out of the ship in

St Helena. Barlow was middle-aged by the time of these incidents, and probably an awkward man to handle, but he was by no means unusual in finding it impossible to develop a satisfactory working relationship with his captain.[41]

Barlow's last thought on captains was that 'all commanders and masters are grown up with pride and oppression and tyranny'.[42] There was clearly some truth in such an assertion, but it needs to be seen in perspective. The nature of a captain's position of absolute authority certainly gave him an awesome power which could well lead to pride, oppression and tyranny. But this power could be and was circumscribed in a number of ways and though tyranny existed it was by no means universal. Most ships indeed seem to have got along with no more than a lot of shouting, the occasional punch or blow from a rattan or a rope's end and a certain amount of unwise abuse of officers by men whose tongues had been loosened by liquor in port. Sometimes, of course, matters went much further than this as will be seen in the discussion of mutiny in the next chapter. But we will start by looking at the very common and virtually insoluble problem of desertion.

CHAPTER ELEVEN

Desertion and Mutiny

CHAPTER ELEVEN

Desertion and Mutiny

'You have heard how frequent
conspiracies are growne aboard
ships, wherefore keep a watchfull eye
and be very carefull and diligent to
prevent such practices in your ship.'

Orders for the *Samuel and Anna,*
1702[1]

An aggrieved or unhappy sailor might go to court, but he was far
more likely to desert his ship and, after sampling the joys of the
shore, try his luck in another one. Desertion was punished by
forfeiture of wages and usually required the abandonment of one's
sea-chest, so it was not undertaken lightly. For all that, it was
common and could be a major problem for masters unable to find
suitable replacements. The collective withdrawal of labour defined
as mutiny was potentially a far greater problem and this too was
sufficiently common in some form or other to keep masters and
other officers alert, watching out for sailors muttering in cliques
and keeping their ears open for the ominous sound of cannon balls
being rolled across the deck at night.

The scale of desertion from merchant ships can be discovered by
using the same muster rolls and paybooks which were used in
Chapter Nine to analyse mortality at sea.[2] If a man 'ran' from his

ship, these documents record the fact. This material shows that no one deserted from whalers, hardly surprisingly since the floating ice floes of the Arctic were not the sort of place that attracted deserting sailors. Very few men deserted in ports in northern or western Europe, but desertion in the Mediterranean was quite common though it was not on the scale of desertion in the American colonies or the West Indies or from slavers and East Indiamen. An average of one in eight men deserted from the crews of the two hundred slavers and West Indiamen examined and about one in fifteen from the fifty East Indiamen. Desertion was also concentrated in particular ships. Despite the high propensity to desert of sailors in slavers and West Indiamen, for example, there were no deserters at all on over 40 per cent of the former and on well over half of the latter.

Lisbon, Cadiz and Leghorn in Tuscany were the favourite places to desert in southern Europe, and Jamaica was much the most popular jumping-off place in the Caribbean, attracting most of the deserters from slavers as well as from West Indiamen. Desertion from East Indiamen might happen anywhere the ships anchored, from the Cape Verde Islands to Canton, but nearly two-thirds of those who ran did so in Bombay, Madras and Calcutta. Most sailors deserted when their ship was lying alongside a wharf or when they were on duty or liberty ashore, but desertion was also feasible when surrounded by water. 'At 1 a.m. missing the pynness from alongside, all hands were called to see who was gon when we found John Whittle carpenter run with a great part of his towells [tools] and likewise a great part of his clooths.' Other deserters swam ashore or to another ship, sometimes with fatal results:

> At 10 p.m. [in the Downs] William Church in attempting to make his escape (as is supposed) by swimming to a ship that lay near us, which was first discovered by his calling out in the water, before a boat could get to his assistance imagine he was unfortunately drown'd as our boat ask'd the ship nearest us whether a man had swam on board and they told them not.[3]

Many men ran simply because they 'had a fancy to do it' or were fed up with shipboard life and wanted to 'go on their rambles' or 'go up and down debauching themselves', many of these being only technically deserters since they returned of their own accord after a few days or weeks on the spree. This was common in Mediterranean ports where mariners often received some pay and even commoner among the crews of slavers who received half their pay once the slaves were delivered and so suffered little financial loss if they deserted. Many were encouraged to do so by captains needing to reduce crews for the homebound voyage. Desertion itself often led to more desertion since, once a few men had gone, the workload for the remainder would increase and make them discontented.

Other men deserted because they were unhappy in the ship or had a grievance. Men who were punished, for instance, were quite likely to desert once the opportunity occurred, like John Salter of the *Judith* who deserted after 'the captain gave him some strips with a caine for loosing a new oare out of the yawle'. This was particularly common in East Indiamen where sailors who were flogged were often later marked as run in the paybook. In general, men whose names appear in logbooks as nuisances or troublemakers often deserted before the end of the voyage, no doubt encouraged by their captains. The logbook of the *Alexander*, for instance, reports the bad behaviour of Peter Nilson which started on his return from liberty in New York 'very much disguised in liquor'. Mutinous behaviour, fighting, abuse of his shipmates and an attempt to steal a boat were eventually followed by his desertion some two weeks after he first began to be mentioned in the logbook. Many sailors claimed they were forced to desert, such as Edward Fentiman, foremastman on the slaver *City of London*. He jumped overboard and swam ashore, following savage beatings from the mate, 'apprehending himselfe to be in danger of his life'.[4]

There were however more positive reasons for desertion. In February 1775, for instance, some forty sailors deserted from the East Indiaman *Godfrey* in the Downs because they had discovered 'there is some transports going out who gives more wages than is given to India'. At so early a stage of the voyage they had nothing much to lose by running, but anyone might take advantage of a good offer, like the carpenter of the *Coast Frigott* who refused to work on the ship in Constantinople and later deserted because he found he could get 'money to drink and debauch with [by working] at day work upon both French, Turkish and English ships' that were anchored in the harbour.[5]

Sailors also found opportunities for financial advantage in Asia where white labour was at a premium. Many deserters found well-paid berths in native shipping or in the 'country ships' owned by Europeans where they met 'with much encouragement', such as the four months' advance of pay which Captain Finch Randall reported being paid in Calcutta to deserters who signed up with country ships. William Spavens and three other men deserted the East India Company in Sumatra with an intent to get to Calcutta 'and there engage in country ships . . . which presented us with a view of accumulating fortunes and being great'. In the event, he accumulated nothing, but other men were more fortunate as Dampier pointed out. 'Oft-times [these] Englishmen are but ordinary sailors, yet they are promoted to some charge of which they could not be so capable any where else but in the East-Indies.'[6]

Great fortunes were less likely to be made in the West Indies and America, but similar opportunities existed for white sailors since there was plenty of local shipping and wages were higher than in England. For the more adventurous, there was the lure of buccaneering or logwood cutting [a raw material for dyeing] in the swamps and forests of central America, an illegal activity which might lead to a Spanish prison but one with charms for a sailor. 'The wood cutters are generally a rude drunken crew, some of which have been pirates, and most of them sailors; their chief delight is in drinking; and when they broach a quarter cask or a hogshead of wine, they seldom stir from it while there is a drop left.' Other sailors simply took the opportunity of a free passage to America to emigrate, as was pointed out in 1789 with reference to deserters from slavers. 'Many of the green men [ie landsmen] that are brought up to trade or husbandry frequently get very good employ and settle in the West India islands.'[7]

However, most of those deserting in America and the West Indies had no intention of staying there, since an easy and profitable way of getting home had been created by the very fact of high desertion rates. When it was time for ships to sail home, their captains were of course likely to be short of crew and so were forced to hire sailors for the run home. Such 'runners' could often command two or three times the normal monthly wages for the same voyage. And so, as Tim Le Goff remarks of French West Indiamen who faced an identical situation, 'one captain's deserter became another captain's necessary replacement'.[8]

Captains had an ambivalent attitude towards deserters. A man who ran had in effect given his services for nothing, as Captain Imy gleefully pointed out when he met his deserted cook in Barbados. 'How now Sparke', he claimed to have said, 'you have spunn a faire thread to lose all your wages (meaneing that the said cooke had forfeited his wages by deserting the ship's service)'. Some deserters in theory lost more than just their wages, since many sailors signed a bond or agreed in their articles to pay a fine to the owners in the event of their desertion. For example, the twenty members of the crew of the *Arabella* agreed in 1717 to pay a £50 penalty if they deserted in the course of a voyage to Madagascar and Buenos Aires, though no example of the successful execution of such a penalty has been discovered. Captains were also no doubt glad to see the back of many deserters, those who habitually got drunk or abusive and disrupted the harmony of the ship. When the mate of the *Edward* deserted in Virginia in 1669, the captain called the company together and said 'I hope wee shall now live in peace and unity together, hee (meaning the mate) being gone', though this hope was not fulfilled since it was the captain himself rather than the mate who was the chief cause of trouble on this ship.[9]

Such instances do not mean that no effort at all was made to recover deserters. Captains might well be worried about the demonstration effects, since when one man ran several others often followed him. And desertion was not always costless. Where replacement crew was difficult to obtain or expensive, captains were likely to go to considerable trouble to recover those who ran. In doing so, they had plenty of allies since authorities ashore would normally co-operate, while merchants and planters were clearly interested in the efficient operation of shipping and had no wish to see ships delayed as a result of crew shortages caused by desertion.

Colonial laws regarding deserting sailors were similar to those enacted against runaway servants and these were reinforced by the Act of 1729 which empowered magistrates to arrest deserters and commit them to up to thirty days' hard labour. The purpose of this punishment was similar to that of confinement in irons aboard, the idea being that the runaway would sooner or later plead forgiveness and return to his ship, though if he proved adamant in his refusal he was rarely forced to do so. Much effort went into the recapture of deserters. Newspapers abounded with notices of deserting sailors and locals could make a living by catching these men on the run, Virginia, for example, offering a reward of five shillings a head to those who brought deserters back from a distance of under ten miles and ten shillings for those who had fled further.[10]

What proportion of deserters were recovered is unknown. Byrn found that only eight per cent of deserters from Royal Navy ships on the Leeward Islands station were apprehended, despite very considerable efforts being made by both the naval and civil authorities. However, local people were almost certainly more sympathetic to deserters from the navy than from merchantmen so the recovery rate of the latter was probably higher, while many returned voluntarily once they had had enough of their 'rambles'. A witness in 1708 claimed a remarkable success rate for the man catchers of Virginia. 'It is usual and customary for masters of ships at Virginia when any of their men leave them there to send a hue and cry after them and then 'tis scarce possible for such mariners to avoid being taken.'[11]

This was no doubt wishful thinking, though logbooks and other sources certainly show that many who ran were later apprehended. 'Last night the cabbin boy run away', reports the logbook of the *Swift* in Maryland, 'but was took up by two men ten miles in the country and brought back'. The paybook of the *Lyon* of Dublin for 1700–01 has entries for no less than seven men who ran away and were recovered in Ireland, America and the West Indies. All had money deducted from their wages for the cost of recovering them, such as John Vickers who was docked five shillings and sixpence 'expended in looking for you when you run away' in New York and a further four shillings and sixpence 'when you runn away the second time' in Antigua. This was simply for the hue and cry. Imprisonment cost much more; the cost to Garrett King of thirty days in a Maryland prison in 1732 was twenty pounds of tobacco a day, a total of some three pounds sterling.[12]

Life was no easier for the runaway sailor in European ports. When seven men from the *Rose Bush* stayed ashore in Leghorn in 1666, 'drinking and idling and soe neglecting their duties aboard', the master complained to the English consul 'of his said men and of the man of the house that harboured them . . . and they all seaven being some time kept prisoners three of them came on board and the captain entertained them', but the other four refused to rejoin the ship despite their spell in an Italian prison. In 1700, some men from the *Hopewell* went ashore without permission in Lisbon and so delayed the ship's departure. Merchants lading on the ship got the vice-consul to commit the men to prison, from which they were discharged on their promise 'to proceed to London and minde their business'. The master paid their prison fees, but no doubt recovered these and other expenses from their wages.[13]

Deserters who refused to return to the ship, even after imprisonment, very often had good reasons to keep away and captains sometimes took precautions lest they might later sue for wages or damages on the grounds that they had been forced to leave the ship. In 1715, for instance, three sailors from the *Mary Frigott* deserted in Lisbon, three in Cadiz and two in Leghorn. In this last port, the master, second mate and carpenter made a declaration before the British consul. 'We do herby further declare that duering ye time of being on board ye said ship Marry frigott that neither I John Feild or James Gamson or Francis Tabby nor any other officer to ye best of our knowlidge have misused ye said persons upon any accompt whatever.' One finds similar declarations in logbooks, as in the journal of the *African* for 5 April 1754. 'Manuel Antonio, a Portuguese sailor, who shipped with us at Liverpool, run away . . . He pretends for ill usage, but every officer on board can witness he never was struck by any one. The true reason it seems by Mr Billinge's account is having been detected stealing some knives and tobacco out of the boat.'[14]

Manuel ran away in Africa, which was not a very popular haven for deserters, though slave ships were sufficiently unpleasant for many men to run away on the coast. Some lived among the Africans for months or years, but most simply shipped aboard the next slaver that arrived and hoped it would prove a more acceptable berth. But Africa was not necessarily any safer as a haven than Europe or America. The Royal African Company clearly had an incentive to round up deserters and the men to do so and so did the local kings and chiefs whose livelihood depended on the smooth operation of the slave trade. When William Lees attempted to desert from the *Duke of Argyle* after being punished, Captain Newton 'was obliged to give the blacks a gallon of brandy to secure him for me in irons', while on his next voyage he 'sent to the King to offer a reward for apprehending my people', though on this occasion without success.[15]

Deserters were no more secure in the Indian Ocean island of Joanna whose economy depended heavily on victualling East Indiamen and whose prince was therefore happy to do the Company a favour. When four men from the *Ankerwyke* deserted there in June 1771, Captain Barwell 'sent an officer ashore to the prince offerring him a reward to find them'. The men were soon rounded up, clapped in irons and later flogged at the gangway. Such a punishment would have been unusual in most merchantmen, but the East India Company tended to be harsher to deserters since European replacements could be difficult to find in Asian waters. They also made considerable efforts to recapture deserters, sending sepoys to search for them ashore or on non-Company shipping and on occasion resorting to diplomacy for the same purpose. In 1770, for instance, the Governor of Bombay made a deal with his French counterpart in Tellicherry, 'as a mutual return of deserters must be for the good of both parties'.[16] The majority of deserters, both in India and elsewhere, retained their liberty but that liberty might be precarious if they did not watch out for themselves.

Sometimes men deserted in such large numbers that their behaviour was akin to mutiny, as in the case of the *Godfrey* in February 1775 when some forty men deserted the ship in the Downs, an action which led to a certain amount of violence before they got clear away.[17] This was not described as mutiny in the logbook, but it seems more mutinous to the outsider than many other actions to which that adjective was applied in contemporary records. The word 'mutiny' could indeed mean anything from a fairly minor questioning of authority to an open revolt.

Mutiny in the latter sense catches one's eye in the records, since it is such a dramatic event. But, once one subjects such revolts to the mundane routine of counting them, they turn out not to have been as common as one might imagine. Marcus Rediker defined mutiny as a 'collective effort, planned or spontaneous, to curtail the captain's power and, in the most extreme cases, to seize control of the ship'. He found evidence of sixty such rebellions on English and American ships in the first half of the eighteenth century, an average of just over one a year, though he is probably correct in believing that there were more than were brought to light by his researches. In about half of the cases, the mutineers succeeded in taking control of the ship and roughly a third turned pirates. The French maritime historian Alain Cabantous found a somewhat higher rate of mutinies in French ships, including those of the navy and privateers. After sifting the evidence, he suggested 'the number of 200 to 250 rebellions for the whole of the French marine between 1680 and 1789', an average of about two a year. Both writers point out that there were more mutinies in some years or periods than others, but overall this ultimate challenge to the authority of captains was surprisingly rare. Sailors muttered a lot, were often abusive or threatening to their officers, but only very occasionally did they resort to real collective violence.[18]

Nevertheless, mutinies did happen sufficiently often to make captains wary at any sign of the forming of cliques or 'cabals' among the men and, more generally, apprehensive of any unusually insolent, abusive or violent behaviour by individuals. The 'Journals Book' of the *Glasgow* records no mutiny in her voyage to Madeira and Virginia in 1735, but Captain George Grear who wrote it up constantly had mutiny on his mind. He noted on the flyleaf that on 15 October Henry Hynes was 'incapable of his duty as mate very much and bred a mutiny on board the ship in the latitude of 43°.25' and gave me very impertinent language'. Two days later, Thomas

Hanshaw addressed several members of the crew, saying that 'he know'd the way to Spain or Portugal . . . and if they would stand by him he would take ye ship by God', but nothing more arose from this incident. At the back of the book, there are further notes about troubles aboard. On the night of 23 September, for instance, 'John Brown made a noise very tumoustly; very mutinous and likewise very drunk . . . likewise deny'd his duty'.[19]

Such troubles frequently happened on ships as 'difficult' and often drunk individuals tested the captain's authority, to see what they could get away with or possibly to gauge the temper of other members of the crew. A strong captain could usually deal with such behaviour quickly and effectively by asserting his authority, as did Captain Blair of the *Vestal Frigate* in May 1760 when faced with serious insubordination from Leif Errickson, a Danish sailor. When the second mate threatened to 'lick' the Dane if he did not stop fighting with a shipmate, he 'answered him very haughtily that he . . . should never strike him while he was able to take his own part, which he hoped his two hands would always enable him to do against any such as him'. Hearing this, the captain quickly came on deck, rebuked the mate for putting up with such insolence and then told Errickson that if he ever attempted to strike an officer he 'would make an example of him to the whole ship's company'. Errickson continued 'to animate and prejudice the people against me with many threatenings of revenge at London and wishing I were in his power', but a threat to clap him in irons for the rest of the voyage was sufficient to stop his bluster and he 'talked nothing more – only what he spoke in Danish or Dutch to some of his countrymen'.[20]

No more is heard of Errickson in the journal and this indeed is the normal scenario in such incidents, a flare-up, an assertion of authority, some muttering and that was the end of it. Muttering and general disobedience by several members of the crew was more alarming, as on the *Elizabeth* on her return from Jamaica in 1691 when 'all the time . . . all or most of the mariners . . . did carry and demeane themselves cross and stubborne [and were] very disobedient to the master and did grumble and mutter att his orders'. In the previous year, a more serious incident occurred on the *St Thomas* when six men refused to allow one of their shipmates to be brought to the capstan to be flogged for 'breeding a great disturbance on board the ship'. This was certainly close to mutiny but, despite the captain's failure to assert his authority, nothing more happened and the six men deserted in Virginia, desertion rather than mutiny being the normal response to discontent.[21]

A real cabal might be signalled by a formal approach by spokesmen for the crew, such as the sailors Rowlands and Hutchinson of the East Indiaman *Godfrey* who led 'some of the people aft and complained that they had not sufficient provisions and that they would not work without they had more nor do any duty'. The captain pointed out that, despite the very slow passage they were making, they still had 'six meat days in a week and on the banyan days two drams a day'. He was however worried about the 'very mutinous' behaviour of these men, but in fact the ship reached Colombo safely without any further trouble.[22]

More sinister than spokesmen was the 'mutinous and seditious paper' known as a 'round robin'. This was a sheet of paper on which two concentric circles had been drawn. Within the inner circle, the sailors would 'write what they have a mind to have done' and between the two circles they would write their names. 'No one can be said to be first, so that they are all equally guilty' and 'no one can be excused by saying he was the last that signed it, and he had not done it without great persuasion'. The origins of the expression 'round robin' are obscure; it was apparently a term of abuse in the sixteenth century and in the seventeenth could be applied to a leader in rebellion. But, by the end of this century, it had undergone a sea change and had become, as the *Gentleman's Magazine* stated in 1731, 'the method used by sailors when they mutiny, by signing their names in an orbicular manner'.[23]

The earliest mention in the sources used here comes from a deposition of 1698 relating to an incident on the *Fleet Frigott*. The captain refused to let the crew go ashore at Tenerife, so 'some of them drew up a paper called a Round Robin and signed the same, whereby they intimated that if the captaine would not give them leave to goe ashore, they would take leave'. Thereafter, round robins appear every now and then, very often in cases where their circulation provided notice of an intended mutiny and enabled captains to take the necessary steps to put it down. In November 1752, for example, Captain Newton was informed by a sailor that 'he had been solicited by Richard Swain to sign what he called a round robin . . . I thought myself very secure of any danger of this kind, as every body has behaved very quiet the whole voyage and I do not remember the least complaint or grievance'. Swain was rapidly put 'in double irons', as was another sailor who said 'in plain terms . . . that he would kill Mr Welsh [the mate] and the doctor, or at least leave just alive'. Newton got rid of his bad apples as soon as he could by transferring them to another ship, whose captain agreed to 'deliver them to the first man of war that offered'.[24]

Captain Nathaniel Uring used rather more violent methods to deal with a suspected mutiny in 1712. He believed that several of his crew were ready to turn pirate and was sure that a round robin had been drawn up and was being circulated. He faced up to the men, beating the supposed ringleaders with his cane one after the other until one of the sailors not in the plot produced the hidden document. This evidence of intended mutiny and piracy was sufficient to keep his crew 'exactly diligent and obedient during the rest of the voyage'.[25] Uring's bravery in facing out the conspiracy no doubt grew in the telling, but quick and decisive action, the assertion of authority and the fact that the captain usually had support from many sailors as well as most officers meant that most mutinies petered out in this fashion. 'Mutiny' was indeed very often no more than a spontaneous reaction to some grievance and might be as short-lived and as quickly forgotten as defiant behaviour by an individual.

When a real mutiny did take place, it might take several forms. In 1669, the whole crew of the *Edward* led by the mate simply took over the ship in Chesapeake Bay, since the captain had ordered a change of course which they believed would result in shipwreck. Other crews adamantly refused to weigh anchor and set sail, maybe because the ship was leaking and considered dangerous or because they wanted to wait for a convoy 'for fear of the Turk', such as the crew of the *Greyhound* who in 1681 refused to sail home with a cargo of currants from the island of Zante.[26]

No violence was offered in the above examples, simply passive resistance, and the sailors had no intention of seizing the ship. But this was not of course always the case and the classic scenario of violent mutiny was always a possibility. Most men carried personal weapons, if only a knife, and ships abounded in other potential weapons, such as handspikes, not to mention the guns and small arms, the latter normally being kept under lock and key in the officers' quarters ready to be distributed to those deemed loyal at the first sign of trouble.

Armed rebellion might end with no one being killed, sometimes with the captain managing to overawe the mutineers, sometimes with the mutineers successful and the captain and those loyal to him put ashore or cast adrift in one of the ship's boats. But such humanity could lead to speedy retribution, as in the slaver *Antelope* in 1749. The master, surgeon and boatswain were put in a boat off the African coast with some food and water and were soon picked up by another slaver which recaptured the *Antelope*. The mutineers were later handed over to HMS *Hunter* and brought home for trial, though they frustrated the course of justice by escaping from the Marshalsea Prison.[27]

Fear of retribution, the heat and violence of the uprising and hatred of particular officers meant that successful mutiny was more than likely to be associated with murder, often several murders. Murder after all carried the same punishment, death, as piracy and these were the two felonies for which captured mutineers were usually indicted. John Wynn, who styled himself 'Captain Power the Bravo' after he and six others armed with cutlasses and pistols had taken over the slaver *Polly* in 1766, shot the chief mate and another man and 'whipped, slashed with cutlasses and beheaded a free black man on board whom he suspected of making a motion to the slaves'. All we know of the mutiny on board the snow *Will* comes from her muster roll, which tells in outline a similar story. She left Liverpool in December 1773 with a crew of 31 and returned in August 1774 with just seven of these men commanded by Elias Harrison, the ship's doctor. One man had died of disease and one had drowned, the captain and four other officers were killed by mutineers on the night of 15 January 1774, thirteen men ran and four were left as prisoners in Madeira. The mutiny of the *Haswell*, on her way to Virginia in 1735, also occurred near Madeira. Led by the boatswain, the crew rose 'and murdered the master and his mates in a most barbarous manner' and then sailed to the island of Marie Galante near Guadeloupe. Here 'a gentleman, who was a passenger in the ship and luckily understanding French, was employed by them as their interpreter, found means to discover their villainy by slipping a paper into the hands of the Governor'. The ship was seized and sent to Martinique where the crew were tried and five men found guilty and sentenced, 'the boatswain and another man to be broke on the wheel, three others . . . to be hanged, which was exactly as they justly deserved'.[28] Mutineers did not have a monopoly of violence.

The motives for mutiny, especially armed mutiny and the seizure of the ship, are not always apparent, since much of what we know comes from the desperate defence of men being tried for their lives. Those who could make a plausible case would obviously claim they were forced into joining the mutineers, as did John Tomlin of the slaver *Plumper* in 1766 who said 'he was obliged to do as the rest of the crew did'.[29] Other recaptured mutineers would be ready with justification of their behaviour – maltreatment, overwork, an unseaworthy ship, shortage of water or provisions, 'a frantick captain' and so on – and these were no doubt important factors in persuading men to join a conspiracy, though not necessarily the motives of its leaders.

Many mutinies were brought to fruition, if not caused, by drink like that aboard the *Pélerin* of Granville which Alain Cabantous said was 'caused entirely by drink and lasted only as long as the crew were drunk'. The mutiny aboard the slaver *Antelope*, by contrast, was caused by the absence of drink according to her surgeon who stated that the captain did not make 'any allowance of strong liquors which it was usual for masters of other ships on the coast to do'. The enraged men broke into the spirits store, got drunk and, from then on, one thing led to another. The motivation of other mutinies was perhaps more rational, such as that aboard the *Deepsey Brigantine* in 1755 when a naval press tender tried to board the ship on its return from Africa. Led by the second mate, the crew mutinied, locked up the captain and first mate and fired on the tender. Eventually, fourteen men escaped in the ship's boat and went ashore in Sussex.[30]

One can have some sympathy with sailors who mutinied as a result of harsh treatment aboard, though desertion was a much wiser course of action since the chances of recapture and punishment were much less than for mutineers. Many mutinies were however simply criminal conspiracies and deserve to be judged as such. The men who betrayed 'the trust in them reposed as mariners' by murdering the captain of the *Dove* and attempting to seize the ship in Leghorn in 1736 seem to have been motivated entirely by gain. They planned to run away with the ship to Spain and there sell the cargo of sugar and tobacco which was valued in the indictment at £1,250, a good booty for any thief though selling pirated goods in a civilized port was not very easy. They were foiled by the bravery of the captain's apprentice, who jumped overboard and swam to another ship to raise the alarm, despite having a knife thrown at him which 'struck one of his buttocks but the informant's trowsers being thick with pitch the knife did not enter them'.[31]

Pirates tend to get a better press than they deserve, often being admired for their laid-back life-style and praised as proto-revolutionaries or democrats rather than condemned as the murderers and thieves that most of them were. In about a third of the mutinies analysed by Marcus Rediker, the mutineers turned pirate, all but one of these cases occurring before the suppression of piracy in the late 1720s. Some of these mutineers may have resorted to piracy because their actions had already placed them beyond the pale and there was little else they could do to earn a livelihood. But many leaders of mutinies had planned to turn pirate before they even took berth on the ship. The Scotsman John Gow, for instance, selected the *George Galley* as a suitable ship for a pirate before he joined her as second mate in 1724. He incited a mutiny, murdered the captain, chief mate, surgeon and clerk, renamed the ship *Revenge* and then went on the rampage before being outwitted and captured in the Orkneys.[32]

Such violent events were however comparatively rare in the

annals of English merchant shipping. This may seem surprising, given the tensions often present on board ship, the ready availability of arms and the temptations presented by rich cargoes or the lazy and undisciplined life of the pirate. Fear of capture and the noose may well have been a major factor in restricting the number of mutinies since, as many of the examples above have shown, mutineers were quite often caught and brought to justice. But maybe, as Alain Cabantous has suggested, sailors were not really the violent and criminal people that they were often portrayed. Life aboard ship required qualities of courage and endurance and sailors were often harshly treated by both the elements and their officers, but there is no real evidence that they were any more criminal than their contemporaries who remained ashore.[33]

The Sailor in Wartime

The Sailor in Wartime

'And their Majestie's ships are better
victualled than most merchant ships
are, and their pay surer, and there
they have no damage to pay; and if
they lose a leg or an arm they have a
pension for it, and their work is not
so hard, neither do they wear out so
many clothes; all of which things
they find in most merchant ships.'[1]

This book has concentrated on sailors serving in merchantmen and
has had little to say about service in the Royal Navy and in
privateers. The focus has also tended to be on the sailor's experience
during peacetime rather than wartime. Such an approach has made
the book easier to write but is somewhat unrealistic. In the first
place, a majority of those who served in the Royal Navy during
wartime had served in merchantmen during peacetime, so that
naval service was common in the career of the typical merchant
seaman. And, secondly, war was by no means a rarity, the major
conflicts alone accounting for over a third of the period. These wars
were so spaced that there was only one period, 1713–39, when the
whole of a typical sailor career of twenty-five years could pass
without the experience of a major war. War, then, had a major
impact on the lives of sailors, whether they willingly or unwillingly

served in the navy or privateers or remained in the merchant service for some or all of the period of conflict.

The most obvious effect of war resulted from what naval historians call the manning problem, a problem of human arithmetic. The numbers of sailors serving in the peacetime navy increased considerably over time, from some 3,000 to 4,000 men in the Restoration period, to around 10,000 between 1713 and 1739 and 15,000 after the Seven Years' War.[2] This rate of growth was greater than that of the total population of English sailors, but the numbers still remained absolutely quite small and naval recruitment faced few problems in peacetime.

Service in the navy had some inherent attractions, such as *esprit de corps* and the belief among man-of-warsmen that they were a better breed than those who chose to serve in merchantmen. But, leaving such intangibles aside, there was little to choose between the two services in peacetime from a purely material point of view. Wages in the navy remained the same for the whole period from 1653 to 1797, but rates in the merchant service were also very stable from the 1680s onwards and pay in the two services was broadly similar in peacetime. An able seaman in the navy got 24 shillings a month from 1653 onwards, nominally a little less than a foremastman in a merchant ship who averaged about 25 shillings a month, but in fact very much the same since the navy calculated wages on the basis of the lunar month of 28 days and merchantmen used the calendar month. And, as Barlow pointed out, naval pay was 'surer', in the sense that it was less subject to deductions for such things as damage and one got it even if the ship was lost.[3]

The possibilities of promotion were at least as good and probably better in the navy than in the merchant service. Food was also said by some to be better on royal ships; it certainly cost more per head if that is any indication of quality. The work was similar, indeed often identical, with the important difference that the huge crews on royal ships meant that each man's load was likely to be lighter than on a merchantman, a differential which grew over time as manning ratios on merchantmen improved or deteriorated, depending on one's point of view. On the negative side, pay in royal ships though 'surer' was nearly always seriously in arrears, less so in peacetime than in wartime, less in the eighteenth than the seventeenth century, but still much worse than in merchant ships despite the well-known desire of owners to delay payment to their men. And finally, discipline was stricter and punishment more severe on ships of the navy, as has been seen, though fear of the lash does not seem to have been a major disincentive to naval recruitment. Merchant captains could be tyrants too. Overall, such considerations meant that, for many sailors, service in a merchantman or a navy ship in peacetime was largely a matter of indifference, many shifting from one service to the other as a berth offered. 'There was no identifiable class of man-of-warsmen', as Nicholas Rodger points out. 'There were simply seamen working at the moment for one particular employer.'[4]

Such indifference changed radically in wartime as the impact of the increase in numbers required by the navy began to be felt. These increases were huge, over 20,000 men being needed during the Second and Third Dutch Wars, five times the peacetime numbers, and over 40,000 in King William's War in the 1690s. Similar demands were made in the 1740s with an average of 43,000 men serving in the navy, while in the Seven Years' War numbers escalated to an average of just under 75,000. For these last two wars, David Starkey has calculated the total demands made on the seafaring community from all sources – merchant shipping, inland navigation, privateers and the navy – and has compared these with peacetime demands. In 1739–48, an average of some 25,000 extra men had to be found, while in 1756–63 over twice as many additional men were needed.[5]

Finding these men was the 'manning problem'. Some people had unrealistic ideas about the number of men who 'used the seas' and believed that virtually any increase in numbers could be met if the search for sailors was conducted vigorously enough. The Admiralty and the navy themselves had no real idea of the total numbers of seafarers, but they knew enough to realize that many of the extra men would have to be drawn from those with no previous experience of the sea. Many thousands of the men who served in the navy in wartime were soldiers and later marines, while thousands more were volunteer landsmen attracted by the pay, the

substantial food and the bounties offered. Others were seduced by
the lure of adventure or an exaggerated idea of the chances of prize
money, while many displayed an almost feudal loyalty by
volunteering to serve in ships commanded by captains drawn from
the local gentry.[6]

Landsmen could be taught to haul on a rope or man the capstan,
but they were not sailors and it was the acquisition of men capable
of sailing their ships that provided the navy with its most
intractible manning problem. In the first flush of war, there were
nearly always considerable numbers of sailors prepared to volunteer
to serve in the navy, but cynics believed that those who volunteered
must by definition be useless and in any case volunteers provided
only a fraction of the men needed. The main problem was money.
Navy pay remained the same in wartime as in peacetime, with the
important difference that arrears of pay were worse in time of war,
sometimes because the government did not have enough money
and sailors' demands were easier to ignore than those of other
creditors, but often as a matter of deliberate policy since it was felt
that at least six months' arrears of pay was necessary to put some
check on the high levels of desertion. 'Their growing wages is a
deposit which detains them', it was remarked in 1758. 'It is a bank
which they do not forget, which keeps them cheerfully together.'
Meanwhile, sailors on merchant ships enjoyed a bonanza in every
war as competition for their services forced wages up to
astronomical levels, 45 to 55 shillings a month for a foremastman in
the 1690s, 50 to 55 shillings in the 1740s and an amazing 60 to 70
shillings a month during the Seven Years' War. Daniel Defoe made
the point succinctly in 1697. 'Who wou'd serve his King and
Countrey, and fight, and be knock'd o' the head at 24 shillings *per*
month that can have 50 shillings without that hazard?'[7]

Money was the most important factor, but service in the navy in
wartime was unattractive to sailors for other reasons as well. War
was likely to be dangerous, as Defoe said, and fear of death or
wounding was one disincentive, though in fact not many sailors
were killed in action. Service in the very crowded conditions of a
man-of-war was also less healthy than in the average merchantman,
especially as many ships spent long periods on the West Indies

station where mortality rates tended to rise in proportion to the time spent there.[8] However, the prospect of dying was something mariners were accustomed to and what sailors disliked most about the navy in wartime was the reduction to almost nothing of their beloved sprees ashore. Leave, though given, was very limited in extent compared to the long periods of idleness enjoyed by merchant sailors between voyages and enjoyment of leave from the navy was curtailed by the fact that it was usually given only to those owed large sums in wages which might induce them to return. In any case, leave was far from universal and sailors suffered very severe restrictions on their liberty, most hated of all being the institution of the turnover by which crews of naval ships coming in to refit or repair were turned over to ships ready to sail, so that a sailor might spend years without setting foot in England.

The reluctance of merchant seamen to volunteer to serve in the navy led in every war to a ritual seen by everyone as unjust and contrary to the very liberties on which English society was supposed to be based. Volunteers would be called for at the beginning of a conflict and, once these started to dry up, further volunteers would hopefully be enticed into the navy by the offer of a bounty of a guinea or two, occasionally as much as five pounds per head. These would draw in a few more men, but very soon the navy would be compelled to resort to force to man its ships. In the early stages of a war or when some particular expedition required a sudden escalation in numbers, resort was often made to an embargo on outward-bound shipping, sometimes for several weeks. Sailors might then be dragooned into the navy, but usually negotiations would be conducted with individual merchants and shipowners to give up some of their crews as a condition of having their ships released and the rest of their men protected. Embargoes were naturally very unpopular with the influential mercantile community and were often not very productive of men, who tended to flee ashore and hide as soon as one was imposed. As a result, the most continuous and, one has to say, the most effective means of manning the navy was the use of press gangs both ashore and afloat.

Naval historians tend to be patriotic men, proud of the

institution they study and eager to think the best of the service. They are therefore understandably embarrassed by 'the paradox of naval servitude in a society so boastful of liberty', as John Bromley put it.[9] However, while regretting the press, they point out reasonably enough that without it England could not have manned the navy, given the political impossibility of any government agreeing to the huge expense of outbidding the merchant shipowners in the market. As it was, the only extra money on offer to sailors were the fairly meagre bounties and so conscription was a sad necessity. From the 1690s onwards, many reformers hoped to make conscription fairer by introducing a system of registration of sailors on the lines of the French *Inscription Maritime* which, in theory at least, shared out naval service amongst the country's sailors on an equitable basis. But, time and time again, the idea foundered on the belief of the sailors themselves that registration was simply a trap to facilitate impressment and on the conviction of the political nation that it must be tyrannical because it had been invented by the French.[10]

The press, then, was a necessity if England was to fight naval wars and historians, while regretting this fact, have been at pains to show that in operation it was not quite so unjust as legend has painted it and not quite as bad as it was made out to be in the classic book on the subject published by J. R. Hutchinson in 1913. Recent work emphasizes the restrictions on arbitrary injustice faced by the press. Civilian authorities were hostile to it more often than not and were likely to move swiftly in response to complaints of injustice, if they allowed the press to operate in their area at all. Individuals who had a grievance were quick to enter into litigation and were often successful, given the widespread hostility to the press. Very large numbers of seamen had protections from the press, nearly 15,000 in 1740 and an astonishing 50,000 in 1757, and, except for obvious forgeries, these were usually (but not always) respected. Press warrants only allowed sailors (broadly defined) to be pressed and very few landsmen were swept up or, if they were, they were quite speedily released. And, finally, the press gangs themselves were supervised by increasing numbers of regulating officers who would release those wrongly impressed, while the correspondence of the Admiralty shows that their officers would go to considerable lengths to right wrongs, if only to avoid the cost and bother of litigation.[11]

The press operated in two main ways. Best known but least effective in producing suitable men for the navy were the press gangs ashore who operated from a 'rendezvous', usually a tavern or inn. They had three main functions, to drum up volunteers, to search for and arrest deserters and, empowered by their warrants, to search for sailors or near sailors who if captured would be forced into the service of the navy. The gangs were made up of sailors from the navy or local toughs and their operations were inevitably violent as raids were made on pubs and other places thought to be the resort of sailors and as sailors threatened with capture fought to defend themselves, often supported by crowds of civilians hostile to the press. Although some civilian authorities supported the gangs, their best allies were often informers working for reward or with a grudge against a particular sailor though, even with accurate information on the whereabouts of sailors, success would depend on surprise and very careful planning. It is pleasant to discover just how difficult the task of the press gangs was, though this does not make their business any more edifying.

The press gangs ashore were expensive and not really cost-effective, since they did not bring in very large numbers of men and many whom they did capture had to be released because they were ineligible or unfit. Much more effective was the press at sea, which was operated from press tenders and other craft manned by sailors from the royal ships. Tenders with armed crews of thirty or forty men would lie in wait for incoming merchant ships, which were boarded and stripped of men, these unfortunates often being replaced by sailors from the tenders known as 'men in lieu' who helped bring the merchant ships into port. Captains and mates of merchantmen had protections from the press and so did many of their crews, such as foreigners and apprentices. At differing times, the entire crews of various types of ship, such as colliers and fishing boats, also had protections. Nevertheless, the fact that so much of England's foreign-going shipping had to return through the narrows of the Channel, and often had to wait for a wind in such roadsteads as the Downs, meant that press tenders could normally be expected to make a good haul of men, all or most of whom were likely to be prime seamen. To be pressed in sight of home was a cruel fate for a sailor returning from a long voyage, as Barlow pointed out. 'It is a very bad thing for a poor seaman when he is pressed in this manner, for if he have a wife and children he is not suffered to go to see them, nor to go and look after his wages, nor to take care of his venture [*ie* private trade], but must leave it to the trust of one whom he knows.'[12] It certainly was a very bad thing, but it was the fate of countless English sailors.

Just to make life a little more unfair for the poor seaman, there was the institution of the 'hot press' or 'sweep' in which only protections sanctioned by parliament were respected. In 1757, these accounted for only about a fifth of all protections, the remainder being issued by the Admiralty, Navy Office and a wide range of other institutions associated with the sea such as the town of Deal, which was said to have sold protections at ten shillings per head to every local sailor.[13] In the brutal game of manning the navy, the 'hot press' was seen as a dirty trick even by its instigators and was only used in emergency, but one way or another the navy got its men.

Sailors were not supine in the face of such tyranny. At the onset of war, some men went into the service of neutral merchant ships, in which they were reasonably but not entirely safe from the attentions of the English press. Some even served in the navies of their country's enemies, particularly during the Anglo-Dutch wars. Other men idled away the war in Mediterranean ports, taking the occasional berth in local shipping. Others deserted the sea altogether and went into hiding in the inland parts of Britain, though such sanctuaries grew less safe as time went on and press gangs began to operate further and further away from the coast.

Sailors also had a variety of tactics designed to avoid the press at sea. Indeed, Admiral Vernon reported in 1745 that 'the greatest part of them will escape, as they are as industrious to avoid [the press] as we can be to execute it'. Ships regularly broke convoy as they entered the Channel, preferring the risk of capture to the attention of press tenders from their escorting vessels, a reasonable preference since returning prisoners of war were normally protected from the press. Men were landed before arrival and the ships brought home by a skeleton crew of those with protections, sometimes augmented by protected sailors from such ports as Deal. Crews fought with or fired on the press tenders, often with the connivance of their captains and often successfully. Men hid from the press, though most hiding-places aboard were only too well known to the gangs, as the sailor-poet John Baltharpe gleefully observed of some men pressed from a fleet of colliers.

> From the Black-Indies-men we gat,
> Brave lusty Seamen, plump and fat,
> Out of the Hold these Men we hurried,
> From down i'the Coals they deep were buried.

And, finally, since the business was inevitably corrupt, there was the possibility of paying off the officer in command of a press gang. This could be expensive, the captain of the slave ship *Amarilla* paying out £5 per man to recover some of his crew pressed in Barbados in 1695. But, on other occasions, it could be remarkably cheap. Robert Kirkland, master of the *Rising Sun* in 1709, paid ten shillings 'in presents to the captain of the man of war' to save John Chin from the press and just six shillings 'in presents of wine' on behalf of Daniel Hilliard, though several other members of his crew were successfully pressed, all receiving their full pay before going aboard the Queen's ship as legally required but not always performed.[14]

We will never know just how many merchant sailors were pressed into the Royal Navy and how many volunteered, since the records are not complete and in any case officers gave false returns to enhance their head money. Volunteer numbers sometimes seem surprisingly high, but these figures were greatly inflated by the fact that, faced with the inevitability of being pressed, many men volunteered in order to get the bounty. 'They are all voluntiers as soon as they find they can't get away', as Admiral Cavendish remarked in 1741. Other men volunteered because the presence of the press gang had made life ashore intolerable, like Edward Coxere at home in Dover during the First Dutch War, 'terrified with the press, for I could not walk the streets without danger, nor sleep in safety'.[15] One way or another, it seems certain that the press or fear of the press was the source of the great majority of the sailors, as opposed to soldiers, marines and landsmen, in England's naval wars of the late seventeenth and eighteenth centuries.

The corollary of this is that a majority of sailors in the merchant service must have served in the navy for at least part of these wars. There is not much long-term biographical information on individual sailors, but what does exist very often shows this dual service. This is true, for instance, of most maritime memoirists, men such as John Newton who served in the navy but deserted, 'generally not liking the service', and William Spavens who also deserted after a few years' service in the Seven Years' War, disappointed at not getting the promotion he felt he deserved. Edward Barlow started as an apprentice in the navy but transferred to the merchant service after a few years. In 1691, he once again tried the navy as an elderly midshipman, but did not stay long once he found that he 'could scarce get my livelihood, having few or no friends to prefer or help me to any place considerable'.[16]

Depositions provide further evidence of men chopping and changing between the two services. John Edmonds, for example, stated in November 1704 that he had used the seas for fourteen years and 'hath served as a boatswain in the merchants' service and as a midshipman in her majestie's service', while Michael Wetherly said in 1716 that he served his apprenticeship in the reign of William III 'and hath ever since used the seas as a foremastman . . . in eight men of war and four East Country ships'.[17]

Wills and probate inventories provide similar evidence. The wills of men who died in merchant ships had often been made on joining a royal ship at some time in the past, some indication of mariners' views on the chances of dying in the navy. Thomas Hayes, for instance, died in an East Indiaman thirteen years after he had made his will on joining the navy in 1693. Inventories often list wages due from both merchant and naval vessels, such as that of William Garrard who died in the merchant ship *Richard and Sara* but was still owed wages for his former service in HMS *Dorsetshire*. They also demonstrate the means of transfer between the two services, as in the inventory of Richard Phinnes who died on the slaver *Olive Tree* in 1707. His widow noted that 'he served about twelve months on board her majestie's ship Kinsale but there is an R [*ie* run] put upon his wages, and believes the same is forfeited'.[18]

Desertion from the navy to the merchant service was very common; indeed the manning problem went through two stages in every war, first to get enough sailors to man the fleet and secondly to try and keep them. Legitimate discharge from the navy during wartime was commoner in the wars around 1700 than in those of the mid-eighteenth century. In the 1690s, the fighting season was from April to September and a third or more of the men were discharged at the end of the season to save money, in time to get a berth on a merchantman sailing in the autumn or winter if they so desired. By the 1740s, however, the navy wanted its men for the duration of hostilities and increased the use of turnovers to try to achieve this. This reduction to very little of the leisure time ashore of England's maritime manpower was one important way in which the country managed to pull a quart of sailors out of a pint pot.[19]

One of the few attractions of naval service in wartime was the chance of prize money and this was loudly trumpeted by officers seeking volunteers. However, the reality rarely matched the expectations. The navy certainly did take prizes, but not on a scale likely to make many able seamen rich given the bias of the distribution system in favour of senior officers. Rather more than a hundred prizes a year were condemned to ships of the navy during the War of the Spanish Succession and the Seven Years' War and about half as many in the war of 1739–48. Such averages meant that many ships took no prizes at all and big crews usually made for payments to individuals in large numbers of shillings rather than pounds even when a ship had considerable success. Benjamin Scolding, for instance, died in HMS *Antelope* in 1705 after having served in her as a mariner for 22 months. His widow received 15/8, 23/6 and 34/- for her husband's share of three prizes taken during this period, a total equivalent to about three months' extra wages. This was certainly better than nothing but hardly sufficient to make much of a dent in the difference between wages in the navy and merchantmen, and HMS *Antelope* had of course been reasonably successful.[20]

The gambling sailor might feel he had a better chance of getting rich by serving in privateers whose prizes were shared out more equitably and among smaller crews than in the navy. Privateers also had the attraction of a relatively light workload as a result of their large crews, coupled with much less severe discipline than in the navy.[21] They were of two main types. The biggest gamble was to serve 'upon the privateering account' in a ship whose only function was to capture and plunder enemy shipping. Service in such a private man-of-war was on the time-old basis of 'noe purchase, noe pay', by which the men got no wages but a sizeable proportion of any prize taken and condemned in the Admiralty or Vice-Admiralty Courts. In the 1690s, the men's share was typically one-third of the total but contracts in the mid-eighteenth century were more generous with many crews sharing 40 or 50 per cent of the net proceeds, the remainder going to those who fitted out the ship. These privateers varied in size from ten or less to several hundred tons but they were all heavily manned, usually with a ton/man ratio somewhere between one and two, and each man had a contracted number of shares in the total take which depended on his rank and experience. In a typical distribution, an able seaman would have one share, ordinary seamen, landsmen and boys half or three-quarters of a share, while the shares of officers and tradesmen would range from two or three shares to seven or eight for senior officers and perhaps twice as many for the captain. In addition to their entitlement to shares, privateersmen might receive 'smart money' for special services or bravery. The articles of the *Lyon Frigate* in 1761 promised one guinea to the first man 'to discover a sail, if an enemy and be taken' and ten guineas for the first five men 'on board an enemy before she strikes and made a prize'. The men were also allowed or simply took a certain amount of plunder at the time of capture, most privateersmen feeling they had a right to the clothing and the contents of the chests of opponents 'of the same degree and station'. They also felt they had a right to any drink they could find, though captains sometimes disagreed and articles often stated that 'all liquors not being of the cargo shall be distributed to the ship's company at the captain's discretion'.[22] Service on a private man-of-war could therefore be a profitable experience, but each month which passed with no 'purchase' meant the sailor had given his service for nothing except his food and had lost the chance to enjoy the high wages offered by merchantmen.

Such considerations meant that service 'upon merchantable account' in a letter-of-marque ship or 'mark' was an attractive alternative. These were normally large merchant ships, often of several hundred tons, which set out on a trading voyage but carried a privateering commission so that they could legally snap up a prize if opportunity offered. Nearly all East Indiamen carried letters of marque as did the larger ships sailing to the Mediterranean, slavers and many others. Their crews received the current rate of wages and in addition a share of any prizes taken, though a much smaller share than those serving for 'noe purchase, noe pay'. Typical crew shares rose from one-sixth in the 1690s to about a quarter in the middle of the eighteenth century and these were distributed amongst the men on the same basis as in a private man-of-war. Since the same commission was given to both types of privateer, it is often only possible to distinguish between them by crew size in relation to tonnage, which was much lower on the letter-of-marque ships. However, it seems probable that 'marks' were commoner than real privateers throughout the period, some of them being very active in their privateering role, others never firing a shot in anger, while some only took out a commission because it provided protection from the press for their crews.

Service in a 'mark' made good financial sense, since it was difficult to earn sufficient prize money to make up for the 'noe pay' in privateers. In total numbers, the privateering 'catch' was quite impressive, nearly a thousand prizes condemned to privateers in the War of the Spanish Succession and about 400 in each of the two wars of the mid-eighteenth century. But many of these prizes, such as coasters and fishing boats snapped up by privateers from the Channel Islands and south-eastern ports, were of very little value and when the totals are divided first by the number of years in the war, secondly by the number of privateers commissioned, and thirdly by the number of men entitled to shares, the average

results are far from being impressive and must have represented
disappointing returns to crews and owners alike.

David Starkey has shown that in the eighteenth century there
was a more or less continuous decline in the privateering catch,
defined as prizes per privateer, and that over half of all privateers
made no prizes at all while many others took only one or two prizes
of moderate value. Privateering was however essentially a lottery
and there were some substantial winners, lucky or effective captains
who did very well indeed for themselves and their crews and
boosted the hopes of the whole privateering fleet. In the war of the
1690s, for instance, the Channel Islands were the most successful
privateering station as they were to be in every subsequent war.
Guernsey sent out 38 privateers which took 192 prizes, an average
of five per ship, but this average was very unevenly distributed with
two captains, John Tupper and John Stephens, having a hand in
almost half of all the prizes condemned. Some letter-of-marque
ships also did very well. In 1712, for instance, the 350-ton *Pompey*
captured seven ships during her Mediterranean cruise, which must
have produced a very satisfactory dividend to her crew of sixty men
in addition to their wages. The rewards of such consistent success
could be matched or greatly exceeded by the capture of a single very
rich prize. Most successful of all was the cruise of the *Duke* and the
Prince Frederick. In July 1745, they captured two register ships
sailing from Callao in Peru to Spain with a cargo consisting mainly
of gold and silver bullion, which was conveyed with much flourish
in a convoy of forty-five armed wagons from Bristol to the Tower
of London. Here was glory indeed for the 399 men in the two crews
who received at least £615 per share for their six months' cruise,
more money than a foremastman was likely to earn in his entire
career.[23]

The dream of such a bonanza drew men into privateering,
though the total numbers of sailors involved was quite small and
the generally disappointing results meant that some men had to be
attracted by bounties as in the navy, while others demonstrated
their view of the likely rewards by insisting on being hired for
monthly wages and not for a share of the prizes. Privateering
activity tended to be confined to a fairly short season and

fluctuated wildly from year to year, usually being most active in the early months of a war when the enemy might be least prepared. Numbers of men in the War of the Spanish Succession hovered around 1,000 or rather less, while annual averages in the two wars of the mid-eighteenth century were around 3,000 men with peaks in 1744–45 and 1757 when 8,000 or even 10,000 men were employed being matched by many years when the privateering fleet had less than 500 men.[24] Between a third and a half of privateering crews were normally landsmen and many others were of foreign origin, so that these private wars made a fairly modest demand on the country's sailors except in peak years. Privateering was also concentrated in particular ports, London, the Channel Islands and the ports of the south-east and south-west throughout the period, while Bristol and later Liverpool became increasingly important in the eighteenth century. The men from England's 'nursery' of seamen on the east coast, by contrast, had very little to do with this branch of the sailor's profession.

The combined manning demands of privateers and the Royal Navy, together with the withdrawal from the sea or at least from England of many sailors anxious to avoid the press, presented shipowners with serious problems in finding crews for their own merchant ships. Overseas trade was usually, but not always, at a lower level in wartime so there might be fewer ships to fit out, thus relieving the problem. On the other hand, many ships unable to find a freight were employed as auxiliaries to the royal fleet or got work with the government transportation service carrying soldiers, military supplies and provisions to Europe or to colonial theatres of war. Government paid slower than merchants, but royal service carried attractive protections from the press. In 1702, for instance, Thomas Braine, master of the *Elizabeth and Mary*, gave up a planned voyage to Virginia, 'findeing that he could not protect his men from the imprest [and] putt his ship into her Majestie's service as a transport ship to transport souldiers and horses'. However, there was usually some overall decline in numbers employed in the merchant service in wartime, David Starkey's figures suggesting a reduction of some 15 per cent in the war of 1739–48 and 10 per cent during the Seven Years' War. This eased the problem a little, as no doubt did undermanning, but there were still very large numbers to be found.[25]

Masters and shipowners did everything they could to protect their men from the press and were quite prepared, as has been seen, to connive at the flight of their sailors on their return from a voyage or even at open violence. But, inevitably, as a war progressed the navy got hold of more and more men and it was necessary to resort to substitutes for the adult English sailors who formed the bulk of crews in peacetime. To encourage this, the rules regarding protection were standardized so that, by the eighteenth century, there were five main classes of substitutes who could be granted protections – those over 55 years of age or under eighteen, foreigners 'for ever', landsmen for their first two years at sea and apprentices for their first three.[26]

All these extra sources of sailors were freely used, though it is difficult to get any exact indication of numbers before the 1740s. It is clear however from crew lists and depositions that there was a huge increase in the numbers of landsmen, that is adults with no maritime experience, serving in the merchant fleet in the wars between 1689 and 1713. Such men were obviously attracted by the high wages and their two years' protection from the press and many no doubt stayed in the service. Old men and boys multiplied aboard ship as well. In 1692, for instance, the 16-year-old Edward Lindsfeild deposed that the coasters plying between Poole and London sailed 'with two, three or four boyes, feareing to carry men least they should be imprest', unless they were very old men such as Edward Round, aged 76, who gave evidence in the same case.[27]

The protection registers were kept more systematically from 1739 onwards and these show that the main source of extra hands in the mid-eighteenth century wars were apprentices and foreigners. In the war of 1739–48, a total of 6,500 foreigners were issued protections 'for ever', about a quarter of the average total numbers employed in the merchant service. During the same period, the three-year apprenticeship protections were running at a rate of between 1,000 and 1,500 a year. Numbers were even greater in the Seven Years' War, with some 2,000 foreigners and 4,000 apprentices gaining protections in the calendar year 1757 and 2,000 and 3,000 respectively in the year from June 1761 to May 1762. Many of these 'apprentices' were no doubt just landsmen by another name, since they got three years' and landsmen only two years' protection, but such numbers show how it was possible to find the sailors needed to man England's foreign and coastal merchant shipping fleet.[28]

Shipowners were permitted to increase the number of foreigners in their crews to a maximum of three-quarters during wartime but there was a very varied response to this concession in different ports. This can be seen by an analysis of Mediterranean passes during the two wars of the mid-eighteenth century. These documents record the numbers of foreigners in the crew of ships seeking this form of protection. Passes were mainly issued to ships sailing south or west, with the result that there are few ships from east coast ports other than London. The registers show that ships sailing from the River Thames nearly all carried their full quota of foreigners, while hardly any ships from ports in the west and south-west of England carried any foreigners at all. This pattern is repeated in the Seven Years' War, with the one difference that during this conflict about a quarter of Liverpool ships were employing foreigners. What evidence there is for other ports suggests that ships sailing from Scottish and east coast ports also carried considerable numbers of foreigners though not on the scale of ships from the Thames.[29]

There seem to be two related reasons for this difference in the employment of foreigners in east and west coast ports. The demands of the navy were far heavier on east and south-east than on west coast ports, a manning discrepancy which had a long history. J. D. Davies has shown that, in the Second and Third Dutch Wars, the majority of sailors in the Royal Navy were drawn from London and the east coast, especially from the Thames and Medway. This pattern was to be continued as a result of the uneven impact of the press in subsequent wars. The press gangs ashore were much thicker on the ground and more effective in London and the south-east, while the gangs at sea concentrated their efforts on ships coming through the narrows of the English Channel and in such roadsteads as the Downs. Bristol, by contrast, was well known for the refusal of local authorities to co-operate with the press, a felicitous situation which was expressed in verse by the Bristol privateersmen:

> Here is our chief encouragement, our ship
>   belongs to Bristol,
> Poor Londoners when coming home they
>   surely will be pressed all;
> We've no such fear when home we steer, with
>   prizes under convoy,
> We'll frolic round all Bristol town, sweet liberty
>   we enjoy.

Liverpool, too, was notorious for violent opposition to the press, both from the crews of incoming ships, often heavily armed and ready to fight, and from the town itself as was remarked during the Seven Years' War. 'There's not a seaport in England where a man fights so much uphill to carry on the Impress Service as at Liverpool.' The result of such disparity of experience was that, after a few months or years of war, London and to a lesser extent other east coast ports simply had to employ very large numbers of foreigners since there were not sufficient English sailors to man the ships, while Liverpool and Bristol could continue to draw on local men and a much higher complement of boys than was normal in peacetime.[30]

Possibly as a result of long experience of having to employ foreigners in wartime, London ships also used far more foreign sailors than other ports in peacetime, a situation which seems to have accelerated after the War of the Spanish Succession. In 1683–84, the register of Mediterranean passes records 1,000 ships of which only 62 had any foreign sailors at all. These ships were nearly all from London or Yarmouth and most of them had only one or two foreigners in their crew. Fifty years later when a continuous series of pass registers begins, the number of foreigners had increased considerably. In 1733–34, nearly every ship leaving the Thames with a Mediterranean pass had foreign sailors in her crew and many had their full quota of a quarter, virtually all East Indiamen, for instance, sailing with a suspiciously standard crew of

75 British subjects and 24 foreigners. The only other ships recording any foreign sailors were a handful from east coast and Scottish ports. Sampling for peacetime years in the 1750s and early 1770s shows that this pattern persisted through the rest of the period, with the exception that quite a few Liverpool ships were employing foreigners in the 1750s. The pass registers do not record the origins of these foreign sailors but it seems probable that they formed part of a common North Sea labour market and were drawn mainly from Scandinavia, Germany and Holland.[31]

The protection registers for the war of 1739–48 are unique in recording the names and the country of origin of practically all the foreigners who received protections. Analysis of these registers shows a clear and predictable pattern. In the early years of the war, not many foreigners were needed and most of these came from the traditional sources of recruitment in Scandinavia. But, as the war went on, more and more of London's sailors were pressed into the navy and foreign sailors came to take their place from further and further away, a polyglot flood of mariners drawn by what must have seemed incredible wages, since there appears to have been no discrimination in pay between British and foreign sailors. And so, with a combination of old and young Englishmen, Swedes and Danes, Germans and Dutchmen, Italians, Greeks and Portuguese, Hungarians and Poles, Cypriots and Maltese, the manning problem was solved.[32]

The composition of the crews of English ships, especially those from the River Thames, was thus completely different in wartime with far greater numbers of youngsters than in peacetime and, in London ships, nearly three out of every four sailors a foreigner. Strangely enough, the evidence suggests that this made very little difference to the operation and general morale of the ships. The merchant service was of course used to training boys to become able seamen and in wartime this process was simply intensified. London ships were also accustomed, as has been seen, to the employment of foreigners and seem to have coped adequately enough with the huge increase in their numbers. Language was not a major problem, most foreign sailors being able to understand sufficient English to do their jobs although they might not be able to speak it 'perfectly' or at all. Swedish and German sailors in the crew of the *Letitia*, for example, were asked about their knowledge of English when giving evidence in a court case in 1747. Their range of understanding was from 'a little' to 'everything that is sayd' and of speaking from 'but little' to 'not perfectly'.[33] Nor do there seem to have been many problems of discipline arising from these multinational crews. Indeed, without the evidence of the pass and protection registers, the historian would be hard-pressed to know that wartime crews were any different from those employed in peacetime.

This is not to say that wartime service was not different. The very existence of the press increased the anxieties of the sailor, who must have feared the approach of any royal ship and could no longer look forward to his landfall with the usual pleasure. It seems probable too that many ships were forced to go to sea short-handed, with a consequent increase in the workload of crews, a situation likely to become critical as ships neared home and lost substantial numbers of men to the press or flight ashore. In 1665, for instance, Thomas Belson, master of the *Endeavour*, deposed that between Plymouth and London seven of the eight members of his crew were pressed, leaving him to bring the ship into port with just one man to assist him. At the other end of our period, the English members of the crew of the *Favourite* were pressed in the Downs on their return from the Mediterranean in December 1776, leaving two Danes and a Swede to do all the work of the ship, 'whereby they were obliged to work night and day', a situation which led to one of the Danes hitting the bottle and the master hitting him savagely with a rope's end.[34]

War also made the life of a sailor much more hazardous. Enemy privateers nearly always took far more prizes than their English counterparts, which meant that English sailors were more exposed to danger of death or wounding if their ships resisted and captivity abroad if they were taken, as was seen in Chapter Nine. Capture was also more likely if the ship was short-handed as a result of the press, a reasonable excuse for striking one's flag without a fight as many cases in the Admiralty Court attest. The movements of enemy predators and the need to wait for convoys also meant there were serious disruptions to the normal seasonal movements of shipping. This might lead to sailing at a dangerous time of the year, thus increasing the risk of shipwreck, or to a long stay in such places as the West Indies, thus increasing the chance of death from tropical diseases. Sailing in convoy was itself a tiresome business, leading to endless heaving to and hanging around for the slowest ship in the fleet, shortening sail at nightfall to prevent scattering, puzzling over the signals and orders of the naval escorts, while the numbers in some convoys, often 100 or 200 sail, greatly increased the danger of collision.

Such disadvantages of wartime service were easily outweighed in the sailor's mind by the very high rates of pay if he could avoid the press, something not easily done by those who sailed from the Thames. A fat wage packet might well be boosted by increased profits on private trade in wartime and, if the ship carried a letter of marque, by a share of prizes like the negro boy given to Thomas Rogers, third mate of the slaver *America* in 1695, as his share of the 170 slaves captured in a French Guineaman. Such plenty had to be grabbed while the time was ripe, for the good pickings ended very abruptly with the return of peace and a grossly overstocked maritime labour market. When Captain Richard Strutton of the *Beakey Galley* arrived in Leghorn in 1697, he discovered that peace had been signed with France and that there were large numbers of Englishmen who had spent the war in the Italian port and were now happy to serve without wages in return for a passage home. He immediately dismissed fourteen of his crew, paying them 'a great deale less than what was due and then he commanded the ship's boat to carry them on shoare, soe they was forced to travell above a thousand miles to Rotterdam towards England'.[35]

Such an abrupt change of fortune was of course commonplace in the lives of men who used the seas. Peace and low wages followed the bonanza of war; storms eclipsed fine weather; Sallee rovers suddenly materialized in empty seas; sailors ashore were robbed of their hard-earned wages in the course of their first debauch; husbands and fathers were pressed in sight of home; men working cheerfully on the yards were gone in an instant 'and nothing but a vacancy' showed their loss. This book has attempted to show the good side of the sailor's life as well as the bad, to emphasize the harmony on board most ships, the reasonably good wages and chances of promotion, the joys of fine-weather sailing when it was a 'wonder how any man can be such a lubber as to stay at land'. None the less, there is no denying that it was a hard, dangerous and uncertain life, like that of Robinson Crusoe, 'a life of fortune and adventure, a life of Providence's chequer work'.[36]

Notes

The notes normally refer only to the surname of the author, or the first word or words of the titles of anonymous works, and the date of publication. For full details of references, see the Bibliography, pp. 256–66.

Chapter One: The Sailor and his World

1. HCA 13/83 f. 385, dep. of John Seagerts, 18 January 1706.
2. Fielding (1776) p. xv.
3. For details of the sources used, see pp. 255–56
4. On whaling see Jackson (1978). There is a large literature on trade and shipping but for valuable introductions see Davis (1962) and Minchinton (1969).
5. Harper (1939) p. 339 shows that, in 1660, 61 per cent of English tonnage was engaged in the coastal trade and inshore fishing. For the end of the period see PRO CUST 17/1–3.
6. The Navigation Laws are discussed in Harper (1939). See also on the employment of foreigners in English shipping pp. 216–20 below.
7. For numbers at the end of the period see Starkey (1990a). The estimate for 1660 is based on ton/man ratios from Harper (1939) p. 321, fn. 3 and tonnage figures from Davis (1962) p. 396.
8. For tonnage estimates, I have relied mainly on Davis (1962) pp. 27, 396, 401 who shows a rise from about 200,000 tons in 1660 to 584,000 tons in 1770–4; valuable data on manning ratios can be found in Davis (1962), Harper (1939) and Shepherd & Walton (1972).
9. For data showing a steady improvement in manning ratios with size see Shepherd & Walton (1972) p. 75; manning ratios in the East India service can be calculated from Chaudhuri (1993) pp. 75–7 whose figures show that the ships were crewed at the rate of about five or six tons per man throughout the period. Slavers had similar manning ratios and these too did not change much across the period. On changes in rig see Davis (1962) pp. 74–80.
10. Tonnage figures from Davis (1962) p. 27 and number of ships

from PRO CUST 17/1–3.

11. HCA 15/34, accounts of *Doncaster Speedwell*; HCA 30/654, accounts of *Content*; HCA 13/80 nf., dep. of Henry King, 9 July 1692; Davis (1962) pp. 217, 399.

12. Voyage and passage times have been drawn from logbooks, muster rolls and occasional references in HCA cases.

13. The English E.I.C. sent out an average of just over eight ships a year in the 1650s and crew size has been assumed to be similar to the 1670s average of 87 men. Bruijn & Gaastra (1993) p. 182 and Chaudhuri (1993) pp. 75–6. In the early 1770s there were 27 ships a year with average crew of 111. Total crews estimated on this basis have been doubled since East Indiamen normally spent nearly two years away from home. It is not quite clear how many English slavers there were in the 1650s, but there were very few. See K.G. Davies (1957) p. 38; Rawley (1981) p. 152. In the years 1772–4 an average of 167 ships cleared annually for Africa (PRO CUST 17/1–3) with average crews of about 30 in Liverpool and Bristol muster rolls.

14. For depositions re the Newfoundland cod fishery see HCA 13/82 fos. 316–17, deps. of Walter Barnaby, Samuel Blackman and John Luscomb, 18 June 1701, and f. 355, dep. of Nicholas Beard, 20 February 1702. For the history of the trade see Lounsbury (1934), Innis (1940), Stephens (1956), Starkey (1992), Russell (1950). The ships which collected salt fish prepared by settlers, known as 'sac' ships, were becoming more important across the period.

15. HCA 13/82 f. 316, dep. of Walter Barnaby, 18 June 1701; for a superb description of whaling in the Arctic see Scoresby (1820) and for a more recent history Jackson (1978). Dates of sailing and return from Liverpool and Hull muster rolls.

16. For instance, in the early 1770s, the twelve largest ports accounted for over 70 per cent of all sailors (PRO CUST 17/1–3).

17. Melville (1929) p. 178; Fielding (1755) p. 220; Defoe, *Review* ii, 47.

18. Fielding (1755) pp. 220–1; Schaw (1939) p. 46; quoted by Cabantous (1995) pp. 55–6.

19. Cremer (1936) p. 213; HCA 13/82 f. 216, dep. of Samuel Wilkinson, 2 January 1700; 13/80 nf., dep. of Richard Collard, 15 January 1691; 13/80 nf., dep. of Christopher Norman, 26 January 1691; 13/81 f. 214v, dep. of John Mitchell, 8 February 1696; 13/83 f. 388v, dep. of Joseph Weymouth, 2 January 1706.

20. BL Add. 24931, journal of *Rochester*, fos. 62, 70, 80, 229–32.

Chapter Two: Bred to the Sea

1. *ON*, Richard Boucher, 23 December 1715.

2. Nicol (1822) pp. 4, 7; Barlow (1934) i, 60; Owen (1930) p. 63.

3. HCA 13/80 nf., dep. of John Robinson, 6 December 1692.

4. HCA 13/80 nf., dep. of Robert Willis, 12 May 1690; 13/83 f. 361, dep. of Thomas Cradding, 28 November 1705.

5. PROB 24/61 f. 354, dep. of Samuel Walker, 27 February 1725; BL Add. 24931, 26 September 1704.

6. *ON*, Joseph Peacock, 17 June 1751; John Higgins, 16 April 1753; Robert Winroe, 13 July 1752. For more on hanged sailors see Linebaugh (1991), esp. pp. 123–38.

7. Davis (1962) p. 153.

8. This analysis is based on all deponents described as sailors who gave their place of birth in PRO HCA 13/75–86.

9. Based on the same sample as above. For a discussion of sailors in London which includes the origins of immigrants see Earle (1994) pp. 74–82.

10. Cremer (1936) p. 39. The discussion of starting ages is based on 220 depositions which gave this information.

11. Compare, for instance, Souden (1985) p. 138.

12. HCA 13/83 f. 211, dep. of Samuel Gunston, 12 December 1704.

13. *ON*, Nicholas Lawrence, 28 May 1753; HCA 13/80 nf., deps. of John Jones and Peter Breton, 11 and 14 January 1692; HCA 13/76 fos. 425 and 431v, deps. of Peter and James Bicknell, 11 and 28 December 1668.

14. On the mathematical schools see Taylor (1954) and (1966) and see also Davis (1962) pp. 124–6. Heal (1931) has biographical information on writing-masters and many details on the schools. Dampier (1906) ii, 108; Uring (1726) p. 2.

15. 2 and 3 Anne c. 6 (1703) and 4 Anne c. 19 (1705); see also Parker (1775) for this and other legislation regarding sailors; for some examples of such pauper apprenticeship see Thomas (1977).

16. For premiums see the registers in PRO IR 1 and see Davis (1962) pp. 117–18; pauper apprentices were not taxed and so do not appear in the registers (see 8 Anne c. ix (1709)) and it seems probable that many masters receiving small premiums avoided the tax; as early as 1685 the master of an East Indiaman could get 100 guineas as a premium, see CLRO MCI 444B, Mongers v. Ely.

17. CLRO MC6/243A, dep. of Richard Haynes, April 1669; MC6/444A, deps. of William Andrews and Robert Milward, 10 July 1685; MC6/467B, deps. of Edward Duckworth, William Reason and Thomas Hanson, 7 March 1687. For other similar cases see MC6/438, /475 and /531.

18. Davis (1962) p. 119; HCA 15/30, indentures of Robert King, 2 January 1708, and Thomas Munnings, 20 January 1707, both bound to Robert Soares of Ipswich.

19. HCA 15/32, indenture of George Atkinson, 21 August 1696; HCA 15/31, indenture of Charles Sadd, 2 January 1697. Some indentures state that annual wages for apprentices were specifically 'in lieu of cloaths' and this may well have been their original rationale. See, for instance, HCA 15/47, indenture of George Lawson of Newcastle, 28 January 1745.

20. Barlow (1934) i, 29.

21. HCA 13/80 nf., dep. of Edward Witt, 2 June 1692; 13/80 nf., dep. of William James, 29 March 1692; 13/82 f. 403, dep. of William Vineard, 22 September 1702; 13/79 nf., dep. of Benjamin Humphreys, 14 April 1690.

22. HCA 13/80 nf., dep. of Thomas Wordsworth, 23 April 1692; 13/80 nf., dep. of Joseph Watson, 12 October 1691.

23. HCA 13/80 nf., dep. of Richard Collard, 15 January 1691; Jackson (1978) p. 50, quoting from J.H. St. John de Crevecoeur, *Letters from an American Farmer* (1793).

Chapter Three: Conditions of Service

1. HCA 13/80 nf., dep. of John Hooper, 25 November 1690.
2. PRO T1/12/15, lists of mariners and seafaring men, January 1691. There are impressive numbers of sailors in these lists, e.g. over 1,000 in both Shadwell and Wapping, but since they were designed to aid impressment they are unlikely to be complete. Cremer (1936) p. 92.
3. HCA 13/83 f. 94v, dep. of Robert Crispe, 11 May 1704. Press (1976) p. 4 found little evidence of crimps behaving in this way in his study of Bristol sailors and I have not found a single instance in the HCA documents.
4. GLRO DLC 249 f. 84, dep. of Anne Harrison, 13 January 1705; PROB 24/58 f. 67, dep. of Mary Ravenscroft, 29 February 1720; Defoe (1728b) pp. 27–31.
5. 2 Geo. II c. 36; see also Parker (1775) pp. 108 ff.
6. HCA 13/85 fos. 75, 79v, 81, deps. of Samuel Atkinson, John Child and John Smith, 24–29 March 1704; 13/73 f. 206, dep. of William Greene, 2 May 1659; 13/81 f. 348, dep. of Samuel Tingcomb, 18 February 1696.
7. For more on the shares in privateers see below pp. 212–13. On the Newfoundland cod fishery see HCA 13/82 fos. 295v, 316–17, 355.
8. HCA 15/53, mariners' contract of *Britannia* of Liverpool, April 1762. These are the only whaling articles found and may not be typical. Most crews of whalers seem to have been on shares in later years.
9. For the custom in voyages to Norway see HCA 13/86 fos. 30 and 151, deps. of Peter Docking and John Hovell, 24 November 1718 and 25 May 1719; HCA 13/80 nf., dep. of Henry King, 9 July 1692. For typical rates for voyages to Norway and in the Newcastle coal trade see Davis (1962) p. 134.
10. On river pay see, for example, HCA 13/75 f. 587, dep. of Thomas Morley, 10 August 1666; 13/82 f. 354, dep. of John Cater, 30 January 1702; for no river pay in wartime see HCA 13/83 fos. 201–2v, deps. of William Canvan and John Edmonds, 20 and 24 November 1704; HCA 13/81 f. 248, dep. of William Dewsto, mate of *Oxenden*, 10 May 1695.

11. For examples see Barlow (1934) i, 205, 251; HCA 13/81 f. 493, dep. of James Berkeley, 7 January 1697.

12. For an early example of the payment of a month's advance on a slaver see Donnan (1930–5) i, 393 – the *Hannibal* in 1693. By the time of the parliamentary enquiries into the slave trade in the late eighteenth century, two months' advance was standard. See Davis (1962) p. 143 for advances in general and see below p. 86 for crew mortality in the slave trade.

13. HCA 13/82 f. 293, dep. of James Jeffries, 3 April 1701.

14. For sailors' wages see Davis (1962) pp. 135–7; Rediker (1987) App. C; for wages ashore in London see Earle (1994) pp. 72–3, Boulton (1996) pp. 288–9 and, in Hull and Newcastle, Woodward (1995) pp. 177, 264, 271. The wholesale price of a sailor's food was 3/- a week according to Davis (1962) pp. 145–6; board and lodging in a sailors' lodging-house in London was 7/- a week. PROB 5/254, inv. of John Hadley; 5/4797, inv. of Richard Eddy.

15. CLRO Orphans Inventory 2330 (I am indebted to John Styles for this reference).

16. For some entertaining descriptions of sailors see Ward (1707) pp. 98–103 and Ward (1927) pp. 268–9; CLRO MC6/208B, dep. of John Gutteridge; for the use of cotton see Lemire (1991); I have also benefited from conversations with John Styles on this subject; for 'open-kneed breeches' see CLRO Orphans 2330 and also illustrations in Phillips (1951) facing pp. 22 and 29.

17. PROB 5/4797, inv. of Richard Eddy; 5/2792, inv. of Edward Boweing; 5/254, inv. of John Hedley; Coxere (1945) p. 80. For more on sailors' clothing and chests see below pp. 63–5.

18. On seamen's sixpences see Davis (1956).

19. HCA 13/81 f. 298v, dep. of John Child, 25 July 1695; HCA 15/31, accounts of *Lyon* of Dublin, 1700–1.

20. Examples from HCA 15/19, journal of *St Quintin*, 1699–1700; 15/31, accounts of *Lyon* of Dublin, 1700–1; 15/55, wage book of *Lyon* of Liverpool, 1761–2; Donnan (1930–5) ii, 271; Barlow (1934) i, 89–91.

21. PRO C24/1223, dep. of Robert Weston, 7 May 1700; HCA

13/80 nf., dep. of Thomas Webber, 7 October 1691; Molloy (1769) p. 357; Parker (1775) p. 286.

22. For the successful attack on the jurisdiction of the High Court of Admiralty by the common lawyers see Holdsworth (1956) i, 547, 553–7; Marsden (1897) p. lxxix.

23. Browne (1802) ii, 85; Prichard & Yale (1992) pp. lxx–lxxx. For agents sueing on behalf of sailors on commission see HCA 13/80 nf., 31 October 1691, dep. of Nicholas Wilkins, and 18 November 1691, dep. of Robert Duncan.

24. Cases can be traced laboriously through the warrant books (HCA 38), libels (HCA 24), books of acts (HCA 3), assignation books (HCA 5) and files of appraisement and sale (HCA 4). HCA 15/47, order dated 27 January 1752 re the sale of the *Faithfull Bankrupt*.

25. E.g. HCA 15/17, petition of John Webster, 20 June 1698; HCA 15/33, petition dated 25 June 1707.

26. Barlow (1934) i, 165.

Chapter Four: Careers at Sea

1. Falconer (1769) s.v. 'Seamen'.

2. CLRO MC6/208B, dep. of John Gutteridge re William Beck; Michell (1978) p. 58, fn. 1; Eaglesham (1977) p. 353 and see p. 265 for alternative shore employment of Cumberland mariners.

3. Sir William Petty claimed in the 1670s that only half of England's sailors were employed at any one time (Ehrman (1953) pp. 110–11); Starkey (1990a) p. 31 calculated from Seamen's Sixpence records that sailors averaged 9.67 months' work a year between 1740 and 1766.

4. For a discussion of crew structure see Davis (1962) pp. 110–13.

5. IOL L/MAR/B/776H, paybook of *Havannah*.

6. HCA 13/75 f. 76v, dep. of John Smart, 8 April 1665; Barlow (1934) ii, 339.

7. Youngsters might be referred to as boy, servant, apprentice or by some 'adult' label such as mariner or foremastman. Only a few sailors under 17 were given such adult labels, but nearly

half of those aged 17 or 18 were and the great majority of those aged 19 or over. HCA 15/48, petition of Elizabeth Thurkell, 17 June 1755.

8. HCA 13/82 f. 334, dep. of John Hammond, second mate of *Temperance*, 18 November 1701. For another comprehensive description of an incompetent seaman see HCA 13/90 f. 302, dep. of Thomas Askew re William Jones, foremastman, 11 December 1745.

9. HCA 13/83 f. 363, dep. of Humberston Clayton, 26 November 1705; 13/85 f. 327, dep. of Charles Newton, 16 May 1716.

10. Based on sixty cases where masters gave this information.

11. HCA 13/76 f. 400v and 13/80 nf., deps. of Peter Walker, 28 May 1668 and 19 August 1692.

12. Based on the muster rolls of 95 ships in the University of Hull Library collection, DTR/3/25–29.

13. HCA 30/664, account-book of *Cadiz Merchant*. For a detailed financial analysis of the indifferent performance of the ship during this period see Davis (1962) pp. 346–57. See also Barlow (1934) ii, 327–50 for Edward Barlow's two voyages to Jamaica on the *Cadiz Merchant*, first as second mate and then as chief mate.

14. HCA 13/76 f. 222, dep. of William Dye, 18 October 1667; HCA 13/83 f. 74, dep. of Samuel Atkinson, 24 March 1704. On the turnover of servants in London see Earle (1994) pp. 84–5.

15. HCA 13/81 f. 550v, dep. of George Marlowes, 9 April 1697; 13/78 nf., dep. of Thomas Collyer, 27 October 1675.

16. HCA 13/79 nf., dep. of Richard Murphy, 9 November 1683; *ON*, Isaac George, 19 July 1738; HCA 13/76 f. 196, dep. of Augustin Hanson, 6 May 1667.

17. Quoted from the 1840 Report on the Merchant Seamen's Fund by Press (1978) p. 34.

18. Barlow (1934) ii, 309.

19. Boulton (1990) pp. 334–6; Lewis (1993) p. 211.

20. Dana (1948) p. 341; HCA 13/83 f. 385, dep. of John Seagerts, 18 January 1706.

21. For the age structure of sailors between 1700 and 1750 see Rediker (1993) p. 300. Similar results were obtained from the

depositions studied for this book.

22. HCA 13/83 f. 334, dep. of Walter Barrett, 29 October 1705; Blane in Lloyd (1965) p. 152; Barlow (1934) i, 28.
23. HCA 13/81 f. 380, dep. of Robert Norman, 2 June 1696.
24. HCA 13/76 f. 146, dep. of Daniel Crosskeyes, 8 February 1667. For some sailor criminals who ended up on the gallows see Linebaugh (1991) pp. 123–38.
25. HCA 13/82 f. 486v, dep. of Thomas Parr, 9 March 1703; 13/80 nf., dep. of John Hooper, 25 November 1690; 13/80 nf., deps. of Arthur Spalding, 9 and 18 April 1692.
26. HCA 13/80 nf., dep. of George Roper, 14 February 1693; 13/77 nf., dep. of John Wilgoes, 6 July 1669.

Chapter Five: Wealth and Possessions

1. Cremer (1936) p. 39.
2. See Earle (1994) pp. 105–6 for some data on the wealth of London occupational groups.
3. The inventories are those of all sailors in PROB 5 whose ship appeared from the index to be in the merchant service, though when they were read at least twelve men were found to be serving in Royal Navy ships. For examples of combined letters of attorney and wills see PROB 11/470/105, will of Thomas Beckwith in favour of his wife Alice, 13 January 1693; 11/432/119, will of Aaron Houseman in favour of John Wilkins, victualler, 27 July 1696.
4. PROB 5/5979 (Houseman).
5. PROB 5/875 (Ansley).
6. Barlow (1934) i, 95.
7. PROB 11/391/84 (Smallbone); for a good example of the clear distinction between 'best clothes' and 'working habit' see HCA 13/88 f. 420, dep. of Robert Reyner, 12 June 1735.
8. HCA 15/48, attestation by the captain and mate of the *Deepsey Brigantine*, 5 August 1755, for the bewigged mutineers; wigs often appear in inventories and see HCA 15/46, libel in Samuel Jones v. Michael Stanley, for a man beaten so savagely with a rope's end that it cut a hole through his wig; PROB 5/3488 (Ellis).

9. PROB 11/383/May 58. Hutchinson was a widower whose home was in Bermondsey.

10. HCA 13/89, dep. of Samuel Bray, 21 February 1738, includes the inventory of Thomas Powell, the producent (plaintiff) in this case.

11. HCA 13/73 f. 560v, dep. of Paul Tucker, cooper of the ship.

12. Barlow (1934) ii, 372–3; Coxere (1945) pp. 84–5.

13. HCA 13/86 f. 205v, dep. of Richard Lamberth.

14. HCA 13/80 nf., 12 October 1691, dep. of Joseph Weston of Poole; PROB 5/3174 (Bundish).

15. HCA 13/73 fos. 373–80, deps. re the seizure of *Lady Frigott*; Barlow (1934) i, 252. Barlow nearly always took a 'venture' on his voyages; for some examples see i, 146, 204, 219, 227, 271, 284.

16. Donnan (1930–5) i, 464; ii, 327, 371; iii, 31, 149 etc. Course (1963) p. 72 for John Chapman.

17. For the private trade allowances in East Indiamen see Sutton (1981) p. 75; Chatterton (1914) pp. 227–8; IOL E/4/996 pp. 47–8.

18. PROB 5/557 and PROB 11/384/131 (Lewis). For other inventories and wills giving a good idea of the variety see PROB 5/177 (Blacon), 11/384/131 (Lewis), 5/565 (Waldo), 5/787 (Parnell), 5/789 (Wood), 5/1212 (Anderson), 5/2594 (Harding), 5/5896 (Richardson).

19. PROB 5/299 (Dennis); 5/565 (Waldo); 5/1768 (Grantham).

20. PROB 5/557 (Lewis); PROB 5/661 (Hopkins).

21. PROB 5/1434 (Tice); PROB 5/1939 (Cole).

22. PROB 5/120 (Delgarno).

23. PROB 5/3844 (Horsey).

24. Such houses were furnished in a very similar way to those discussed in Earle (1989) pp. 290–300.

25. For some examples see PROB 5/955 (Beckwith), 5/1977 (Bedient), 5/4020 (Mann), 5/6068 (Holman).

6. PROB 5/2460 (Westcoat).

Chapter Six: Sailors at Work

1. Dana (1948) p. 20.
2. Newby (1956).
3. The following logbooks were those mainly used: *Alexander* (HCA 15/53); *Ankerwyke* (IOL L/MAR/B/126B–D); *Asia* (IOL L/MAR/B/24C); *Aurora* (HCA 30/715); *Blakeney* (HCA 15/55); *Briton* (HCA 16/59/17A); *Calcutta* (IOL L/MAR/B/308C and E); *Charming Sally* (HCA 16/67/695); *Experiment* (HCA 15/56); *Favourite* (HCA 16/65/577); *George* (HCA 30/715); *Glory* (HCA 16/59/18A); *Hooper* (HCA 30/715); *Royal Charlotte* (HCA 16/62/313); *Swift* (HCA 16/63/392); *Thomas and Betsey* (HCA 16/64/524); *Trecothick* (HCA 16/62/307); *Warren* (HCA 30/715). References will give the ship and the date. Books on seamanship were also useful, especially Villiers (1953) and Harland (1984).
4. This description of fitting out and loading is based mainly on *Swift* and *Charming Sally*, which are particularly informative on this stage of the voyage, many logbooks not starting till the ship's departure or when it was actually at sea.
5. *Charming Sally*, 29 January 1776.
6. *Swift*, 18 November 1773.
7. Barlow (1934) i, 164–5.
8. *Warren*, 4 January 1778
9. Barlow (1934) i, 60.
10. HCA 15/39, journal of *Glasgow*, 23 September 1735.
11. *Blakeney*, 22–24 July 1764; ibid., 28–29 December 1763; *Alexander*, 16 July 1762.
12. These incidents from *Swift*, 21 January 1775; *Aurora*, 12 January 1777; *George*, 28 September 1775.
13. HCA 13/76 f. 360, dep. of Edward Everson, 7 March 1668; *Alexander*, 5 June 1762; *Briton*, 21 August 1771.
14. Cremer (1936) p. 192.
15. *Swift*, 15 August 1774; PRO T/70/1211, log of *James*, 12 April 1675.
16. This section on slave ships is based mainly on *Blakeney*, *Glory* and the voyages of John Newton in Martin and Spurrell (1962).
17. *Trecothick*, 1 April 1774.

18. *Alexander,* 17 July 1761; *Hooper,* 29–30 September 1777.
19. *Swift,* 3 March – 4 April 1774.
20. *Alexander,* 8, 22 September 1761.
21. Kent (1973) p. 57 and see Chapter 3 of his book for a discussion of the eighteenth-century timber trade.
22. Martin and Spurrell (1962) p. 25; *Blakeney,* 27 April 1763.
23. Middleton (1953) pp. 282–3.
24. *Alexander,* 26 July 1761; *Thomas and Betsey,* 17 March – 7 April 1776.
25. Dana (1948) p. 343; *Swift,* 14 July 1774.
26. Liverpool custom is quoted in mariners' contracts for that port; e.g. in that of the *Blakeney* attached to her logbook.
27. HCA 16/59/95.

Chapter Seven: Life Aboard Ship

1. Gawdy (1906) pp. 59–63.
2. Lindsay (1874) p. 497, fn. 1.
3. For heights between decks see Rediker (1993) p. 160; HCA 15/48, attestation dated 5 August 1755 by the master and mate of *Deepsey Brigantine*; Teonge (1927) p. 248.
4. HCA 1/57 fos. 1–2, dep. of Richard Walker; BL Add. 24931, journal of *Rochester,* 22 July 1704. See also CLRO MC6/452A, dep. of Francis Hanson, 15 May 1686, for the dangers of 'moone blasts' when sleeping on deck. They could twist the mouth and swell the ears.
5. Phillips (1732) p. 174.
6. HCA 16/65/577, log of *Favourite.*
7. De Saussure (1995) p. 226.
8. HCA 4/10, inv. of *Welcome,* 5 May 1676. The inventories in HCA 4 contain a mass of detail on ships' equipment.
9. Dixon (1982) p. 166; Schaw (1939) p. 53.
10. HCA 15/14, accounts of *Rose* of Boston, 1684–8; and 15/18, accounts of *Richard and Elizabeth,* 1697–8; HCA 15/32, accounts of *Providence.*
11. HCA 15/15, accounts of *Viner Frigott,* 1676–8; 15/33, accounts of *Upton Galley,* 1701–3.

12. Schaw (1939) p. 39.

13. Rogers (1936) p. 154; Beaglehole (1962) ii, 241–2; Uring (1726) p. 186; Barlow (1934) i, 200.

14. Rogers (1936) p. 151; Beaglehole (1962) i, 233; Compton (1891) p. 65; Uring (1726) p. 249; BL Add. 24931, 20 May 1704.

15. HCA 15/48, Anthony Robinson v. William Dodsworth, master of *Anne and Mary*; HCA 16/59/17A, log of *Briton*.

16. HCA 16/63/392, dep. of Henry Forster.

17. Barlow (1934) ii, 462; BL Add. 24931, 3 June 1704 and 7 March 1705.

18. Barlow (1934) i, 254; Dampier (1906) i, 104.

19. These and other examples in this section come from HCA 15/19, journal of *St Quintin*, 1699–1700; HCA 15/31, accounts of *Lyon* of Dublin, 1701–2; HCA 15/38, ship's book of *Suffolk*, 1731–2; HCA 15/43, accounts of *Lawson Snow*, 1740–2; HCA 15/47, accounts of *Mediterranean*, 1748–9; HCA 15/55, wage book of *Lyon Frigate* of Liverpool, 1761–2.

20. Cremer (1936) p. 86; Chatterton (1933) p. 159.

21. HCA 13/80 nf., 19 October 1691, dep. of John Skruton.

22. HCA 13/89 f. 137; Ward (1707) p. 96; Schaw (1939) p. 66.

23. Schaw (1939) pp. 73, 47, 66, 68.

24. Phillips (1732) pp. 180–2, 174–5; Cremer (1936) p. 66; Dampier (1906) i, 365. Hugill (1969) pp. 10, 33 says there were no shanties in our period. Their heyday was in the nineteenth century.

25. BL Add. 24931 f. 248, 15 September 1705.

26. IOL L/MAR/C/12, inv. of Thomas Loveday, 17 September 1664, and cf. inv. of Ralph Egerton, 12 May 1664, whose library aboard the *London* contained 37 named books on astronomy, maths, history, navigation and religion. HCA 13/84 f. 481, dep. of Samuel Stubbs.

27. Quotations from Rogers (1936); BL Add. 24931, journal of *Rochester*; L/MAR/B/308C, logbook of *Calcutta*; HCA 15/53, logbook of *Alexander*.

28. BL Add. 24931, 6 February 1704; HCA 13/89 f. 118 (Marshall); PRO SP 94/218, letter from Consul Cayley dated 26 February 1724.

29. Martin & Spurrell (1962) p. 32; Fielding (1755) pp. 102–3.
30. Barlow (1934) i, 82; Nicol (1822) pp. 69–70.
31. HCA 16/64/524, log of *Thomas and Betsey*, 27 February 1775; IOL L/MAR/B/126B, log of *Ankerwyke*, 23 June and 30 December 1771; Barlow (1934) i, 254, 256.
32. Beaglehole (1962) i, 207. Captain Cook restricted himself to remarking that 'the People were none of the soberest'.
33. HCA 15/38, ship's book of *Suffolk*; Barlow (1934) i, 181. For more elaborate examples of the ceremony, including mock baptisms, see Lydenberg (1957) and Henningsen (1961). Also Falconer (1769) s.v. 'Ducking'.
34. Beaglehole (1962) i, 176–7; Martin & Spurrell (1962) p. 9, fn. 4.
35. Barlow (1934) i, 162; HCA 16/62/313.
36. HCA 1/59 f. 9v, inf. of John Brede; BL Add 24931, journal of *Rochester*, 26 September 1704.
37. HCA 13/85 f.44; Barlow (1934) ii, 540; HCA 15/31, accounts of *Lyon* of Dublin; HCA 15/15, accounts of *Viner Frigott*; Uring (1726) p. 327.
38. BL Add. 24931 f. 195; cf. HCA 13/89 f. 135, dep. of Samuel Bray of the *Pearl Galley* who claimed that the reason for the captain's victimization of Thomas Powell was the latter's refusal to buy brandy from him when they crossed the Equator since he had a bottle in his own store.
39. HCA 13/90 f. 21, dep. of Charles Johnson, 31 March 1744; Barlow (1934) i, 151, 159–60; HCA 13/80 nf., 29 November 1691, dep. of Samuel Vivian, mate of *America*.
40. Rogers (1936) p. 189; Dampier (1906) i, 304 and see i, 86 for rum punch; for another good description of punch see De Saussure (1995) pp. 100–1. For the introduction of lemon juice into the navy's grog see Carpenter (1986) p. 95 and see p. 184 for the poor performance as an anti-scorbutic of lime as opposed to lemon juice in tests done in 1918.
41. For two examples see HCA 16/63/392, log of *Swift*, and HCA 15/53, log of *Alexander*.
42. HCA 16/63/392, log of *Swift*, 18 December 1774. The mate died of his injuries two days later and was buried in Bayonne.

43. BL Add. 24931, 29 April 1705 (f. 162) and 5 August 1705 (f. 226); Coxere (1945) p. 27.

44. HCA 30/715, logs of the brigs *Martha* and *Hooper*.

45. HCA 13/82 f. 228v, dep. of Richard Gartrell.

46. Schaw (1939) p. 66; Martin and Spurrell (1962) p. 75; HCA 1/57 fos. 128–9v, inf. of Elizabeth Hughes, and 1/58 f. 1, inf. of John Esterby re the same case.

47. Barlow (1934) i, 163–4, 193; Ovington (1696) p. 42.

48. Capp (1989) pp. 256–7; J.D. Davies (1991) pp. 92–3; Rodger (1986) pp. 80–1. For an alternative view see Gilbert (1976–7).

49. Fayle (1929) pp. 113 and 177–8.

50. HCA 1/58 fos. 56v–57, inf. of Robert Gregory, and fos. 57v–58, inf. of Christopher Pike, the carpenter.

51. Defoe (1719) p. 97. For a discussion of the beliefs of sailors see Rediker (1993) ch. 4, 'The Seaman as Plain Dealer'.

52. PROB 24/24 f. 333, dep. of David Forrester, 16 November 1685; PROB 11/400/130, will of Charles Wood, 5 March 1687; PROB 11/535/212, will of Robert McCenny, 24 September 1713. For the wills of non-sailor Londoners see Earle (1989) pp. 319–20.

53. HCA 13/78 nf., deps. of William Kingsmead and Christopher Blackett, 1–2 June 1677, and see other depositions in the same case. HCA 13/78 nf., dep. of William Hersee, 12 June 1678. Such questions were quite often asked in the church courts in the late seventeenth century, e.g. GLRO DLC 249 fos. 354, 356, 358.

54. PRO T70/1216, 9 January 1681; T70/1211, 28 March 1675; Garstin (1925) p. 52; HCA 13/73 f. 367, dep. of John Pendleton, 8 October 1659; Chatterton (1914) pp. 182–3. For examples of prayers and sermons on East Indiamen see IOL L/MAR/B/126, logs of *Ankerwyke*, and the journal of the *Rochester* in BL Add. 24931.

55. Coxere (1945) p. 88; Martin & Spurrell (1962) p. 47; Fielding (1755) pp. 219–20; HCA 1/52 fos. 36–8, inf. of Henry Jenkins, Rogers' servant and Henry Jackson, cooper.

56. BL Add. 24931, 1 July 1705 (f. 199).

57. HCA 15/53, log of *Alexander*, 8 December 1762; HCA 13/132, answer of John Perryman, master of *Neptune*, 25 April 1684,

and personal reply of Edward Man, 28 April 1684. Man, the mate, was in command because Perryman was sick.

58. Barlow (1934) i, 257–61 and see also i, 55 and ii, 471; for other examples of witches and similar phenomena see Bent (1893) p. 127; Rogers (1936) pp. 223–4; BL Add. 24931 fos. 257–8; Spavens (1796) p. 73; for 'Pongo' see Bassett (1885) p. 212 and *passim* for a wonderful collection of sailors' superstitions.

59. Dampier (1906) i, 480; Teonge (1927) pp. 30, 138 and see in general Bassett (1885) and Rediker (1993) pp. 179–84.

Chapter Eight: The Perils of the Sea

1. Lines by Edmund Waller quoted on title page of Falconer (1720).

2. This statement is based on data from Garcia-Baquero (1976) i, 380–94; Hardy (1835); Bruijn *et al.* (1987) i, 75, 91; Richardson (1991) p. xviii; Jackson (1972) p. 166; Press (1978) p. 94, fn. 4.

3. Wrecks reported in *LL* have been included if the name of the ship and/or master appears to be British or if the ship was sailing on a route reserved for British and colonial shipping.

4. *LL*, 23 February 1770 (*Mary*).

5. 'Causes' (1867) p. 573; see also Murton (1884) and *Report* (1836); HCA 13/82 f. 7v, dep. of Robert Stevens re *Lindsey*, 7 June 1698.

6. IOL L/MAR/B/546B, log of *Huntingdon*, 14–16 April 1774; HCA 13/73 f. 86, dep. of Joseph Bond, boatswain of *Anne*, 26 February 1659.

7. As for note 6.

8. See *Report* (1836) pp. 375–6 for an early nineteenth-century attempt to calculate mortality in shipwrecks from *LL* data. Well over half of the *LL* reports for the early 1770s make no comment on the deaths or safety of the crews, so this estimate is very much guesswork.

9. *LL*, 4 June 1771 (*Nonsuch*); Foster (1913) pp. xx, 182 (*Little William*).

10. *LL*, 17 November 1775 (*Cranbrook*); 27 November 1772 (*Jolly Bacchus*); 13 April 1770 (*Expedition*).

11. Barlow (1934) ii, 331; *LL*, 22 December 1775 (*Fanny*).

12. In *LL*, 1771–5, 78 per cent of the European wrecks occurred between October and February inclusive and 86 per cent of the wrecks in which high mortality was reported.

13. HCA 13/83 f. 315, dep. of Stephen Crosskeys of the *Benbow*, 13 October 1705; *LL*, 14 January 1772 (*Margaret*).

14. Beaglehole (1962) ii, 81; Uring (1726) pp. 333–4.

15. *LL*, 21 November 1775.

16. Grandchamp (1937) p. 485; Defoe (1725–7) p. 148. There is a large literature on the Moslem corsairs, but for some general books see Fisher (1957), Earle (1970) and, for Sallee, Coindreau (1948).

17. Hebb (1994) p. 139.

18. Coxere (1945) pp. 52–67; Barlow (1934) i, 57, 153.

19. For details of expeditions against the Barbary corsairs and for treaties see Fisher (1957) and Coindreau (1948) pp. 148–205.

20. HCA 13/76 fos. 411, 469, 551, deps. of John Jessop, John Chapman and William Alford, 17, 19 and 22 November 1669; quoted by Mathiex (1958) p. 89.

21. Bromley (1987) pp. 37–8.

22. PROB 24/60 f. 156, dep. of John Morgan, 12 November 1722; PRO SP 89/31 f. 200 (1726); 89/36 f. 264 (1728); 89/38 fos. 183–97 (1735); 89/44 f. 252 (1746); Starkey (1990b) pp. 276,278; Troughton (1788); PRO SP 71/16 f. 107v, Capt. Paddon to the Earl of Dartmouth, Cadiz, 3 October 1713. Many thanks to David Hebb for this last reference.

23. HCA 13/79 nf., dep. of Thomas Avery, 29 February 1684.

24. HCA 13/82 f. 344, dep. of Marmaduke Crampton, 24 December 1701; 13/82 f. 312v, dep. of Robert Bradenham, 30 May 1701; see Ritchie (1986) for this phase in the history of piracy.

25. Rediker (1993) p. 256 and see ch. 6 for a general discussion of the pirates during this period; see also Cordingly (1995) and, for a contemporary account, Johnson (1724).

26. Ritchie (1986) p. 236; Rediker (1993) p. 283.

27. Hebb (1994) p. 139; Bruijn (1975) pp. 407, 409 for the Dutch Wars; Delumeau (1975) for the French wars and Bromley (1963) for the War of the Spanish Succession; Cordingly (1995) p. 132 for the estimate of ships taken by Roberts.

28. HCA 13/83 f. 159, dep. of John Campion, master of *Berkeley Galley*, 10 August 1704.

29. HCA 13/79 nf., dep. of Joseph English, 5 April 1690; for the law on insuring wages see Eaglesham (1977) p. 261; HCA 13/80 nf., dep. of William Dransfeild, 7 May 1692. The insurance was effected by an English merchant in Cadiz and the premium deducted from the men's wages.

30. BL Add. 24931, journal of *Rochester*, 17 January 1703; HCA 13/81 f. 348, dep. of Samuel Tingcomb, 18 February 1696; PRO SP 98/24, English consul in Livorno to Secretary of State, 17 March 1719; HCA 15/17, log of *Eagle*, 31 March 1697.

31. Bromley (1987) p. 213; HCA 13/81 f. 396, dep. of John Yemes, mate of *Eagle*, 16 July 1696.

32. Uring (1726) p. 3; HCA 13/83 f. 510v, dep. of Bartholomew Biggs, 25 March 1707. For the use of a vice see 13/83 f. 463, dep. of George Gilbert, 16 November 1706.

33. HCA 13/89 nf., dep. of Abdel Hamel del Ally, 8 May 1685.

34. Delumeau (1975) pp. 274–6 has figures for captures and ransoms from 1695 to 1763; HCA 13/83 f. 463, dep. of George Gilbert, 16 November 1706 (custom of not paying more than a third of value); HCA 15/53, Francis Burt & Coy. v. the *Charming Nancy*; HCA 15/29, petition of Susanna Williams, 5 February 1705; HCA 13/83 f. 400, dep. of William Bashley, 8 May 1706 and cf. fos. 403 and 411, deps. of William Redford and John Filpott on the same day, and 13/84 f. 534v, dep. of Nurse Hereford, 9 September 1712.

35. *CSPD* (1702–3) p. 624; ibid. p. 583, Mornay to Nottingham, 9 February 1703. Scattered information on conditions can be found in the volumes of the *CSPD*; see indexes under 'prisoners of war' and 'Commissioners for Sick and Wounded and Exchange of Prisoners'. See also PRO ADM 97/98, 99, 102 and other documents in this class for correspondence relating to prisoners. For English policy towards prisoner exchange see Anderson (1960).

Chapter Nine: Medicine and Mortality

1. Barlow (1934) i, 214.
2. Defoe (1697) p. 124; Flavel (1682), introduction A3.
3. The analysis is based on 54 ships employed by the East India Company in 1771–4 whose pay ledgers are in IOL L/MAR/B and 578 ships sailing out of Liverpool, Bristol and Hull whose muster rolls are in PRO BT 98/33–35, the Merchants' Hall Bristol and the University of Hull Library DTR/3/25–29.
4. Crew mortality in ships sailing to North America or in European waters was well under 20 per 1,000 man years worked, while in slave ships it was 275 per 1,000 man years. For age-specific mortality rates for young adults and infant mortality in eighteenth-century London see Landers (1993) pp. 136, 170, 172.
5. Defoe (1728) p. 134; Scoresby (1820) ii, 340 and see ii, 199–378 for his description of whaling. See also Starbuck (1878) p. 114 for further confirmation of the low mortality in whaling.
6. IOL L/MAR/B/126C, log of *Ankerwyke*; Barlow (1934) ii, 465; IOL L/MAR/B/589B, log of *Caernarvon*, 27 March and 19 May 1720.
7. IOL L/MAR/B/126B, log of *Ankerwyke*, 21 June 1768; /126C, log of *Ankerwyke*, 16 June 1772.
8. IOL L/MAR/B/308E, log of *Calcutta*, 1 September 1771; Barlow (1934) ii, 445–6; cf. IOL L/MAR/B/126D, log of *Ankerwyke*, 3 March 1775.
9. Dana (1948) p. 40.
10. Donnan (1930–5) i, 135. Crew mortality (*ie* deaths in the course of the voyage) in the 97 slave ships in the muster roll sample was 23.8 per cent. This is higher than figures calculated for other European slavers, e.g. 17.9 per cent for 70 Dutch ships, 18.3 per cent for 439 ships from Nantes. See Postma (1979) p. 260; Klein & Engerman (1979) pp. 263, 268; Stein (1980) pp. 35–41. The high English figures are however confirmed by contemporary estimates, e.g. *HCSPEC* vol. 69 (1789) pp. 145–8; vol. 82 (1791–2) pp. 289–92.
11. For disease and mortality in eighteenth-century West Africa see Lind (1768) ch. 2; Aubrey (1729); Newton (1788); *HCSPEC*

vol. 68 (1788–9), especially the evidence of Captains Knox, Macintosh and Littleton; Lloyd (1961) and Scott (1939) ii, 982–1010. See Press (1976) p. 13 for blind sailors in Bristol.

12. Boxer (1969) pp. 218–19; Van Royen (1989) p. 24; Bruijn *et al.* (1987) i, 143, 162–4; for mortality in the East Indiamen of other countries see Bruijn & Gaastra (1993) pp. 91, 135, 202–3. Most rates, except those of the Dutch, were around 10 per cent and the Dutch rates varied enormously in different decades. Barlow (1934) i, 243.

13. Bruijn *et al.* (1987) i, 67, 162; death by disease was even lower in the English ships since 22 of the 69 deaths which make up this percentage of 1.15 were of men who were drowned and two were 'killed'. Dutch mortality rates on the passage to the Cape were much lower in the early eighteenth century, only 1.9 per cent in the decade 1710–20, for instance.

14. On the history of the understanding of the nature of scurvy and of progress in its prevention and cure see Carpenter (1986); IOL L/MAR/B/272H, log of *Devonshire*, 1 November 1773.

15. Lind (1768) ch. 3. French East Indiamen also had lower mortality on ships sailing to China. See Haudrère (1989) iv, 1267.

16. HCA 13/80 nf., 31 January 1692, dep. of James Nixon; 13/81 f. 595v, 1 September 1697, dep. of Thomas Christian; 13/83 fos. 79v and 81, deps. of John Child and John Smith, 28–29 March 1704.

17. Cook (1992) p. 14; Gemery (1980) pp. 185–6; Lloyd (1965) p. 167. See also Crewe (1993) ch. 2 for statistical material on mortality aboard Royal Navy ships on the West Indies station, 1739–48.

18. Lloyd (1965) pp. 51–3.

19. Donnan (1930–5) i, 409; Scott (1939) i, 15; HCA 16/59/18a, log of *Glory*, 2–3 December 1770.

20. Scott (1939) i, 105–7; Rogers (1936) p. 192; for an example of rapid recovery from sickness see IOL L/MAR/B/126B, log of *Ankerwyke*, September 1769 onwards. There had been very serious sickness and mortality from Bengal to the Cape but, after sending the sick ashore for two weeks, there was no more

mention of sickness and no further deaths.

21. Barlow (1934) i, 213–14.

22. For a study of these medical chests and the medical guides produced for ships with no surgeon see Gordon (1993). I am indebted to Dr Jordan Goodman for this reference.

23. Aubrey (1729) p. 27; Falck (1774) p. 55; Lloyd (1965) p. 49; Dampier (1906) i, 485–6.

24. Falck (1774) p. 149 quoted by Gordon (1993) p. 141.

25. HCA 15/41, accounts of *India Merchant*, September 1729; HCA 15/36, obligation dated 28 March 1718, signed by George Drummond; HCA 16/63/392, log of *Swift*, 20 December 1774.

26. Abbott (1802) p. 139; cf. Justice (1705) p. 454 and see Morris (1946) pp. 252, 257.

27. HCA 15/33, accounts of *Upton Galley*, 1701–2; HCA 15/31, accounts of *Lyon* of Dublin, 1700–1.

28. PRO PROB 11/478/191, will of William Watson, 27 October 1702; HCA 15/31, accounts of *Lyon* of Dublin; PRO PROB 5/299, inv. of Benjamin Dennis, and 5/5109, inv. of Alexander Reid.

29. Ritchie (1986) p. 76; Hickey (1960) p. 269; PRO PROB 11/400/130, will of Charles Wood, 5 March 1686; BL Add. 39946 pp. 12–13.

30. Martin & Spurrell (1962) p. 31; Phillips (1732) vi, 196; Barlow (1934) i, 214.

Chapter Ten: Discipline and Punishment

1. Abbott (1802) pp. 125–6.

2. Capp (1989) pp. 213–30; Davies (1991) pp. 95–9; Baugh (1965) pp. 225–6; Rodger (1986) ch.6, numbers of lashes on pp. 220, 227; Byrn (1989). Rodger (1992) thought that discipline in the navy became much harsher in the late eighteenth century.

3. Byrn (1989). I have calculated the monthly rate of floggings from the data in Appendix B (pp. 211–20). Dening (1994) pp. 113–24 found much higher rates of flogging in his analysis of punishment on fifteen Royal Navy ships that entered the central Pacific, 1767–95, with 21 per cent of all sailors being flogged.

4. Davis (1962) p. 154; Rediker (1993) ch. 5, especially pp. 211–22, quotation from p. 221.

5. Rediker (1993) pp. 206–12.

6. Abbott (1802), preface A3. This is the clearest book on the subject which I have seen. See, especially, Part II, ch. 4, 'Of the behaviour of the masters and mariners'. Although rather late in time, it merely expounds in more detail on what was said by earlier writers such as Molloy (1st. ed. 1676) and Justice (1705).

7. Marsden (1885) p. 23. The case was Davis v. Rotch. For the colonial vice-admiralty courts see Morris (1946) pp. 230, 256–7, 266–7.

8. Abbott (1802) pp. 125–7; Justice (1705) p. 456; Molloy (1769) p. 358; PP (1860) xiii S.C. on Merchant Shipping Q.2998. I am grateful to Dr Valerie Burton for this reference.

9. Barlow (1934) ii, 451–3.

10. Number of cases based on arrests during the 1730s and early 1770s in HCA 38/62–66 and /77–78.

11. Based on HCA 3/71–72, the Books of Acts for 1733–40. For the two deaths see HCA 3/72 f. 354 (Marchant v. Yates) and f. 410 (Powell v. Hardwick).

12. The judgment in Anderson v. Blinstone in HCA 3/72 f. 120, Terrill v. Ingo in 3/71 f. 460, Cortis v. Hart in 3/71 f. 249 and Drew v. Hardwick in 3/72 f. 428. For other successful actions for damages in the Admiralty Court see Marsden (1885) pp. 311–15.

13. HCA 13/82 f. 337, dep. of John Higgins, 27 November 1701; HCA 13/88 f. 426v, dep. of James Dowie, 1 October 1734.

14. HCA 13/84 fos. 3–3v, deps. of Giles Lone and John Allen, 19 January 1703.

15. HCA 13/78 nf., dep. of Robert Stones, 26 August 1681; 13/88 f. 393, dep. of William King, 18 July 1734; 13/76 f. 518, dep. of Antony Phippard, 21 September 1669.

16. HCA 13/88 f. 406, dep. of William Underwood, 19 February 1735; 13/89 f. 39, dep. of Walter Deniston, 8 November 1736.

17. HCA 13/79 nf., dep. of John Clarke, 4 May 1688; 13/82 f. 226, dep. of Jacob Dunn, 21 February 1700. Williams complained of his treatment to an English merchant in Seville who

convened a sort of informal court martial consisting of merchants and captains of other English ships. These gentlemen heard Williams' evidence against his captain and 'blamed the said Scott for abuseing [Williams] and cry'd out shame on him'. HCA 13/82 f. 227, dep. of Thomas Jones, 22 February 1700.

18. HCA 24/139, Yorkson v. Curling, 3 May 1737; HCA 13/80 nf., dep. of John Coulson, 27 December 1690; 13/89 f. 159, dep. of William Lisle, 9 May 1739.

19. Examples in this and the next paragraph from HCA 13/88–89.

20. HCA 13/82 f. 336v, dep. of George Martin, 27 November 1701; HCA 24/139, Hance v. Jeffery, 22 November 1736; HCA 13/78 nf., dep. of Robert Stones, 26 August 1681; 13/88 f. 437, dep. of Hugh Crawford, 18 October 1735.

21. BL Add. 24931 f. 232. According to Charles Abbott (1802) p. 126, there was no legal requirement for a master to get the consent of anyone else before giving punishment but it was a sensible precaution, both to prevent acting in temper and hot blood and 'to secure witnesses to the propriety of his conduct'.

22. IOL L/MAR/C/12, consultations relating to Peter Lord and Thomas Fling, 13 February and 28 November 1665.

23. IOL L/MAR/B/94C, log of *Duke of York*, 1 July 1723. Cf. IOL L/MAR/A/LXXI, journal of *London*, 15 August 1673, 3 and 11 March 1674 for consultations relating to theft.

24. The logbooks searched were three successive voyages of the *Ankerwyke*, 1767–76 (IOL L/MAR/B/126 B–D), two of *Calcutta*, 1764–6 and 1770–2 (L/MAR/B/308 C and E), two of *Godfrey*, 1771–6 (L/MAR/B/464 B–C), two of *Lord North*, 1770–6 (L/MAR/B/494 A–B), *Devonshire*, 1772–4 (L/MAR/B/272H), *Caernarvon*, 1720–1 (L/MAR/B/589B), and *Duke of York*, 1720–1 (L/MAR/B/94B).

25. Byrn (1989). Analysis based on all ships with less than 20 guns in App. B, pp. 211–20. It is of course a bit problematic to compare East Indiamen from the 1720s to 1770s with Royal Navy ships from the 1790s to 1810s when it is well known that naval discipline was getting more severe. However, even if

Royal Navy punishments were at half the rate, the contrast would still be striking.

26. IOL L/MAR/B/494A, 22 September, 25 November 1771 and 25 February 1772. It was quite common for men who had been punished to be later transferred to Royal Navy ships.

27. IOL L/MAR/B/464C, 18 April and 9 May 1775; /464B, 18 June and 20 October 1771; /308E, 4 November 1771.

28. IOL L/MAR/B/464B, 13, 16, 26 December 1772; /94C, 8, 19, 28 September 1723.

29. Martin & Spurrell (1962) *passim* and p. 88 for the carpenter.

30. Martin & Spurrell (1962) pp. 12, 14–19. A flogging might also continue until the offender promised submission, e.g. HCA 13/80 nf., 20 October 1692, dep. of John Braddyl re the whipping of Herman Hinde, steward of the *Sarah*.

31. CLRO MC6/467A, deps. of Archbell Smith and Edward Muckleston, 8 and 26 February 1687.

32. Cremer (1936) pp.226–7.

33. Cremer (1936) p. 235; HCA 13/73 f. 367 (*Peace*); 13/82 f. 228v, dep. of Richard Gartrell, 2 March 1700, re John Soule.

34. HCA 1/58 fos. 13–27 for the evidence and 1/20/39 for his conviction and sentence.

35. These two examples from HCA 13/81 f. 680v, dep. of Anthony Wilkinson, 3 February 1698; and IOL L/MAR/B/126B, log of *Ankerwyke*, 30 November 1768. Such authorities in port might also question the behaviour of the master, as in the case mentioned in n. 17 above.

36. Phillips (1732) p. 174.

37. For change of voyage see above pp. 34–35; BL Add. 24931, journal of *Rochester*, 25 January 1704; Dampier (1906) i, 509.

38. Dana (1948) p. 41; HCA 15/11, extract from journal of the *Francis*; HCA 16/64/52, log of *Thomas and Betsey*, 1 June 1776.

39. HCA 13/77 nf., 26 August 1670, dep. of William Watson.

40. HCA 13/77 nf., 28 July 1670, dep. of Peter Paulson; Rediker (1993) p. 240 suggested that sailors encouraged these divisions between masters and mates since they tended to loosen discipline.

41. Barlow (1934) ii, 352, 355, 357, 529, 539, 544, 546.

42. Barlow (1934) ii, 553.

Chapter Eleven: Desertion and Mutiny

1. IOL L/MAR/C/18 f. 1, orders for the *Samuel and Anna* on a voyage to Borneo in 1702.
2. See Chapter Nine, note 3 for more details of the sample used.
3. HCA 16/62/307, log of *Trecothick*, 9 April 1774 in Jamaica; IOL L/MAR/B/126D, log of *Ankerwyke*, 9 January 1775.
4. HCA 24/36, dep. of John Salter; HCA 15/53, log of *Alexander*, 5, 6, 21 October 1761; HCA 24/136, dep. of Edward Fentiman.
5. IOL L/MAR/B/464C, log of *Godfrey*, 12, 14 February, 18, 19 March 1775; HCA 13/80 nf., dep. of Thomas Cullington, 30 October 1691.
6. IOL E/4/997 pp. 1055–6; IOL L/MAR/C/18 f. 49, 26 November 1704; Spavens (1796) pp. 75–8, 85–6; Dampier (1906) ii, 42.
7. Uring (1726) p. 355; *HCSPEC* vol. 89 (1789) p. 161.
8. Le Goff (1994) p. 21; for some comments on English run wages see *HCSPEC* vol. 88 (1788–9) pp. 120, 246, 264, 285.
9. HCA 13/83 f. 185, dep. of William Imy, 25 October 1704; HCA 15/34, subscription dated 4 January 1717; HCA 13/76 f. 518v, dep. of Robert Hannay, 21 September 1669.
10. Morris (1946) pp. 230, 246–9; Abbott (1802) p. 124; Rediker (1993) pp.100–6; Middleton (1953) p. 275.
11. Byrn (1989) pp. 161–5; HCA 13/84 f. 38, dep. of Thomas Crutchley, 18 September 1708.
12. HCA 16/63/392, log of *Swift*, 14 April 1774; HCA 15/31, accounts of *Lyon* of Dublin; HCA 15/39, wages book of *Josias*.
13. HCA 13/76 f. 135, dep. of William Grainger, 7 February 1667; 13/82 f. 223v, dep. of John Peters, 16 February 1700.
14. HCA 15/31, undated declaration but March 1715; cf. HCA 15/12, 'noatt', dated 29 August 1678, by the English consul at Cadiz, regarding the desertion of Joseph Barnes, boatswain of the *Hannah and Elizabeth* 'without the least cause or provocation'. For the *African* see Martin & Spurrell (1962) p. 92.

15. Martin & Spurrell (1962), journal of *Duke of Argyle*, 18 November 1750, and *African*, 5 October 1752.

16. IOL L/MAR/B/126C, log of *Ankerwyke*, 25, 26, 28 June 1771; IOL E/4/998 p. 721. Rewards were also offered, as in the American colonies. Captain Randall of the *Samuel and Anna*, for instance, offered 20 rupees [about £2.10.0] per head for the recapture of 14 of his men who deserted in Bengal in 1704. L/MAR/C/18 f. 50. Cabantous (1984) p. 131 says that from 1729 the East India Company imposed a £5 fine on captains for every sailor who had to be engaged to replace a deserter, which must have acted as a major incentive for recapture.

17. IOL L/MAR/B/464C, log of *Godfrey*, 12, 14 February 1775.

18. Rediker (1993) pp. 227–8 and see pp. 227–35 for a general discussion of mutiny; Cabantous (1984) pp. 10–11, 195.

19. HCA 15/39, journals book of *Glasgow*.

20. NMM BRK/13, journal kept by William Falconer, 14 May 1760.

21. HCA 13/80 nf., deps. by Joshua Ingle and Robert Kenton, 20 and 25 February 1692; 13/80 nf., dep. of John Coulson, 27 December 1690.

22. IOL L/MAR/B/464B, log of *Godfrey*, 4, 5 November 1771.

23. Uring (1726) pp. 259–62; on round robins generally see Rediker (1993) pp. 234–5; see also *OED* s.v. 'Round Robin'.

24. HCA 13/81 f. 679, dep. of Christopher Young, 31 January 1698; Martin & Spurrell (1962) pp. 69–72.

25. Uring (1726) pp. 259–62 and see Rediker (1993) pp. 229–30.

26. HCA 13/76 fos. 518 and 518v, deps. of Antony Phippard and Robert Hannay, 21 September 1669; HCA 15/12, statement by Thomas Pellegrini, English vice-consul in Zante, 19 March 1681.

27. HCA 1/58 fos. 2v–11, re the mutiny on the *Antelope*. For the escape from prison see HCA 1/20/35.

28. HCA 1/58 fos. 106v–108, exam. of Peter Jordan, 19 September 1766; PRO BT 98/34, muster roll of snow *Will*, late Joseph Spencer, now Elias Harrison, from Madeira; *CSPAWI* (1734–5) no. 578, Governor of Virginia to the Duke of Newcastle, 26 May 1735.

29. HCA 1/58 f. 111, exam. of John Tomlin.
30. Cabantous (1984) p. 51; HCA 1/58 fos. 6v–11, exam. of William Steele; HCA 15/48, attestation of Elijah Goff, master of *Deepsey Brigantine*, 5 August 1755.
31. HCA 1/57 fos. 1–10v; HCA 1/19/45, 47 and 50. Two men were hanged for the murder of the captain and one for piracy. See also Rediker (1993) pp. 232–3 for the mutiny on the *Dove*.
32. Rediker (1993) pp. 228, 308–9; Cordingly (1995) pp. 149–51.
33. Cabantous (1984) pp. 147–9, 193–5.

Chapter Twelve: The Sailor in Wartime

1. Barlow (1934) ii, 426.
2. For the Restoration navy see Davies (1991) pp. 12, 69 and, for the eighteenth century, Lloyd (1968) pp. 286–8. See also Starkey (1990) for detailed estimates for the period after 1736.
3. Lloyd (1968) pp. 91, 248–9; Rodger (1986) pp. 124–7; Barlow (1934) ii, 426.
4. Rodger (1986) p. 113; on differences in the cost of food between the navy and merchantmen see p. 117.
5. Davies (1991) p. 13; Ehrman (1953) p. 110; Starkey (1990).
6. Here and in the following paragraphs I have drawn on an extensive literature about manning, especially Lloyd (1968) chs. 6–9; Capp (1989) ch. 8; Davies (1991) ch. 4; Ehrman (1953) ch. 4; Baugh (1965) ch. 4; Rodger (1986) ch. 5; Gradish (1980); Hutchinson (1913). Policies changed in detail from war to war, but in essence both the problem and the solutions adopted were remarkably consistent.
7. Quotation from Pares (1937) pp. 38–9; wartime pay levels from Davis (1962) pp. 135–7; Defoe (1697) p. 329.
8. For statistical data on mortality in individual naval ships on the West Indies station 1739–48 see Crewe (1993) ch. 2.
9. Bromley (1982) p. 159.
10. A registration act was passed in 1696 but the system proved unworkable. Bills to reintroduce registration failed in 1706, 1720, 1740 and 1758. For the pamphlet literature associated with reform see Bromley (1974), which has an excellent

introduction. The subject is also discussed at length in the works cited in note 6.

11. Hutchinson (1913); on the numbers of protections see Baugh (1965) p. 187 and Gradish (1980) pp. 66–7. Apart from the authors already cited see Hinchcliffe (1967) for Admiralty response to supposed irregularities by the press.

12. Barlow (1934) i, 146. Ships coming into the West Indies were also visited by press tenders, who in the middle of the eighteenth century would take one man in five from West Indiamen and one in three from slavers. Pressing ashore in the colonies was however strongly resisted by colonial governments. See Pares (1937).

13. Gradish (1980) pp. 66–7.

14. Vernon quoted by Baugh (1965) p. 158; Baltharpe (1959) p. 12; Donnan (1930–5) i, 414; HCA 15/32, wages book of *Rising Sun*; cf. HCA 15/31, accounts of *Lyon* of Dublin, and HCA 15/43, accounts of *Lawson snow*, which also have payments for saving sailors from the press.

15. Cavendish quoted in Baugh (1965) pp. 167–9; Coxere (1945) pp. 24–5.

16. Martin & Spurrell (1962) p. x; Spavens (1796) p. 63; Barlow (1934) ii, 425 and for a summary of the ships in which Barlow served see ii, 554–9; cf. Cremer (1936) and Coxere (1945), both of whom served in the navy for a while, but mainly in the merchant service.

17. HCA 13/83 f. 202v, dep. of John Edmonds, 24 November 1704; 13/85 f. 342, dep. of Michael Wetherly, 17 July 1716. It was also very common for men deposing about their last merchant voyage to state that they were currently in the navy.

18. PROB 11/488/126 and 5/2644, will and inv. of Thomas Hayes; PROB 5/5971, inv. of William Garrard; 5/4128, inv. of Richard Phinnes.

19. Ehrman (1953) pp. 110, 120; Baugh (1965) pp. 147–8; Starkey (1990a) pp. 31–3, 38.

20. For numbers of prizes see Starkey (1990b) pp. 99, 137, 178; PROB 11/482/125, inv. of Benjamin Scolding; cf. HCA 13/84 fos. 99–100, 16 November 1708, deps. of James Mason,

foremastman on HMS *Pembroke*, who sold his share in two prizes for ten shillings, and of John Philpott, midshipman, who sold his share for twenty shillings.

21. The following section on privateering relies mainly on Starkey (1990b); Powell (1930); Bromley (1987); Meyer (1981) and (1983).

22. Starkey (1990b) p. 71; HCA 15/55, articles of *Lyon Frigate*, 11 May 1761.

23. Starkey (1990b) pp. 99, 137, 178.

24. Numbers for 1702–63 from Starkey (1990b) App. 2 and annual averages from Starkey (1990a) p. 29.

25. HCA 13/82 f. 542, dep. of Pieter Vandermore, 24 April 1703; percentage reductions calculated from Starkey (1990a) p. 29.

26. See, for example, ADM 7/393 f. 3, 'Rules for granting protections', 1740.

27. HCA 13/80 nf., deps. of Edward Round and Edward Lindsfeild, 28 and 29 May 1692.

28. ADM 7/393–5, 397 for protections from the press; Starkey (1990a) p. 29 for total numbers needed.

29. PRO ADM 7/83–4, 89.

30. J.D. Davies (1991) p. 68; Lloyd (1968) p. 138; Rodger (1986) pp. 169, 175.

31. ADM 7/75, 80, 89 and 96. Mediterranean passes for 1683–4, 1733–6, 1754–5 and 1769–72.

32. PRO ADM 7/393–4.

33. HCA 13/91 fos. 7, 8, 10, 21.

34. HCA 13/75 f. 229, dep. of Thomas Belson, 13 May 1665; HCA 16/65/577. Papers in Salomon v. Johnson attached to logbook of the *Favourite*.

35. HCA 13/81 f. 269, dep. of Thomas Rogers, 4 June 1695; HCA 15/16, petition of Judith Leach.

36. Dana (1948) p. 40; Schaw (1939) p. 73; Defoe (1972) p. 220.

Sources and Bibliography

Manuscript sources

The most valuable sources have been the records of the High Court of Admiralty (HCA) in the Public Record Office. The main focus has been on the deposition books (HCA 13/63–91) for the period 1650 to 1750. These provide information not just on the court cases in which the witnesses were giving evidence but also contain much biographical information about sailors, as well as incidentally throwing light on virtually every aspect of seafaring life. A sample of 1,900 officer and sailor witnesses who gave their place of birth in their depositions was drawn from HCA 13/75–86 for more detailed study and this has been used for analysis of age structure, age at going to sea, careers, literacy and residence as well as place of birth.

The miscellaneous material in HCA 15, 16 and 30 has also been invaluable, especially for ships' articles, account books, logbooks and apprenticeship indentures, though there is a bit of everything in these splendid collections. Other classes which proved useful were the criminal indictments and examinations (HCA 1), books of acts (HCA 3), libels (HCA 24) and warrant books (HCA 38).

The analysis of wealth and possessions in Chapter Five is based mainly on the inventories and copy wills of sailors in PRO PROB 5 and 11 and these documents have also produced much other incidental information. Other important sources from the Public Record Office include the registers of protections from the press and Mediterranean passes (both in ADM 7), customs data on the number of ships, ship clearances and sailors in the early 1770s (CUST 17/1–3), the muster rolls of Liverpool and the ports of the

Tyne (BT 98) and the papers of the Royal African Company (T 70) which include some logbooks.

The most important sources outside the Public Record Office which have been used were the logbooks and paybooks of East Indiamen in the India Office Library (L/MAR/B), the Bristol muster rolls in the Merchants' Hall at Bristol, the Hull muster rolls in the Hull Trinity House collection in the University of Hull Library and the interrogatories relating to sailor apprentices in the Corporation of London Records Office (MC6). Occasional material has also been collected from other classes in the Public Record Office and India Office Library and from the Greater London Record Office and the National Maritime Museum. Detailed references to these and other sources used will be found in the Notes.

Bibliography

The works listed are those which have been referred to in the Notes. Place of publication is London unless otherwise stated. Where there is a second publication date in parentheses, the second one has been consulted. For abbreviations see p. 225.

Abbott, Charles, *A Treatise of the Law relating to merchant ships and seamen* (1802)

Alsop, J.D., 'Sea surgeons, health and England's maritime expansion', *MM* lxxvi (1990)

Anderson, Olive, 'The establishment of British supremacy at sea and the exchange of naval prisoners of war, 1689–1783', *English Historical Review* lxxv (1960)

Aubrey, T., *The Sea-Surgeon, or the Guinea Man's Vade Mecum* (1729)

Baltharpe, John, *The Straights Voyage, or, St. Davids Poem* (1671; ed. J.S.Bromley, Oxford, 1959)

Barlow, Edward, *Journal of his life at sea* (ed. B. Lubbock, 1934)

Bassett, Fletcher S., *Legends and Superstitions of the Sea and Sailors* (New York, 1885)

Baugh, Daniel A., *British Naval Administration in the Age of*

Walpole (Princeton, NJ, 1965)

Beaglehole, J.C. (ed.), *The Endeavour Journal of Joseph Banks, 1768–1771* (1962)

Bent, J.T. (ed.), 'Extracts from the diaries of Dr. John Covel, 1670–1679' in *Early Voyages and Travels in the Levant* (1893)

Blane, Sir Gilbert, *Observations on the diseases of seamen* (1785)

Boulton, Jeremy, 'London widowhood revisited: the decline of female remarriage in the seventeenth and eighteenth centuries', *Continuity and Change* v (1990)

Boulton, Jeremy, 'Wage labour in 17th-century London', *EcHR* xlix (1996)

Boxer, C.R., 'The Dutch East-Indiamen: their sailors, their navigators and life on board, 1602–1795', *MM* xlix (1963)

Boxer, C.R., *The Portuguese Seaborne Empire, 1415–1825* (1969)

Bromley, J.S., 'The British Navy and its seamen after 1688: notes for an unwritten history' in Palmer & Williams (1982)

Bromley, J.S., 'The Channel Island privateers in the War of the Spanish Succession' (1950), reprinted in Bromley (1987)

Bromley, J.S., *Corsairs and Navies: 1660–1760* (1987)

Bromley, J.S., 'The French privateering war, 1702–13' (1963), reprinted in Bromley (1987)

Bromley, J.S., 'The Jacobite privateers in the Nine Years War' (1973), reprinted in Bromley (1987)

Bromley, J.S., 'A letter-book of Robert Cole, British Consul-General at Algiers, 1694–1712' (1974), reprinted in Bromley (1987)

Bromley, J.S., *The Manning of the Royal Navy: selected public pamphlets, 1693–1873*, NRS, cxix (1974)

Browne, Arthur, *A Compendious View of the Civil Law* (1802 ed.)

Bruijn, J.R., 'Dutch privateering during the Second and Third Anglo-Dutch Wars' in Mollat (1975)

Bruijn, J.R. *et al.*, *Dutch-Asiatic Shipping in the seventeenth and eighteenth centuries* vol. i (The Hague, 1987)

Bruijn, J.R. & Gaastra, F.S., *Ships, Sailors and Spices: East India Companies and their shipping in the 16th, 17th and 18th century* (Amsterdam, 1993)

Byrn, J.D. Jr, *Crime and Punishment in the Royal Navy: discipline on the Leeward Islands Station, 1784–1812* (Aldershot, 1989)

Cabantous, Alain, *Les Citoyens du Large: les identités maritimes en France (xviie–xixe siècle)* (Paris, 1995)

Cabantous, A., *Dix Mille Marins Face à l'Océan* (Paris, 1991)

Cabantous, A., *La Vergue et les Fers: mutins et déserteurs dans la marine de l'ancienne France (XVIIe–XVIIIe s.)* (Paris, 1984)

Capp, Bernard, *Cromwell's Navy: the fleet and the English revolution, 1648–1660* (Oxford, 1989)

Carpenter, Kenneth J., *The History of Scurvy and Vitamin C* (Cambridge, 1986)

'The causes of wrecks', *Journal of the Royal Statistical Society* xxx (1867)

Chatterton, E.K., *The Old East Indiamen* (1914, 1933)

Chaudhuri, K.N., 'The English East India Company's shipping (c.1660–1760)' in Bruijn & Gaastra (1993)

Clarkson, Thomas, *The History of the Rise, Progress . . . of the Slave Trade* (1808)

Cohn, R.L., 'Maritime mortality in the eighteenth and nineteenth centuries: a survey', *IJMH* i (1989)

Coindreau, Roger, *Les Corsaires de Salé* (Paris, 1948)

Compton, H. (ed.), *A Master Mariner, being the life and adventures of Captain Robert Eastwick* (1891)

Cook, G.C., *From the Greenwich Hulks to old St. Pancras: a history of tropical disease in London* (1992)

Cordingly, David, *Life Among the Pirates: the romance and the reality* (1995)

Course, A.G., *The Merchant Navy: a social history* (1963)

Coxere, Edward, *Adventures by Sea* (ed. E. Meyerstein, New York, 1946)

Cremer, John, *Ramblin' Jack: the journal of Captain John Cremer* (ed. R. Bellamy, 1936)

Crewe, Duncan, *Yellow Jack and the Worm: British naval administration in the West Indies, 1739–48* (Liverpool, 1993)

Crowhurst, Patrick, 'Bayonne privateering, 1744–1763' in Mollat (1975)

Dampier, William, *Voyages* (ed. John Masefield, 1906)

Dana, R.H., *Two Years before the Mast* (1840, 1948)

Davies, J.D., *Gentlemen and Tarpaulins: the officers and men of the Restoration Navy* (Oxford, 1991)

Davies, K.G., *The Royal African Company* (1957)

Davis, Ralph, *The Rise of the English Shipping Industry in the 17th and 18th centuries* (1962)

Davis, Ralph, 'Seamen's sixpences: an index of commercial activity, 1697–1828', *Economica* n.s. xxiii (1956)

Defoe, Daniel, *Atlas Maritimus and Commercialis: or, a General View of the World* (1728a)

Defoe, Daniel, *An Essay upon Projects* (1697)

Defoe, Daniel, *A General History of Discoveries and Improvements* (1725–7)

Defoe, Daniel, *Robinson Crusoe* (1719, 1972)

Defoe, Daniel, *Some Considerations on the Reasonableness and Necessity of Encreasing and Encouraging the Seamen* (1728b)

Delumeau, J., 'La guerre de course française sous l'ancien régime' in Mollat (1975)

Dening, Greg, *Mr Bligh's Bad Language: passion, power and theatre on the Bounty* (Cambridge, 1994)

De Saussure, C., *A Foreign View of England in 1725–1729* (Ipswich, 1995)

Dixon, Conrad, 'Pound and pint: diet in the merchant service, 1750–1980' in Palmer & Williams (1982)

Donnan, E. (ed.), *Documents illustrative of the history of the slave trade* (4 vols, Washington, DC, 1930–5)

Duffy, Michael *et al.* (eds.), *The New Maritime History of Devon* vol. i (1992)

Eaglesham, Annie, 'The growth and influence of the West Cumberland shipping industry, 1600–1800' (Unpublished Lancaster Ph.D., 1977)

Earle, Peter, *A City Full of People: men and women of London, 1650–1750* (1994)

Earle, Peter, *Corsairs of Malta and Barbary* (1970)

Earle, Peter, *The Making of the English Middle Classes: business, society and family life in London, 1660–1730* (1989)

Ehrman, John, *The Navy in the War of William III* (Cambridge, 1953)

Elder, Melinda, *The Slave Trade and the economic development of eighteenth-century Lancaster* (Halifax, 1992)

Falck, N.D., *The Seaman's Medical Instructor* (1774)

Falconer, Richard, *The Voyages, dangerous adventures and imminent escapes of Captain Richard Falconer* (1720)

Falconer, William, *An Universal Dictionary of the Marine* (1769)

Fayle, C.E. (ed.), *Voyages to the East Indies: Christopher Fryke and Christopher Schweitzer* (1929)

Fielding, Henry, *Journal of a Voyage to Lisbon* (1755)

Fielding, Sir John, *A Brief Description of the Cities of London and Westminster* (1776)

Fisher, Sir Godfrey, *Barbary Legend: war, trade and piracy in North Africa, 1415–1830* (Oxford, 1957)

Flavel, John, *Navigation Spritualized: or, a new compass for sea-men* (1682)

Foster, William, *The English Factories in India, 1642–1645* (Oxford, 1913)

Garcia-Baquero, A., *Cadiz y el Atlantico, 1717–1778* (Seville, 1976)

Garstin, Crosbie (ed.), *Samuel Kelly: an 18th-century seaman* (1925)

Gawdy, Philip, *Letters* (ed. I.H. Jeayes, 1906)

Gemery, Henry A., 'Emigration from the British Isles to the New World, 1630–1700' in Paul Uselding (ed.), *Research in Economic History* vol. v (Greenwich, Conn, 1980)

Gemery, Henry A. & Hogendorn, Jan S. (eds.), *The Uncommon Market: essays in the economic history of the Atlantic slave trade* (New York, 1979)

Gilbert, A.N., 'Buggery and the British Navy, 1700–1861', *Journal of Social History* x (1976–7)

Gordon, Eleanora C., 'Sailors' physicians: medical guides for merchant ships and whalers, 1774–1864', *Journal of the History of Medicine and Allied Sciences* xlviii (1993)

Gradish, Stephen F., *The Manning of the British Navy during the Seven Years War* (1980)

Grandchamp, P., 'Une mission délicate en Barbarie au XVIIe siècle', *Revue Tunisienne* xxx (1937)

Hadley, G., *History of the town of Kingston-upon-Hull* (1788)

Hans, N., *New Trends in Education in the Eighteenth Century* (1951)

Hardy, Charles, *A Register of Ships employed in the service of the Hon. the United East India Company* (1835)

Harland, John, *Seamanship in the Age of Sail* (1984)

Harper, L.A., *The English Navigation Laws* (New York, 1939)

Haudrère, Philippe, *La Compagnie Française des Indes au xviiie siècle (1719–1795)* (Paris, 1989)

Heal, Ambrose, *The English writing masters and their copy books* (Cambridge, 1931)

Hebb, D.D., *Piracy and the English Government, 1616–1642* (Aldershot, 1994)

Henningsen, Henning, *Crossing the Equator: sailors' baptism and other initiation rites* (Copenhagen, 1961)

Hickey, William, *Memoirs* (ed. Peter Quennell, 1960)

Hinchcliffe, G., 'Impressment of seamen during the War of the Spanish Succession', *MM* vol. 53 (1967)

Holdsworth, Sir William, *A History of English Law* vol. i (1956)

Hugill, Stan, *Shanties and Sailors' Songs* (1969)

Hutchinson, J.R., *The Press-Gang Afloat and Ashore* (1913)

Innis, Harold A., *The Cod Fisheries* (New Haven, 1940)

Jackson, Gordon, *The British Whaling Trade* (1978)

Jackson, Gordon, *Hull in the Eighteenth Century* (1972)

Jackson, Gordon, 'Scottish sailors', paper given at the Conference on European Sailors at The Hague, 19–21 October 1994

Johnson, Captain Charles, *A General History of the Robberies and Murders of the most notorious Pyrates* (1724)

Justice, Alexander, *A General Treatise of the Dominion and Laws of the Sea* (1705)

Kent, H.S.K., *War and Trade in Northern Seas* (Cambridge, 1973)

Klein, H.S., *The Middle Passage: comparative studies in the Atlantic slave trade* (Princeton, NJ, 1978)

Klein, H.S. & Engerman, S.L., 'A note on mortality in the French slave trade in the eighteenth century' in Gemery & Hogendorn (1979)

Landers, John, *Death and the Metropolis* (Cambridge, 1993)

Le Goff, T.J., 'The labour market for sailors in France', paper given at the Conference on European Sailors at The Hague, 19–21 October 1994

Lemire, Beverley, *Fashion's Favourite: the cotton trade and the consumer in Britain, 1660–1800* (Oxford, 1991)

Lewis, Fiona, 'The demographic and occupational structure of Liverpool: a study of the parish registers, 1660–1750' (Unpublished Liverpool Ph.D., 1993)

Lind, James, *An Essay on Diseases incidental to Europeans in Hot Climates* (1768)

Lindsay, W.S., *History of Merchant Shipping* (3 vols, 1874)

Linebaugh, Peter, *The London Hanged: crime and civil society in the eighteenth century* (1991)

Lloyd, C.C., *The British Seaman, 1200–1860: a social survey* (1968)

Lloyd, C.C. (ed.), *The Health of Seamen* (NRS, cvii, 1965)

Lounsbury, R.G., *The British Fishery at Newfoundland, 1624–1763* (Yale, 1934)

Lydenberg, H.M., *Crossing the Line: tales of the ceremony during four centuries* (New York, 1957)

Marsden, R.G., *Reports of Cases determined by the High Court of Admiralty* (1885)

Marsden, R.G. (ed.), *Select Pleas in the Court of Admiralty* vol. ii (Selden Society, 1897)

Martin, B. & Spurrell, M. (eds.), *Journal of a Slave Trader, 1750–4* (1962)

Mathiex, Jean, 'Sur la marine marchande barbaresque au XVIIIe siècle', *Annales* xiii (1958)

Melville, Herman, *Redburn: his first voyage* (New York, 1849, 1929)

Meyer, W.R., 'English privateering in the war of 1688 to 1697', *MM* lxvii (1981)

Meyer, W.R., 'English privateering in the War of the Spanish Succession, 1702–1713', *MM* lxix (1983)

Michell, A.R., 'The port and town of Great Yarmouth and its economic and social relationships with its neighbours on both sides of the seas, 1550–1714' (Unpublished Cambridge Ph.D., 1978)

Middleton, A.P., *Tobacco Coast: a maritime history of Chesapeake Bay in the colonial era* (Newport News, Va, 1953)

Minchinton, W.E. (ed.), *The Growth of English Overseas Trade in the 17th and 18th centuries* (1969)

Mollat, Michel (ed.), *Course et Piraterie* (2 vols, Paris, 1975)

Molloy, C., *De Jure Maritimo et Navali* (9th ed., 1769)

Morris, Richard B., *Government and Labor in Early America* (New York, 1946)

Morse, H.B., *The Chronicles of the East India Company trading to China, 1635–1834* (5 vols, Oxford, 1926–9)

Murton, W., *Wreck Inquiries* (1884)

Newby, Eric, *The Last Grain Race* (1956)

Newton, John, *Thoughts upon the African Slave Trade* (1788), reprinted in Martin & Spurrell (1962)

Nicol, John, *Life and Adventures* (1822)

Ovington, J., *A Voyage to Suratt in the year 1689* (1696)

Owen, Nicholas, *Journal of a Slave-dealer* (ed. Eveline Martin, 1930)

Palmer, Sarah & Williams, Glyndwr (eds.), *Charted and Uncharted Waters* (1982)

Pares, R., 'The manning of the navy in the West Indies, 1702–63', *TRHS* 4th ser. vol. xx (1937)

Parker, Sir Thomas, *The Laws of Shipping and Insurance* (1775)

Phillips, Hugh, *The Thames about* 1750 (1951)

Phillips, Thomas, 'A Journal of a voyage made in the *Hannibal* of London, Ann. 1693, 1694' in A. Churchill (ed.), *Collection of Voyages and Travels* vol. vi (1732)

Plumb, J.H., 'The new world of children' in Neil McKendrick *et al.*, *The Birth of a Consumer Society* (1982)

Postma, Johannes, 'Mortality in the Dutch slave trade, 1675–1795' in Gemery & Hogendorn (1979)

Powell, J.W.D., *Bristol Privateers and Ships of War* (Bristol, 1930)

Press, Jonathan, 'The economic and social conditions of the merchant seamen of England, 1815–1854' (Unpublished Bristol Ph.D., 1978)

Press, Jonathan, *The Merchant Seamen of Bristol, 1747–1789* (Bristol, 1976)

Press, Jonathan, 'Wages in the merchant navy, 1815–54', *Journal of Transport History* 3rd ser. ii (1981)

Prichard, M.J. & Yale, D.E.C. (eds.), *Hale and Fleetwood on*

Admiralty Jurisdiction (Selden Society, 1992)

Rawley, J.A., *The Transatlantic Slave Trade* (New York, 1981)

Rediker, Marcus, *Between the Devil and the Deep Blue Sea: merchant seamen, pirates and the Anglo-American maritime world, 1700–1750* (Cambridge, 1987, 1993)

Report of Select Committee into the Causes of Shipwrecks, HC 1836 (567) xvii (1836)

Richardson, David (ed.), *Bristol, Africa and the eighteenth-century slave trade to Africa: iii, the Years of Decline, 1746–69* (Bristol Records Society xlii, 1991)

Richardson, David, 'The eighteenth-century British slave trade: estimates of its volume and coastal distribution in Africa', *Research in Economic History* xii (1989)

Ritchie, Robert C., *Captain Kidd and the War against the Pirates* (Cambridge, Ma, 1986)

Rodger, N.A.M., 'Devon men and the navy, 1689–1815' in Duffy *et al.* (1992)

Rodger, N.A.M, 'Shipboard life in the Georgian Navy, 1750–1800: the decline of the old order?' in L.R. Fischer *et al.* (eds.), *The North Sea* (Stavanger, 1992)

Rodger, N.A.M., *The Wooden World: an anatomy of the Georgian Navy* (1986)

Rogers, Francis, *Journal* in Bruce S. Ingram, *Three Sea Journals of Stuart Times* (1936)

Russell, Percy, *Dartmouth: a history of the port and town* (1950)

Schaw, Janet, *Journal of a Lady of Quality . . . 1774 to 1776* (ed. E.W. Andrews, New Haven, 1939)

Scoresby, W., *An Account of the Arctic Regions with a history and description of the northern whale-fishery* (Edinburgh, 1820)

Scott, H.H., *A History of Tropical Medicine* (1939)

Shepherd, J.F. & Walton, G.M., *Shipping, Maritime Trade and the Economic Development of Colonial North America* (Cambridge, 1972)

Souden, David, 'Migrants and the population structure of later 17th-century provincial cities and market towns' in Peter Clark (ed.), *The Transformation of English provincial towns, 1600–1800* (1985)

Spavens, William, *Narrative* (1796)

Spooner, F., *Risks at Sea. Amsterdam insurance and maritime Europe, 1766–1780* (Cambridge, 1983)

Starbuck, Alexander, *History of the American Whale Fishery* (Waltham, Ma, 1878)

Starkey, David J., *British Privateering Enterprise in the eighteenth century* (Exeter, 1990b)

Starkey, David J., 'Devonians and the Newfoundland trade' in Duffy *et al.* (1992)

Starkey, David J., 'War and the market for seafarers in Britain, 1736–1792' in L.R. Fischer & H.W. Nordvik (eds.), *Shipping and Trade, 1750–1950* (Pontefract, 1990a)

Stein, Robert, 'Mortality in the eighteenth-century French slave trade', *Journal of African History* xxi (1980)

Stephens, W.B., 'The West-Country ports and the struggle for the Newfoundland fisheries in the seventeenth century', *Transactions of the Devon Association* lxxxviii (1956)

Sutton, Jean, *Lords of the East. The East India Company and its ships* (1981)

Taylor, E.G.R., *The Mathematical Practitioners of Hanoverian England* (Cambridge, 1966)

Taylor, E.G.R., *The Mathematical Practitioners of Tudor and Stuart England* (Cambridge, 1954)

Teonge, Henry, *Diary* (ed. G.E. Manwaring, New York, 1927)

Thirsk, Joan & Cooper, J.P. (eds.), *Seventeenth-century Economic Documents* (Oxford, 1972)

Thomas, E.G., 'The Old Poor Law and maritime apprenticeship', *MM* lxiii (1977)

Troughton, Thomas, *Barbarian Cruelty* (Exeter, 1788)

Tryon, Thomas, *The Way to Health, Long Life and Happiness* (1683)

Uring, Nathaniel, *Voyages and Travels* (1726)

Van Royen, P.C., 'Manning the merchant marine: the Dutch maritime labour market about 1700', *IJMH* i (1989)

Villiers, Alan, *The Way of a Ship* (1953)

Ward, Edward, *The London Spy* (ed. A.L. Hayward, 1927)

Ward, Edward, *The Wooden World Dissected* (1707)

Willan, T.S., *The English Coasting Trade, 1600–1750* (Manchester, 1938)

Woodward, Donald, *Men at Work: labourers and building craftsmen in the towns of northern England, 1450–1750* (Cambridge, 1995)

Index